Every dramatist's dream: his name and his play's title in lights on a New York marquee, and a line at the box office, even on a rainy day.
(*Theatre Collection, New York Public Library*)

LIFE
AMONG THE
PLAYWRIGHTS

LIFE
AMONG THE
PLAYWRIGHTS

Being Mostly the Story of
The Playwrights Producing Company, Inc.

JOHN F. WHARTON

Photographs selected by Betty A. Wharton

Quadrangle / The New York Times Book Company

Copyright © 1974 by John F. Wharton. All rights reserved, including the right to reproduce this book or portions thereof in any form. For information, address: Quadrangle/The New York Times Book Co., 10 East 53 Street, New York, N.Y. 10022. Manufactured in the United States of America. Published simultaneously in Canada by Fitzhenry & Whiteside, Ltd., Toronto.

Library of Congress Catalog Card Number: 73-89269

International Standard Book Number: 0-8129-0442-7

Design by: Tere Lo Prete

To All Those Persons Who Have Ever
Enjoyed a Theatrical Performance
and
Especially to That Silent Majority Among Them
Who Have Thought of Writing a Play of Their Own
This Book Is
Affectionately Dedicated

Acknowledgments

If the title page of this book followed theatrical precedent, it would read: "Book and Captions by John F. Wharton, Pictures by Betty A. Wharton." Mrs. Wharton searched out almost all of the pictures from the files of the Theatre Collection of the New York Public Library at Lincoln Center where she works as a staff member. Invaluable help was given her by fellow staff members. My own debt to that staff is also great; to Paul Myers, Curator, and especially to Dorothy Swerdlove, First Assistant. I would like also to mention Maxwell Silverman and Gilbert Bledsoe. And my thanks to Don Madison and Carmen Memberg of the Photographic Services for their patience and efficiency in providing the many prints needed for the illustrations. The entire staff of the Theatre Collection helped, clearing up doubtful points in both research and allied fields—so much so that I do not see how a definitive book on any phase of the American theatre could be written without their assistance.

Also, my thanks to Mrs. Maxwell Anderson, Robert Anderson, Robert Ardrey, Mrs. S. N. Behrman, Mrs. Howard Cullman, Mrs. William (Mary) Frank, Miss Lotte Lenya, Mrs. Anita D. Littell and Mrs. Robert E. Sherwood for permission to use letters and photographs. Also, to Yale University as legatee under the will of Carlotta Monterey O'Neill for permission to use the letter from Eugene O'Neill to Robert E. Sherwood, to Samuel Taylor for permission to use the Prologue from *Sabrina Fair*, to William Koppelmann of Harold Freedman Brandt & Brandt Dramatic Department, Inc., and to Miss Jeanne Newlin of the Harvard Theatre Collection for their help in obtaining various permissions.

Special mention should also be made of friends such as Richard F. Shepard of *The New York Times* and of my legal associates, Messrs. Zelenko (who is also trustee of Elmer Rice's writings), Taylor, Davidson, Breglio and Miss Joan Daly, all of whom read the manuscript and checked facts.

Help and encouragement came from many other sources. Albert Leventhal, who edited one of my former books and who now heads Vineyard Books, read the first few chapters and insisted that I go on to completion. Nearly twenty friends in various fields of work read

the manuscript and gave me encouragement. In the academic world—
in addition to Mr. Myers and Miss Swerdlove—Norris Houghton,
State University of New York, and Robert C. Schnitzer, Columbia
University. In the world of the theatre: Judith Abbott, Robert An-
derson, Arthur Cantor, John Cromwell, Robert Kimball, Arthur
Miller, Mr. and Mrs. Worthington Miner, Joseph Papp, Natalie
Schafer, and Victor Samrock, the Company's general manager
throughout its entire life.

Nor must I omit my editors and publishers—Messrs. Geltman, Mc-
Leroy, Hamparian, Rebecca Sacks and Creon Psome.

Inge Morath went out of her way to make possible the use on
the jacket of her photograph of Mrs. Wharton and me. Indeed, all of
the photographers were most cooperative.

Finally, someone who went far beyond the call of duty in innumerable ways—my secretary, Antoinette Scaffidi. Patiently and tirelessly,
she not only typed and retyped, but also found the papers which I
continually misplaced, set up necessary files, and coordinated the
preparation of the entire manuscript.

As I re-read the foregoing, I am astonished at the number of people
to whom I owe a debt of one kind or other. If have omitted anyone,
my heartfelt apologies.

John F. Wharton

Contents

LIFE
AMONG THE
PLAYWRIGHTS

Background for an Experiment

Peculiar Problems of the Playwright

Some years ago a charming and brilliant lady, a leader in a special branch of psychiatry, made what I first considered to be a strange request. She wanted help on a book she proposed to write showing what stimulated a certain successful dramatist to write his plays. I begged off and quoted a couplet written by the columnist Franklin P. Adams. A contributor had sent in a poem he had composed, saying that some time ago he could not write because he was in love; now he had fallen out of love and couldn't write because of *that*. "What's the use of love, anyway?" was his concluding line.

Mr. Adams printed the poem and below it his own comment.

> Be passion dead, unborn, or hot,
> Some people write and some do not.

The lady thought my letter rather flippant; perhaps, in the circumstances, it was. But as I thought more about it I became convinced that Mr. Adams was making a more profound comment than first appeared to be the case. For the playwright has certain problems peculiar to his profession which you should ponder deeply if you ever decide—as you well may—to try your hand at writing a play. These problems make the odds against the dramatist so great that I, for one, believe only a powerful subconscious compulsion keeps a dramatist at work. He can honestly say, as did Martin Luther when he finished his famous theses, "Here I stand; God help me, I cannot do otherwise." Some people have this compulsion, some do not.

Statistically, it has been estimated that ten thousand full-length plays are written every year in the United States. Less than 5 percent of these are ever given serious consideration for production, and only 10 percent of those will achieve any kind of success. Moreover, many of the productions are acutely disagreeable experiences for the playwright, largely because the producer may assume a position of domination that is infuriating. But such is the desire to see your play produced—greater, at that moment, than even sexual desires—that the producer can sustain his position. And in the end, failure is the preponderant result, and that is even more devastating. All in all, it *must* be a compulsion that stimulates a human being to write a play.

However, if you ever find yourself gripped by that particular compulsion, I urge you to go ahead. At worst, you will get it out of your system. At best, you may be gloriously surprised. Authors have won the Pulitzer Prize with their first Broadway production. You may be the next one.

In any event, you will be in a much better position than were the unestablished playwrights and, to some extent, the established ones, during the first quarter of this century. During that period Broadway was dominated by aggressive, ruthless, frequently uneducated, men who controlled theatres or money, or both, and treated all but the most distinguished authors as second-class citizens. They unblushingly traded on the dramatist's desire for production to obtain terms which now seem outrageous. They would have thought of themselves as the Lords of the Broadway Manor and the dramatists as serfs, if they had known what a Lord of the Manor was.

Eventually, the dramatists rebelled. Out of the rebellion came a unique experiment; it eliminated the producer. It was developed by five out-of-the-ordinary playwrights: Robert E. Sherwood, Maxwell Anderson, S. N. Behrman, Sidney Howard, and Elmer Rice. All except Behrman had been awarded the Pulitzer Prize for drama.

Sherwood was the acknowledged leader of the group. The word *charisma* had not come into fashion in 1938, when the experiment was developed. If it had, Sherwood would have been said to have it in plenty. Born of a distinguished New York family, he entered Harvard University but left in 1917 to join a Canadian regiment fighting in World War I. Everything about Sherwood was "noticeable," beginning with his height—six feet, eight inches. His manner of speaking was unusual; he would pause in the middle of a sentence, sometimes for an inordinate length of time; Sam Behrman once said that you could read a large part of *War and Peace* before he resumed. But no one ever stopped listening.

No one knew, in 1938, that he would win two more Pulitzer Prizes for drama, and still another for biography, nor that he would become a confidant of Franklin D. Roosevelt, spearhead of an anti-Hitler campaign, and serve a term as head of the Office of War Information. But such was the admiration and liking for him that no one would have been surprised by a prophecy of such things to come.

He was no saint. He drank what he wanted when he wanted it; at parties this habit frequently led him to get up and sing the old burlesque song, "When the Red, Red Robin Comes Bob, Bob, Bobbin' Along." The theatre community was astonished to learn that he had fallen in love with the wife of his good friend, Marc Connelly, courted and won her, and married her after she and he obtained divorces. Lynn Fontanne once asked him how he could have courted the wife of such a close friend. He replied, "Well, Lynn, I guess. . . . [long pause] I was just ruthless."

When President Roosevelt appointed him to the Office of War Information, government rules required that he be investigated before he could act. The chief investigator saw a number of people, including myself, who were lavish with their praise. Finally he asked one man, "Isn't there *anyone* who will have something bad to say about this man?" "Well," said the man, after thinking a bit, "you might try Marc Connelly—but I'm not sure even he will be as damning as you might expect."

Elmer Rice was the direct opposite of Sherwood in almost every way. He had little or no charisma; it was only after you knew him well that you came to admire him and love him. His real name was Reizenstein. He came from a poor New York Jewish family who could not afford to send him to a doctor to have his eyes examined, let alone to a dentist to have his teeth straightened. He was short and dumpy; to put it bluntly, homely. He had a bad habit of repeating stories over and over again. But when you came to know him well, you found in him loyalty, sympathy, and desire to help; also, indefatigable energy in fighting against what he deemed evil—particularly censorship.

Sidney Howard came from the Far West; from a family, I judge, not unlike an eastern upper-middle-class family. He was almost as much a natural leader as Sherwood. He was handsome and attractive to both men and women. He gave endless time and energy to helping younger playwrights; at the same time, as president of The Dramatists Guild (the dramatists' union), he led both young and old playwrights in a pitched battle against producers and theatre owners. To me, his outstanding quality was that on very first meeting you knew he was adult in every sense of the word. His plays reflected this maturity.

Maxwell Anderson also came of middle-class stock; his father was a small-town minister. He once told me that he never quite knew how he came to write plays. To me, playwriting seemed to be his natural métier. He had a wonderful inquiring mind; some of the plays he abandoned dealt with more fascinating subjects than the ones he finished. His looks can be best described by a phrase of a lady who said he looked like a lovable tame bear. But he could be as violent as the wildest of wild bears. Unlike Sherwood, Rice, and Howard, he had no interest in The Dramatists Guild; indeed, he resented the fact that he was subject to its rules even when the rules were to his own advantage. He was attractive to women, but two of his three marriages were unsuccessful. He was mercurial, at times a bit paranoid; I never knew just where I stood with him.

S. N. Behrman grew up in a Jewish household in Worcester, Massachusetts. The family was poor, but money was considered secondary to scholarship and creativity. He was the only one of the five founding playwrights who remained married to one woman all his life; he was equally constant in his devotion to one man—his agent, Harold Freedman. We all loved Sam; we enjoyed his never-failing, ebullient wit; we felt that he had great personal fondness for all of us. But, from the beginning, I doubted whether he really wanted to join the organizers, and it was no surprise to me that he eventually defected.

The company which these men formed, called The Playwrights Producing Company, Inc., was the acme of the rebellion against producers which had simmered and then boiled up many years before.

The Older Playwrights' Rebellion

Elmer Rice's first play, *On Trial*, adapted the movie flashback to the stage; it was an enormous success in the 1914–1915 season. Later he wrote *The Adding Machine*, a nonrepresentational play which added greatly to his artistic stature. He was, as a result, well known in, and well acquainted with, the Broadway theatre of those days. It was dominated by theatre owners, most of whom also produced plays, and by their satellites who held themselves out only as producers—they used the term *Manager*. The Shubert Brothers, Charles

Robert E. Sherwood.
(*Theatre Collection, New York Public Library*)

Frohman, Klaw and Erlanger, George Tyler, William A. Brady, and David Belasco were all prominent. Elmer was full of stories about the woeful state of playwrights in those days; no wonder rebellion began to simmer.

"Most of the theatre owners and producers were arrogant, tricky, and inartistic," he once said to me. "Here's a simple story which illustrates their business ethics. Lee Shubert had an interest in a play of mine and we were negotiating with two bidders for the foreign rights. I received a letter from one of them making a firm offer if, and only if, it was accepted by return mail. The amount was much less than the amount the other bidder was talking about *if* he decided to go ahead at all. I asked Lee what to do. He replied instantly, 'Don't accept by letter. Phone him and say yes. Then you can deny you said it if the other offer comes through.'

"Even the more honest ones," he continued, "were not averse to some sort of trickery that might save them a dollar or two. Take Bill Brady—Pop, as we called him. He once produced a play with an unusually large number of bit parts, for which little-known actors were hired. The critics praised the play and production, many of them mentioning the excellent performances of the unknowns. Pop waited a week or two until he felt sure that the names of the praised bit players were completely forgotten, then fired them all and hired even cheaper actors to take their places. He figured that audiences would remember only that the critics had said these parts were well played and would therefore think the cheaper actors were excellent. That this procedure caused the author to gnash his teeth was a matter of complete indifference to Pop.

"Pop was, as a rule, the stingiest producer I have ever known," he continued. "When I hear talk today about shoestring productions, I wish there was a record of some of Pop's presentations. He got a revival of *Little Women* started at a cost of two hundred dollars. It looked it. Sometimes he overreached himself. He owned the Playhouse Theatre and he tried to keep *something* playing there all the year round. One summer he got together a production using worn-out old sets and worn-out old actors; it was so bad that on one Wednesday it achieved a record: nobody, I mean *nobody*, bought a ticket for the matinee; at three o'clock they dismissed the cast. I've

Dudley Digges (perhaps best remembered for his portrayal of the fear-ridden Harry Hope in *The Iceman Cometh*) as he appeared in Elmer Rice's fifty-year avant-garde play *The Adding Machine*. I say "fifty-year" because the picture rights were sold fifty years after its first run.

(*Vandamm*)

never, before or since, heard of a New York performance which drew not a single customer.

"On the artistic side, he could display ignorance for which the word *colossal* is far too mild. He apparently had no idea of how a play came to be written. He once asked me if I had seen a play of his which had flopped in one week; it happened that I had; I didn't like it and said so. That didn't concern him at all; what he wanted was something involving the four sets—which *were* nice. Pop assured me they were as good as new and asked if I would write a play that fitted them. He was obviously disappointed and bewildered when I refused."

Elmer thought for a moment, and then continued. "He was a curious man. He wasn't always just a penny-pinching meddler. He produced *Street Scene* when every other manager who read it assured me that no audience existed for a drama about poor people in America. What's more, to my surprise, Pop gave me a reasonably free hand in money and production. He admitted once that he didn't really understand the play; he simply had faith in me. No author can really dislike a man who feels that way about him. But I think I was the exception that proved the rule."

The Customs of the Times

Elmer's stories were no exaggerations; quite the contrary. He had become an "established playwright" with his first production. The unestablished playwright was subjected to really contemptuous treatment. He frequently could get no more than a flat payment for his play; if royalties were to be paid, they might be 1 or 2 percent of the gross box office receipts, a tiny sum; and the producer often held up payment for weeks or months; if things went badly, he might never pay at all, certainly not unless he were sued. Somewhere along the line producers had gained the right to a 50 percent participation in stock and amateur rights, which they administered, often dishonestly. When motion picture rights became important, producers simply took the same 50 percent and the same power of administration and often used it to the dramatist's disadvantage. A newcomer might be required to give a producer an option to acquire all picture rights for a small sum, perhaps $1,000. If the play were a failure, the option was not exercised; if a hit, it was exercised, and the producer might make thousands on the sale to a movie company. If an author didn't agree to such terms, a producer might pay him a small advance for exclusive stage rights to his play and then hold up production indefinitely; the

Although Clyde Fitch became a leading dramatist, at the turn of the century his deal with the actor-manager Richard Mansfield was such that he received only $1,500 for writing one of Mansfield's greatest successes, *Beau Brummel*. (*Theatre Collection, New York Public Library*) (*Sarony*)

play would die on the vine unless the author agreed to the producer's terms.

Dealings in movie rights became an acute sore spot with many authors. But two other features were an abomination to *all* authors. First, a producer selected the cast and director for the play, often not telling the playwright until the first rehearsal who had been selected. Second, and more galling to an author, was the producer's power to change the script if he, in what he considered to be his God-given wisdom, thought he could improve it. Unfortunately, God had not been generous in supplying producers with artistic talent. But they had the power, and power, as usual, tended to corrupt, creating delusions of grandeur and creative talent.

Playwrights submitted to such treatment because it was the custom of the times; there seemed to be no alternative. However, there was probably another reason; no American dramatist was writing what we call today "important plays." The effect of this is not generally understood.

If a play has no importance, any producer's interest in it has one basis, and *only* one basis; will it make money? But an important play, such as *Death of a Salesman*, has an additional basis; a top-flight producer *wants to do it* even if he thinks it a bad monetary risk. (Frequently, as was true of *Salesman*, it turns out to be immensely profitable.) This puts the producer and the author on equal footing when it comes to negotiating terms.

If money is the only factor involved in play production, we are quickly back into that situation described by Wordsworth:

> The good old rule
> Sufficeth them, the simple plan,
> That they should take, who have the power,
> And they should keep who can.

This was pretty much the rule during the first quarter of this century. The appearance of important plays by American dramatists was one factor that helped to change it. In my fifty years of work in the theatre I have seen scripts I thought had money-making possibilities go unproduced. I have never read a well-written script of importance that failed to find a producer; some producer appeared who *wanted* to do it, and he did it.

"Important play" is a phrase hard to define, although, like the phrase "state of happiness," everyone knows what it means. For our purposes, we might say that an important play is a play that gives a new insight into some social situation (*A Doll's House*) or delineates a fascinating individual (*Oedipus*) or is lifted out of the ordinary by great creative imagination and superb writing (*The Tempest*).

The nineteenth century was not distinguished by important plays. Some theatrical historians attribute this to the influence of a remarkable, now barely remembered, Frenchman named Eugène Scribe. He is reputedly the author, or co-author, of some *four hundred* plays, and he tossed off a few opera libretti in between times. He believed that ingenuity of plot was all-important; his plays lacked characterization, and hence they had little or no depth. Many dramatists followed his rules, adding, whenever possible, startling stage effects. By the end of the century, a number of dramatists—Ibsen was outstanding—had challenged the Scribean principles, and important plays began to appear in England and on the Continent. But the notion was slow in taking root in America. One reason was, undoubtedly, that most plays reflect the culture of the society in which they are written, and the culture of American society in my formative years, from 1895 to 1920, was a curious culture indeed.

American Victorianism

The dominant feature of that society was a sort of American Victorianism that would be hard for anyone born after 1920 to believe; I grew up in it and *I* find it hard to believe as I look back today. Never before nor since were there so many high moral principles combined with such distortions, delusions, and warped interpretations, all overlaid with a naive smug idealism that today seems, not entirely correctly, to have been downright hypocrisy and the acme of prudery.

Children were told that even a white lie was sinful; yet parents unblushingly lied to the same children on sex matters; they actually told them—yes, they did—that the stork brought babies; later on, when a girl knew better, she was told that if a man kissed her, she would have a baby. "Nice women" when married were supposed to submit to, but not enjoy, sex. Indeed, sex was considered sinful to a degree that would have astonished even St. Paul, whose declaration that it was better to marry than to burn was taken quite seriously.

The popular religions were pure Salvationism; Man's goal in life was to make himself worthy of heaven. Unhappily, the real goal of almost everyone was to be able to live like the very rich people—with big houses, fine clothes, good food, servants, and no need to work.

There were, however, many admirable, even if naive, standards. It was taken for granted that democracy and the Christian brotherhood of man should (and would) sweep the world. We really believed that in World War I we were fighting to make the world safe for democracy, as President Wilson told us. We also believed—can you believe it today?—that democracies never wanted war. A real antiwar movement began in those days and had at least the effect of making jingoes everywhere (including America) give lip service to the cause of world peace. The honest crusaders for peace realized that defensive wars were necessary; the jingoes thereupon began to declare every war to be defensive.

One famous expression of smug idealism perhaps sums up, as well as anything can, the feelings of pre–World War I Americans:

> God has marked the American people as His chosen nation to finally lead in the regeneration of the world. This is the divine mission of America, and it holds for us all the profit, all the glory, all the happiness possible to man. We are trustees of the world's progress, guardians of its righteous peace.
>
> *Senator Albert J. Beveridge of Indiana*

It is hardly surprising that such a culture should fail to produce very many important plays.

The Twenties

After World War I, the men and women who had grown up in this prewar culture began to question many phases of it. Consequently, change was in the air, and Broadway was no exception. Playwrights began to appear who were destined to make the Broadway theatre the most important theatre in the world. "Important plays" by American playwrights began to appear in increasing numbers; not all of them succeeded, but even the failures demanded respect. Such plays sought to present three-dimensional characters who were motivated by realistic forces and whose dialogue had style and sharpness. Adult subjects were sought and used.

Eugene O'Neill tackled among other things, racism (*All God's Chillun Got Wings*), capitalistic greed (*Marco Millions*), and the plight of the unskilled laborer (*The Hairy Ape*).

Maxwell Anderson, with Laurence Stallings, began a crusade against naive conceptions of war (*What Price Glory?*); the theme was further developed by Sidney Howard (*Paths of Glory*) and became a burning subject with Robert E. Sherwood (*Idiot's Delight, There Shall Be No Night, The Rugged Path*). Anderson also attacked injustice (*Winterset*) and political chicanery (*Both Your*

Houses). He further astonished Broadway by using, successfully, blank verse when he felt the subject warranted it.

Sidney Howard brought an adult picture of sex to Broadway (*They Knew What They Wanted*), wrote the first serious gangster plays (*Lucky Sam McCarver, Ned McCobb's Daughter*), and showed that heroism was not limited to fighting battles but could be as great in fighting disease (*Yellow Jack*). He also exposed the seamy side of evangelism (*Salvation*). Rice wrote the first Pulitzer Prize drama portraying American lower-income groups (*Street Scene*). Behrman began to try adult conceptions of psychological forces (*The Second Man*) and developed a style of dialogue and wit surpassing anything else of its kind.

There were many plays by less well-known authors which dealt with important subjects.

The Criminal Code depicted the horrors of our prison system; *The Racket* exposed the hookup between politicians and racketeers; *Wings over Europe* predicted, in 1928, that when and if atomic energy became a reality, politicians would be interested primarily in the military aspect. No one believed this; the play failed. (Nor would the public believe, in 1934, Rice's mild indictment of Naziism in *Judgment Day*.)

Dramatists with such interests, even before becoming established, resented bitterly the arrogance and power of the theatre owner–producers. As early as 1920 they began to stimulate the older established playwrights to action. All playwrights resented the impertinence of the Lords of Broadway in changing scripts; clearly, the idea that Lee Shubert *could* change a Eugene O'Neill script *was* ridiculous (it never actually happened). Authors had observed that actors, stagehands, and musicians had begun to protect their positions by unionization. The playwrights decided to try a somewhat similar course, and organized what they called The Dramatists Guild.

The birth of The Dramatists Guild has been described elsewhere; the details need not be repeated here. In brief, a document called a Minimum Basic Agreement between Authors and Managers (producers) was concocted, and the Guild members announced that they would permit their plays to be produced only by producers who signed this Agreement. Since the document provided, along with many other things, that the producer could not, without the author's consent, change a script, nor sell motion picture rights, and had to have the author's approval on director and cast, the producers' resistance to signing it was something that could be *truly* described as colossal. But the dramatists stuck to their guns, and in 1926 a tough, able negotiating committee finally forced the leading producers to sign.

The Lords of Broadway remained true to their false colors even after signing. One committee member was Arthur Richman, an extremely successful dramatist of that time, and the first Dramatists Guild president. Arthur told me that just before the signing meeting broke up the producers' spokesman announced that it would be a long, long time before any producer who was present would produce a play by anyone on the Negotiating Committee. The other producers exhibited complete approval. As Arthur left the room, a producer sidled up to him and whispered, "Arthur, I hear you have a new play. Will you give me the first crack at it?"

However, all was not easy sailing for the new Dramatists Guild, and it probably owed its continued existence to the fact that leading playwrights accepted terms as president and *worked at the job*. Rice, Howard, and Sherwood all took on this responsibility. Ten years after the 1926 agreement, a new organization of theatre owners and producers went to the mat with the Guild and for a time threatened to destroy it. But Sidney Howard, who was then president, held his forces together; a new agreement was signed and The Dramatists Guild grew steadily in power until a new producer, years later, attacked it under the antitrust laws. It is still powerful, but not quite so arrogant and self-satisfied as it was in the forties. It then posed as the defender of playwrights' artistic rights. Sherwood once remarked to me that it was really a group of copyright owners determined to get the most out of their property rights.

But some of the leading authors were still dissatisfied. They resented any producer. Rice became his own producer and rented a theatre in addition. He was not too successful; in a fit of pique he once announced that he was retiring from the theatre altogether. Sherwood, Howard, Anderson, and Behrman all drifted to the Theatre Guild, then at the height of its glory as a producer of important plays. The first three, particularly Sherwood, found even the Theatre Guild unsatisfactory. I never discussed this at any length with Sherwood, but he made it clear that he thought their ideas of production were more often an irritation than a help to a serious playwright. This antipathy apparently increased with time.

The Theatre Guild produced his play *Idiot's Delight* with two stars, Alfred Lunt and Lynn Fontanne, in the star roles. Sherwood felt that a bad producing job was being done; so did Lunt. As usual, innumerable conferences were called to discuss possible changes; Lunt and Sherwood became more than ever convinced that the Guild members and the director they had chosen simply did not understand how the play should be presented.

According to Sherwood, a climax came in a hotel room with a door with an open transom. The Theatre Guild members were arguing with him about what was wrong and what should be done. He thought their ideas spelled disaster. Footsteps were heard outside the door; then the sound stopped. The discussion became more heated. Suddenly the footsteps were heard again, this time in departure; also, Mr. Lunt's voice was heard saying agonizingly, "Oh, *shit!*" Sherwood was emboldened to demand that Lunt be given directorial power; the play became a smash hit and was awarded the Pulitzer Prize. Sherwood began ruminating on how to free himself entirely from producers. The stage was being set for a new experiment.

Alfred Lunt in *Idiot's Delight*. It does not look like a scene from a bitter antiwar play, but it is. The play was one of Sherwood's most successful mixtures of comedy and propaganda.
(*Vandamm*)

II

The Experiment Begins

A Not Too Contented Lawyer

In the theatre anyone who earns his living in some other field is known as a private person. A private person who is enchanted with the theatre is known as a theatre buff. I became a theatre buff at the age of eleven after seeing a road production with Victor Moore as the slangy, youthful hero of *Forty-five Minutes from Broadway*. *The Wizard of Oz*, with Montgomery and Stone and *The Little Minister* with Maude Adams tripled my enchantment. However, it never occurred to me that I would be anything but a private person. Broadway—not to mention the fast-growing Hollywood—seemed as far away as the moon. I was growing up in typical American Victorianism, the youngest child of a typical middle-middle-class family in the typical middle-middle-class suburb of East Orange, New Jersey. There theatrical folk were looked on askance; my mother explained to me that it was "unnatural" to work at night and sleep by day. She urged me to become a lawyer; I agreed, *faute de mieux*. But I still dreamed dreams of the world of the theatre; it was the chief source of my fantasy life.

A surprisingly large number of my fantasies have come true—perhaps this is the case with all people—and this was such a one. The playwright John Van Druten once told me that he believed if you wished for anything hard enough, you would get it, but probably in

A typical startling stage effect from *The Wizard of Oz* which enchanted young and old. The Scarecrow (Fred Stone) has been cut to pieces. The Tin Woodman (David Montgomery) and Dorothy put him together again. The Tin Woodman first threw a false head through the opening; Stone's real head then appeared; its first demand was an arm to scratch itself. A false arm was then thrown through the opening. And so on, until finally Stone stepped out of the frame.
(*Byron*)

some unexpected and violent way. The event that led me into the theatre was a severe illness, which was to have unpredictable ramifications.

I was living and working in New Jersey, apparently slated to be a small-town lawyer. Our family doctor and his confreres were at a loss to discover the cause of my ailment. Prior to this, one of my sisters and I had consulted, as a specialist, a youngish man named Joseph Eastman Sheehan who had offices both in New Jersey and New York. She told him my symptoms; he correctly diagnosed the case as a kidney infection without even seeing me. He *was* a bit of a genius; he became a pioneer in plastic surgery.

The incident planted in my mind the idea that perhaps I should consider New York as well as New Jersey. The notion grew after Sheehan dropped his New Jersey office and I had to go to New York to see him. Incidentally, I learned from my acquaintance with him that genius in one line can be accompanied by strange deficiencies in others, for he was the closest thing to a male Mrs. Malaprop that ever existed. He might casually spout such an aphorism as "No rose without a bud," and he once told a friend of mine who consulted him that he would like to go over him with a fine toothbrush. But he did save my life, and plastic surgery has certainly added enormously to the happiness of many people.

My illness was a rare type of infection. Together with my convalescence, it took almost a full year. During that time I read every play I could get my hands on, as well as numerous books relating to theatrical production. This background was to stand me in good stead when I met prospective clients; there was an immediate rapprochement.

My reading was not limited to the theatre. Friends brought me all kinds of books. One day a former college classmate brought me a book which he felt sure would amuse me. It had, he said, curious and funny explanations for many common idiosyncrasies. He thought I would get some good laughs out of it. It was *The Psychopathology of Everyday Life* by Sigmund Freud. I immediately became an avid reader of all of Freud's books, and quickly made friends with Freud's other early admirers—not a very large group.

As a convalescent measure, I was sent to a mountain resort where I met a young actor named Walton Butterfield who eventually brought me into an ever widening circle of theatrical friends. When World War I broke out, I enlisted in naval aviation, but a recurrence of my illness kept me out of active service—a fortunate thing, for I should undoubtedly have killed myself and my instructor on my first flight. I then went to work for the British Ministry of Shipping in New York. I lost interest in New Jersey; a married sister gave me the money to live in New York and attend Columbia Law School. There I met Louis Weiss; he was an ardent Freudian devotee, and this started a friendship which increased to the point where we eventually formed the law firm of Weiss and Wharton.

Our first client, and our only one—which soon went bankrupt, to our dismay—was a motion picture producing corporation manned mostly by a group of young Yale graduates who had known Weiss at college. Our first case involved an unusual situation. The corporation's main actor was a young man named Glenn Hunter, who had recently become a Broadway star. Hunter was given a considerable

Maude Adams. Both her voice and her laugh were unforgettable. Her admirers were fanatical. In the depths of the 1930s depression, she organized a road tour of *The Merchant of Venice* in which she played Portia. It sold out everywhere. The critic George Jean Nathan wryly suggested that the owners of empty New York theatres should run special trains to the tour in order to show gawkers the forgotten sight of full houses. (*Sarony*)

sum of money for some purpose connected with his first picture; he dutifully used most of the funds for the purpose intended; but $3,000 (a very large sum in 1923) was not so used. When pressed for an explanation he said that he had used it "for a night with Jeanne Eagels," the most beautiful actress of the day, who had herself just become a star in the play *Rain.*

It seemed an unlikely explanation; Hunter was no "ladies' man," Miss Eagels was not in the business of selling sex. Someone suggested that we ask the seemingly slandered Miss Eagels if there was any truth in the story. Her reply was prompt and clear. "Of course it's true. I don't object to that sort of thing with my good friends now and then, but that young man! Just because he had a *little success* the same time I became a star, he seemed to think he was entitled to it. So I made him pay—$3,000!"

The corporation went bankrupt, but one member, Dwight Deere Wiman, became my close friend and my first theatrical client. He became a producer and through him I began to meet other producers and also playwrights, actors, and backers; my theatrical practice expanded rapidly. Among these new clients was a young producer named Alexander McKaig who, in some mysterious way, had interested John Hay Whitney in backing him. Whitney retained me to represent him in theatrical work. Later I represented him and some of his family when they took their fling in motion pictures, backing David Selznick and Merion Cooper in independent producing companies. This involved regular trips to Hollywood.

Hollywood was then *the* film capital, and at first I found it completely exciting and glamorous. It also paid well. I had every reason to be contented. But the gilt soon rubbed off. Film folk were, I discovered, all too often glib talkers with little substance to support the talk. The dominant men who ran the business were aggressive, tricky, uncultured, conceited, much like the Broadway producers of the 1920s. Although the Selznick corporation was to win lasting fame by producing *Gone with the Wind*, I wanted no part of it at all. I longed for Broadway. Hence, I was delighted to receive a letter from Sherwood asking me to represent a company to be set up for playwrights to produce their own plays.

Jeanne Eagels, beautiful and talented, burst into stardom as the prostitute in *Rain* at the age of twenty-eight. Her success was followed by the swiftest tragic deterioration of any star in the history of the American theatre. She died at the age of thirty-five.
(*Straus-Peyton*)

Preorganization Problems

Now and then I have run across stories saying that the decision to form this company sprang full blown from a luncheon meeting of Anderson, Howard, Rice, and Sherwood. I have no doubt such a luncheon took place, but someone—Sidney Howard, I think—told me that the idea was first put forward to the group by the playwright Philip Barry.

Barry had a curious career. His light comedies—*Paris Bound, Holiday, Philadelphia Story*—met with enormous success; his more serious plays, such as *Here Come the Clowns* and *Hotel Universe*, were rejected by the public with discouraging promptitude, although they garnered a small band of enthusiastic admirers. At the time that he approached other playwrights with his idea, he was, according to Howard, working on an avant-garde morality play which would have cost a fantastic amount to produce. His insistence that this be produced by the new company led to other disagreements, and, despite the esteem in which he was held, it became impossible to include him in the group. There was no personal rancor; after Barry's death Sherwood finished a half-written play and the Company invested in the production.

I never had the opportunity to work with Barry, but an incident connected with the star actor of his play *The Animal Kingdom* has always stuck in my mind. It still strikes me as the prime example of a celebrity with one-way pockets. The actor was Leslie Howard, an attractive but parsimonious young man. He had to leave the play for a Hollywood engagement; no substitute could be found, so the play had to close. On the last night he said good-bye to the cast, told them he had to rush off, but had arranged a little backstage party for them. When they gathered, there were chairs, a table, and on the table glasses and one bottle of Scotch whiskey. It *was* a fine old Scotch.

Everyone had a drink and left. One actor chatted a bit with the stage doorman. "It's been a nice run," said the latter. "You've all been very nice to us men. So much so that the crew chipped in with me and bought Mr. Howard a bottle of fine old Scotch."

In any event, the first I heard of the playwrights' project was Sherwood's letter, and, feeling as I did about the theatre, I was naturally delighted. Yet I nearly blundered out of any connection with the project; only luck and Sherwood's determination to bring me into it carried me through. To begin with, in a spirit of quixotic honesty, I answered the letter with one which pointed out only the difficulties of such a project—the problems that would arise when two playwrights were seeking the same star, or director, or theatre; as I think back, it was *not* a document calculated to win five new clients. But it worked out well. Sherwood shortly wrote again saying that they had discussed my letter and felt they could handle such problems (which proved to be true). He again asked me to meet with them and I readily agreed.

Later on, I ran into a real mess—caused by Selznick. I was at swords' points with him at the time, for a number of reasons. The most important was the fact that he was frittering away the company's money through inability to find a project; he tried to conceal this and was furious when I pointed it out to Mr. Whitney. But, from my personal angle, the major problem was my refusal to subscribe to the instructions he gave his lawyers—when he had made an oral commitment, they should so haggle over minor points in the papers that he could get out of his commitment any time before he signed.

He had made an oral commitment to buy the picture rights to Anderson's play *The Star Wagon*. His West Coast lawyer had dutifully kept the deal juggling; Selznick suddenly went cold on it and used as an excuse that it might be held to plagiarize a suddenly released movie, *Turn Back the Clock*. I was disgusted and refused to act for Selznick in the dispute that followed, but Anderson, in a suspicious mood, decided that I had tricked him. Selznick, on his side, was furious that I would not act for him; I believe—I have no evidence—that Anderson heard of this and his suspicions were allayed; possibly Sherwood talked him out of them. In any event, he agreed to go forward, and wrote me a charming letter:

April 22, 1938

Dear John:

When I saw you the other day I realized that you had been from the first more deeply concerned about your own good faith than I could possibly be, and my misgivings must have seemed both heartless and thoughtless. My excuse must be that I didn't know you very well, that legal ethics are often baffling and sometimes disillusioning to the layman and that one learns to be astonished at nothing in a business deal. In the last analysis there is nothing to rely on but personal probity and from now on I shall rely on you implicitly.

Sincerely,
Max

However, my relationship with him continued to be an up-and-down one; an episode—years later during the production of *Anne of the Thousand Days*—was to be an unbelievably startling display of

what is called "artistic temperament." I was not the only one to have such a relationship; at one time he suddenly began to feud with Elmer Rice to an extent which nearly wrecked the company then and there. But for the moment, all was well.

The new venture needed financing, and here, again, I skirted around trouble. Whitney was then greatly interested in the theatre and had been a substantial investor in a number of plays. At my first conference with the group, it was suggested that he should be approached. I arranged a meeting for him to meet the five playwrights and it went very badly. Out of it, surprisingly, came a compliment. I had assumed that one major reason why the five had come to me was the belief that I could get them Whitney backing; Sherwood informed me that they had thought I was a Whitney employee and had only suggested the idea of getting his backing in order to get me! He could certainly be extremely tactful when he wanted to be; no wonder he was a leader.

In the meantime, I went to work on the legal necessities. I drew up a memorandum of agreement providing for the relation of the playwrights to the company and each other. It had three major points: (1) each author would submit all his plays to the Company for production, (2) the Company would produce any play that could be done for less than $25,000 (which was then a normal budget for a drama), although this obligation did not apply to past unproduced plays, (3) the author was to have the final say in all production matters within the budget.

When the memo had been signed, we held an informal meeting at which it was decided to make a public announcement. Behrman, who had been a press agent, was absent, and, to our embarrassment, we discovered that none of the rest of us knew how to issue a newspaper release. We prepared a document and I sent a copy of it to every New York newspaper, marked for the attention of the Theatre Department. I knew enough to avoid giving any paper the jump on the others and arranged for the copies to arrive late Saturday or early Sunday. Consequently, we got full coverage on Monday and became the center of the talk of Broadway.

By and large, the reaction was astonishment. True, playwrights in business were not altogether new in theatre history; one William Shakespeare was a theatre owner as well as an author. But in the

Mercurial Maxwell Anderson. His wide-ranging mind made him the most prolific of the five playwright-founders. His prize-winning *Both Your Houses* foreshadowed the Watergate scandal of 1973. (*Vandamm*)

1930s the New York theatre had broken into three important divisions—authors, producers, and theatre owners—and very few authors had ventured into the producing or theatre-owning fields. And the notion that *five* of the most prominent, and therefore the most demanding, playwrights could work together was another startling feature.

Some of the talk was downright unfavorable. The wiseacres' tongues began to babble at once. It couldn't be done! It had been tried once before and had failed. (There *had* been a somewhat similar attempt in the 1920s.) Five prominent playwrights would tear each other apart in jealousy. Creative writers couldn't possibly conduct the business side of producing. And so on, and on, and on, always ending with the assurance that the company would be out of business within, *at most*, two years. A prediction that the company would last over twenty years would have been laughed down hilariously.

Well, the Company continued for twenty-two years. It survived the untimely death of one of its founders. It survived the ravages of the war years; it survived the sudden catastrophic rise in production costs. It was only after death had reduced the number of playwrights to two that the Company wound up its affairs.

But being the center of talk did not of itself produce the capital we wanted, one hundred thousand dollars. We finally agreed that each playwright should invest $10,000 and we would try to raise another $50,000 outside. I did know about money-raising and set out to help in this, but Sherwood outdistanced me and raised the bulk of the $50,000 very quickly. The final list of backers included some impressive names:

Dorothy Schiff, who became the owner and publisher of the *New York Post*

Alicia Patterson Brooks, who became the publisher of the successful newspaper *Newsday*

Howard S. Cullman, a well-known public figure, for many years head of the Port Authority of New York

Harold K. Guinzburg, a well-known book publisher, head of the Viking Press

Averell Harriman, who became a Governor of New York State and an Ambassador-at-large

William S. Paley, President of Columbia Broadcasting System, Inc.

Raymond Massey, the famous stage, screen, and TV star.

The backers, including the five playwrights, received a preference stock in the amount of their investment and a Class A Stock giving them 50 percent of the profits. A Class B Stock, entitled to the other

50 percent, was issued, at $1.00 per share, to the five and, on their insistence, to me. Two other people were given small amounts of Class A stock: Victor Samrock, who began as general manager and gradually became, in effect, a co-producer on the business side, and William Fields, our press representative, a curious, tempestuous man whom I never understood to the day of his death.

Every theatre lawyer learns very quickly a strange fact about playwright clients: they will fogive, sometimes quite readily, a mistake about financial terms, but heaven help you if you make a mistake involving the title of their play, even in the size of the type or its position on the page. Hence, I was not surprised that no one paid much attention to the stock structure I proposed but that everyone entered a lively discussion of the Company name. I cannot reproduce the oral discussions, but the following excerpts from letters and wires are illuminating.

At a meeting in New York on March 8 the name The Playwrights' Theatre was selected. This promptly resulted in a telegram from Sidney Howard, who was in Hollywood:

NAME SEEMS DREARY AND SLIGHTLY PRETENTIOUS TO ME BUT OK
IF OTHERS LIKE IT

Whereupon there came a letter from Max from New City, New York:

By the way, another organization has been making announcements under the name of the Playwrights' Theatre, and it may be we've lost our name, since they're first out with it. I'm sorry, for I like that name.

On May 12 I wrote to Max:

I regret to say that the name "The Playwrights' Theatre, Inc." is not available. The unavailability is due to a conflict with other names. In the circumstances, I am afraid that we shall have to think up another title. I am writing everyone on this and asking them to put their minds to work. At least Sidney will be pleased, because he never liked the other title.

Max replied:

So far I haven't been able to hit on any title for our venture that sounds acceptable even to my ears. However, I'm glad the old one is unavailable if Sidney didn't like it. There should be a certain unanimity toward the label.

Bob, who was in England, wrote on May 23:

> The corporate name that I like best is "The Writers' Theatre." But perhaps we can't use that, either. I also have had a persistent though inexplicable partiality for the name "The New City Theatre"—which (aside from the fact that it's Max Anderson's home town) doesn't mean a thing. I shall try to think of some others and send them; but please don't settle on anything without letting me know.

The next day a wire arrived from Sam, who was in Hollywood:

> WHY CAN'T WE USE THE DRAMATISTS OR THE AMERICAN DRAMATISTS FOR A NAME?

To which I replied on May 31:

> BELIEVE NAME DRAMATISTS PREEMPTED BY DRAMATISTS GUILD. WHAT WOULD YOU THINK OF THE AUTHORS THEATRE?

Sam did not reply.

On June 3 I wrote the following in a letter to Bob who was still in England:

> I had a meeting with Elmer, Sidney and Max yesterday and we came to certain conclusions on the name without having the benefit of your suggestions.
>
> Everyone felt that regardless of what name we choose, our organization will be popularly known as "The Playwrights." In view of this we decided to try first for "The Playwrights' Company, Inc." If this proves unavailable, we shall ask for "The American Playwrights, Inc.," and if both of these fail, we shall in desperation take "The Playwrights Producing Organization."

Bob wrote to me on June 15:

> The Playwrights Company, Inc. seems to me an ideal name, and I hope it is available. As an alternative, I like American Play-

MAXWELL ANDERSON · S. N. BEHRMAN · SIDNEY HOWARD · ELMER RICE · ROBERT SHERWOOD · JOHN F. WHARTON
DIRECTORS

VICTOR SAMROCK

BUSINESS MANAGER

THE
PLAYWRIGHTS
PRODUCING
COMPANY,
INC.

MURRAY HILL 4-2065

230 PARK AVENUE

NEW YORK CITY

Our first letterhead. Can you find the word "producing"?

wrights—without the definite article, as *The* American Playwrights might be construed as a slap at Eugene O'Neill, George Kaufman, etc.

On June 20 I was finally able to write to Bob:

The only name which turned out to be reasonably satisfactory and available was The Playwrights' Producing Company, Inc. We are having a form of letterhead prepared which subordinates the word "Producing" to the other word.

And on July 1 we received notice that a Certificate of Incorporation of The Playwrights Producing Company, Inc. had been filed in Delaware.

Elmer had the last word in this momentous decision. From Camp Curry, Yosemite Park, California, he wrote:

I'm glad to know that the corporation has been organized and that we are ready for business—though I do wish we had been able to use *a less stodgy name.*

And that was that.

By July 1 Sherwood had finished *Abe Lincoln in Illinois*, which Rice was to direct, with Raymond Massey as star; Anderson had prepared, with his close friend, Kurt Weill, a musical, *Knickerbocker Holiday;* Behrman's play *No Time for Comedy* was finished; Rice and Howard were working on new scripts. We were ready to go. Of course, there remained some problems of casting and direction, but authors of such prominence had no problems in interesting stars and top-flight directors. At least, so I assumed.

CHAPTER

III

The Experiment Proves Workable

The Mysteries of a Script

The five authors gave each other various reasons for the formation of the Playwrights Company. One of these was the announced belief that they could get constructive criticism from other playwrights, whereas comments from nondramatists were only irritating. I was, therefore, not a little surprised and flattered when all of them asked me to read, and comment on, their scripts.

However, it was, I sensed, a delicate situation. I had been reading scripts for less eminent authors for fifteen years and had done some nondramatic writing myself. I had learned that what authors really want from *any* reader is a statement that the work is superb. Once that is said, a criticism here and there is acceptable. It so happened that I was greatly impressed by the first Playwrights' scripts, and I could easily apply this technique. It worked. No matter how eminent a playwright may be, he is insecure and wants praise. Probably Ibsen waited nervously for the opinion of the first readers of *A Doll's House* and *Hedda Gabler*.

Whatever value my opinion may or may not have had, I learned some things from reading these scripts—particularly from Sherwood. First of all, there is no such thing as a finished script until it has been tested before an audience; in Sherwood's case, before a New York audience. This was one of the reasons for his almost unbroken run of successes from *Reunion in Vienna* through *There Shall Be No Night*, with three Pulitzer Prizes out of seven plays. He read every review, even if he had contempt for the reviewer, and checked the audience reaction on every scene which received unfavorable comment. And he really *checked*. Less important playwrights could listen to titters of laughter during a comedy scene and tell you that the audience "rolled in the aisles." Not Sherwood. If he expected roars of laughter and didn't get *roars*, he admitted to himself that something was wrong, and he went to work to change it. Similarly, if any scene evoked too many coughs or too much restlessness, out it came.

The first point I ever discussed with him involved acting. *Abe Lincoln in Illinois* moved me immensely, but the meaning of the prayer which Lincoln delivered in Act II, Scene 4, was not entirely clear to me. I somewhat naively asked Sherwood if he was relying on the actor to make it clear. A look almost of horror crossed his face. "It is hard enough to get an actor to convey to an audience a mean-

The prayer scene from *Abe Lincoln in Illinois*, a vitally important scene on which Sherwood worked unceasingly, even *after* the New York opening.
(*Vandamm*)

ing which you think you have made absolutely clear; I wouldn't dream of expecting him to clarify what I've written."

Actually, I had put my finger on a sore spot. He had written this prayer, on the back of a restaurant menu, first of all; the whole play had developed from it; but it was *not* entirely clear just what it meant. True to form, when he found audiences showed confusion, he rewrote the scene—several times—even after the play had opened in New York and received almost universal acclaim. (Mr. Massey did help; he was superb in his handling of this difficult sequence.)

But that was all much later. During the late spring and early summer of 1938 Bob was in England. On May 20 he wrote me a letter about a talk with Elmer Rice, and then suddenly went into a startling story about the problems arising from Massey's success in the London production of *Idiot's Delight*.

May 20, 1938

Dear John,

Elmer has been here for four days and sails tomorrow on a slow boat, arriving about June 1st. He has finished two acts of his play [*American Landscape*] and expects to have the last act completed before he lands. I have read the two acts. It's a remarkable play and I think it stands a chance of being a conspicuous success *provided* an obvious element of confusion is cleared up. I am certain that this can be done, and done with the utmost ease. I discussed this at length with Elmer and told him precisely what I thought and made the suggestions which occurred to me.

Elmer and I talked about various aspects of the organization set-up but didn't reach any new conclusions. We just agreed that everything looks wonderful. Elmer's report to you on your memos seems to agree pretty much with what we said when you, Max, Sid and I met before I sailed.

The situation as regards Massey has been frightfully complex—not to say appalling—and for the first ten days after my arrival I had it so terribly on my mind that the sinus returned. However, it has largely straightened out. *Idiot's Delight* is, alas, a hit of incalculable proportions, and he has made an immense personal success in it. His partner in the management and the lessees of the theatre have been fighting hard to prevent him from leaving. But Massey himself has been just as firm in his determination to be in New York for rehearsals Sept. 5th. It has ended up with him making the most overwhelming concessions —giving up all his interest in the show, guaranteeing them

against loss which might immediately follow his departure, etc.
I've agreed to drop my royalties and go on a profit sharing basis.
So now it is all settled; except that they face the formidable job
of finding a replacement for Massey. I cabled Harold to look up
Kent Smith but he has just signed with Katharine Cornell. Lee
Tracy would be marvelous, of course, if reliable and obtainable.
If you have any ideas on this subject, you'd help me a lot by
cabling them. This, of course, is all extraneous: The main point is
that Massey will play Abe and, having seen him in *Idiot's Delight*, I'm more certain than ever that he'll do a superb job. Elmer
seems to agree emphatically.

I hoped the sketches from Jo Mielziner would arrive before
Elmer's sailing, but as soon as they do come I shall make any
notes that occur to me and shoot them right back. The construc-
tion can be done in the summer. It should be emphasized to Jo
that he is to supervise all the lighting and that Elmer is not the
kind of director who wants to interfere in that.

I hope to hear news of Max's play, also of how Sid is progress-

Jo Mielziner, a genius with no
conceit whatsoever, creative, practical, experimental. Like all experi-
menters, he tried things which mis-
fired; unlike most, however, he
admitted the failures and came up
with something better. If we had
ever decided to ask a scenic artist to
be a member, Jo would have received the first invitation.
(*Theatre Collection,
New York Public Library*)

ing. I may get a play done this summer. At the moment, I feel terribly tired. The sinus isn't bad and I am taking a series of treatments that seem sensible.

Give my best to Mrs. Wharton.

Yours,
Bob

P.S. I hope Vic Samrock or you have booked the theatre in Washington for the week of October 2d. It will mean a lot to *Lincoln* to open there, and as there will be a rush of try-outs at that time it's none too soon to make sure of it.

Rehearsals of *Abe* went smoothly. I recall only one unhappy spot, which came from the willingness of the company and the set designer, Jo Mielziner, to try an experiment. Mielziner had established, as early as the 1920s, an extraordinary reputation. (It has held good for fifty years.) You could count on him not only for brilliant artistry but also for certainty that the ordinary mechanical problems of scene shifting and changing were solved; his designs would work. But he was, and still is, ready to try experiments, knowing that experiments do *not* always work. In this case he persuaded us to try playing behind a loosely woven cloth called a scrim; he felt that by cutting off all light, the stage would be a blank to the audience, and scenic changes could be made without wasting the time required to lower and raise a curtain. It was a fine idea for a multiscene play, it had only one fault; it didn't work. Somehow, there was enough light left for the audience to see the stagehands as ghostly figures rushing madly about and stumbling over each other. The experiment ended after one trial.

The scrim had had its most disrupting effect just before the scenes with Mary Todd began, and the rest of the play was somehow clouded by this during this particular run-through. The Mary Todd–Lincoln relationship took on, in that one performance, a wrong emphasis. Present at the run-through was the talented actress-authoress Ilka Chase, who could wield a caustic pen and tongue. She did not like the play, told my wife that she had recently seen the hit musical *I Married an Angel*, and suggested calling this play *I Married a Republican*. I sadly replied that there probably never would be a play which pleased everybody; when I hear such remarks I always think of Tolstoy's diatribe against "that silly, stupid play, *King Lear*."

Sherwood was never entirely happy about some of the scenes with Mary Todd. I think he might have cut them down if Elmer had not turned up a true comment made by Mr. Lincoln: "Miss Mary Todd, with two *d*'s; mighty impressive, considering one was enough for

Abe (Raymond Massey) and Ann Rutledge (Adele Longmire) in *Abe Lincoln in Illinois*.
(*Vandamm*)

God." The line always brought a healthy laugh; Sherwood was given great credit for having discovered it or invented it—somewhat to Elmer's annoyance. In any event, the line did serve to keep Bob thinking about the character.

He asked me one day what I thought of a new curtain line for the scene in which she learns that Lincoln is to be nominated for president. He suggested that she suddenly exhibit a burst of great love, admiration, and excitement, ending by a speech something as follows: "We'll be in the nation's capital, think of it, Abe; we'll be able to meet all the famous people of all sorts, artists, musicians—[Pause]—we'll be able to go to the theatre!" I thought the line would be quite a smasher; so did Bob, but he finally said he thought it was too slick.

I asked him how he defined the word *slick*. After a bit of rumination, he replied that it was the use of a speech or an action which would be instantaneously effective but would, after the audience thought about it, lack real motivation and hence would seem obviously contrived. Slickness, he added, was the trouble with a lot of

Hollywood movies of the era; it turned thinking people against them. I was to have occasion to remember this when a film producer became a partner in one of our plays.

Abe Lincoln's tryout began in Washington. It was an instant hit. Everything went well during the tryout—so well that I, with my natural tendency to worry, began to have fears for New York. The New York dress rehearsal confirmed those fears; I could not attend but sent a number of people from my law office. They all reported that Mr. Massey had lost his voice; his portrayal of the role was, therefore, meaningless.

Mr. Massey was conserving his strength; on opening night his voice was quite all right. But near the end another disaster threatened. An elderly lady in the first row—some say it was Sherwood's mother, who was rather deaf—began talking very loudly during a crucial scene. I shall never forget my horror nor my sense of relief when she quieted down and the scene came to an end.

The audience was enthusiastic. I put away my fears and congratulated everyone; when I praised Mielziner, he reciprocated. I insisted

Lincoln bids farewell to Illinois and leaves, never to return. Mielziner suggested a way to open the stage on both sides while also producing an effect of the train moving away. We could not afford it, but it would have been sensational.
(*Vandamm*)

that I had little or nothing to do with the success. "Don't be so bashful," he replied. "You'll get plenty of blame when the first flop comes along. Take all the bows that are offered to you." It was good advice; I've been inclined to follow it ever since.

Despite the enthusiasm and the excellent critical notices, the ultimate test—the box office—was slow in responding. Fortunately, Samrock had sold a few benefits, so no one saw a half-filled theatre; the word went around that we had a big hit. Eventually, business did pick up and capacity became the rule, not the exception.

Bob received letters of praise from a host of famous people—Carl Sandburg, Sherwood Anderson, Mrs. Roosevelt, to name only a few. But I think the letter which meant the most to him was this one:

Dear Robert Sherwood,

I have just finished *Abe Lincoln in Illinois* and I want to tell you how moved I was by it and what a splendid piece of work I think you have done. It has exactly the qualities a Lincoln play should have, deep sincerity and simplicity without ever losing the mystery of his character. In my opinion, it is the only true Lincoln play ever written. My enthusiastic congratulations! And here's wishing you the same fine achievement in all your future work!

Yours very sincerely,
Eugene O'Neill

O'Neill, at the time, had withdrawn from the theatre. He had no play produced from 1934 to 1946. Would that he could have been a member of our Company!

Maxwell Anderson's *Knickerbocker Holiday* taught me once and for all that you can twist a script just so far—and not very far at that. This script was something very rare in those days—and today—a drama with music; Kurt Weill was the composer. Weill was later to become a member of the Company, but we never really appreciated his genius until after his death.

The original version led up to a dramatic confrontation scene between Peter Stuyvesant, representing Old World authoritarianism, and Brom Broeck (the younger man), representing New World rebellion against that concept. The key of the whole play was in the song "How Can You Tell an American?"—the answer being that "authority repels him as a lad and never goes down at all." There was also a love story that gave Weill scope for some delightful melodies. Anderson had no difficulty in obtaining Joshua Logan as director; Logan was just establishing himself as one of Broadway's top directors. But trouble was on the way.

Anderson, Lotte Lenya, and
Kurt Weill.
(*Collection of Lotte Lenya*)

The part of the hero, the young rebel, was written with Burgess
Meredith in mind. He could project all the qualities necessary to
make an attractive rebel. But, despite the eminence of Anderson,
Logan, and Weill, he refused the part. (I began to see why even top-
flight playwrights were insecure.) A frantic search for an alternate
began, with no success; there was no other young star with a good
enough voice. All of us wracked our brains and memories; I can't
recall who came up with the suggestion that the part of Peter
Stuyvesant be built up and given to Walter Huston, but this was
accepted as a solution. It wasn't.

Huston was an outstanding personality. But if there was one thing
he couldn't portray, it was any sort of Hitlerian authority; audiences
all adored him for his kindly, lovable qualities. Hence, the original
idea was thrown completely off balance, and the play really never got
back on an even keel. It was saved by Huston's draw and the fact that
Weill hastily composed a new song for which Anderson wrote
charming lyrics. It was titled "September Song" and quickly became
a minor classic. Someone once told me that in this song Weill had
shamefully plagiarized himself; if so, it was a plagiarism devoutly to
be desired. Huston revelled in it; later on, he appeared in a play which
had only a halfhearted success in New York, but went very well on
the road. Huston usually received such curtain applause from road

An example of what prevented audiences from taking seriously
Walter Huston's Stuyvesant as a threat to democracy.
(*Life Magazine*)

audiences that he obliged by singing "September Song" to everyone's delight. He never asked anyone's permission to use the song; his producer never paid a royalty; such was the liking for Huston that no one in the Company ever thought of objecting.

Because it was a musical, *Knickerbocker Holiday* went into rehearsal before *Abe Lincoln*. It was *not* a promising beginning. No one was happy about the two young leads; the attempt to twist the original idea began to cause trouble early in the game. I still have a clear picture of Max at the end of the first run-through; he stood shaking his head and saying, "My, my, we certainly do go to pieces in the last act." He was right; we did. The script had been twisted too far.

To add to the tribulations, as the day for the tryout opening in Hartford arrived, so did a fine late summer flood. Just how Victor Samrock managed to get the cast, the scenery, and the playwrights there on time, none of us ever quite understood; Victor was regarded with a certain awe from that time on.

This was the first musical with which any of the playwrights had ever been concerned, and their reaction to the problems showed up the difference between dramas and musicals. If you strengthen one act of a drama, the whole play usually benefits. If you strengthen one act of a musical, you may make the other acts look very much poorer. If you then begin tinkering too much with the other acts, you may wreck the whole show. The playwrights came perilously near to taking this course, but Weill and Logan restrained them. However, no one could solve the essential wrong twist.

The script of Elmer Rice's play *American Landscape* really puzzled me. It was a strange semi-fantasy; an American family of realistic characters was surrounded by reincarnated ancestors whenever death was approaching the head of the living family. Since the ancestors included such unexpectedly bizarre figures as Moll Flanders and Harriet Beecher Stowe, the illusion was doubly confusing. However, Rice was the man who, at an early age, had introduced the movie flashback to the stage; he had written the avant-garde *Adding Machine*, which was years ahead of its time: *Street Scene*, which won him a Pulitzer Prize, was the first American drama to use only lower-strata characters theretofore deemed too unglamorous for the stage. With these recollections in mind, I could only say—and feel—"wait and see." I believe the playwrights all felt the same way. Nobody made any constructive comment.

But we never did see. The play ran into a unique problem which proved insoluble. The full meaning of the drama was expressed in a long speech by the leading character, the longest speech I ever read in a manuscript; longer than the protagonist's last act speech in O'Neill's

The Iceman Cometh. All of the playwrights insisted that this speech needed editing, that it was too diffuse; Rice agreed and said he would cut and revise it after the first run-through. At that point, Arthur Byron, who was to deliver the speech, admitted that his memory was failing and dropped out of the play. The cutting had to wait while we scrambled for a successor.

It was worse than the *Knickerbocker Holiday* scramble, for time was running out. Every recognized star was considered. Walker Whiteside, an early 20th Century star, was called in. He was about eighty; according to Rice, their interview revealed such outmoded histrionics that they never got to a discussion of the play. Finally, the part was given to Charles Waldron, who fancied himself a star and demanded and got star compensation, but who utterly lacked the sympathetic quality needed. By the time agreement with him was reached, the play was booked to open. Rice, therefore, had to cut a speech which he had never heard delivered to an audience—even a run-through audience. He did the best he could, but it was not good enough. *American Landscape* was the Company's first failure.

I didn't learn much from reading *American Landscape*, but I learned one thing from the production; the days when one man could both write and direct a play were coming to an end; the demands on him as writer and as director were too great. If things went awry on the writing side, there wasn't time to rewrite and to re-direct. Adding the duties of a producer made it even worse. But Rice stuck to his guns despite the arguments of the rest of us—much to his own loss.

Knickerbocker Holiday opened in New York four days after the *Abe Lincoln* opening. It was a mild success, running 166 performances in New York and, later, some 70 or 80 on a road tour. Although *American Landscape* failed, we had had two out of three successes and felt firmly established as a major producing company. However, we had one more hurdle to get over; I more or less bore the brunt of it. It involved Behrman's play *No Time for Comedy*.

This play had given us trouble from the start. Soon after the public announcement of the Company's formation, people began telling me that Behrman was offering the play to producers who he thought could get him some star or director he wanted, utterly disregarding the memo he had signed requiring him to have the Company produce it. The wiseacres began to chuckle, then laugh loudly; the Company, they said, was breaking up before it got started. Actually, I doubt if Sam ever read the memo. Luckily, someone in the Company sent the script to Katharine Cornell; she expressed great interest; Behrman's interest in the Company revived.

But we weren't out of the woods.

Katharine Cornell as Jo in *Little Women*. Very few people who were enchanted by the cute youngster playing Jo suspected that she would grow up to be an actress unrivalled in projecting charm and dignity. (*Theatre Collection, New York Public Library*)

Word came back from the Cornell office that since Miss Cornell was her own producer, she wished to be *sole* producer. This word, as I suspected, came from her business adviser, Stanton Griffis, who went about denigrating the Company, saying that it was simply a bunch of boys with some plays to sell, trying to get better than usual terms.

I knew Griffis well, and I knew he was a tough trader and a skillful one. One of his techniques was to tell everyone how hard-boiled his adversary was and how he was being worn down by the other's persistence. He would then make an insultingly small offer and pretend that he went *that* far only because he was worn out. It so happened that I was at that time engaged in a trading match with him where he was using this technique; I was representing a television company seeking financing from a bankers' consortium of which he was the driving force. I recall a luncheon with him to discuss the *No Time for Comedy* deal, which took place at a downtown lunch club frequented by investment bankers. One after another stopped at our table to ask if we had settled this or that point in the television deal. They were, naturally, bewildered when Griffis said, "Don't bother us with unimportant things like millions of dollars. We're talking *art*."

Griffis finally offered to let the Company have a 10 percent participation in the production. (Behrman, as author, would, of course, get his usual royalties.) Everyone was outraged and insulted; fortunately, knowing Griffis, I could persuade them to hold out and look a little deeper into the situation. It was clear to me that Miss Cornell wanted to do the play, and I had ascertained she had no interest at the time in any other. Hence, I simply did not believe that she was, as Griffis intimated, holding out for the lion's share of the money. But I was pretty nervous; I knew that if we lost Miss Cornell, we would pretty surely lose Sam Behrman.

Katharine Cornell
(*Vandamm*)

Luckily, I was right. What was holding her back was not anything to do with terms; she was worried about casting the male lead. So was her husband, Guthrie McClintic, who always directed her plays. One day they announced that Behrman's agent, Harold Freedman, had found a brilliant, although little known, actor for the part; after that there was no more quibbling on terms. Griffis sheepishly bowed out and a 51–49 percent deal was quickly agreed upon. Oddly enough, I never got to know the actor who saved the day, but I have never ceased to admire him. He is now known as Lord Olivier.

The television deal heated up at about this time. It was one of the most strenuous of my legal career; when it finished, I was exhausted

Miss Cornell and the future Lord Olivier in *No Time for Comedy*.
(*Vandamm*)

and took off for a vacation. I never saw any rehearsals of Sam's play, and I was not present at the New York opening. Sherwood wrote me a charming letter confirming that it was another hit; when I returned to New York we had three successes running simultaneously. Happiness fairly radiated throughout the office.

In December, Max had written a piece for *Stage Magazine* which expressed the way we all felt then; the same attitude continued through the rest of the season.

By Maxwell Anderson

"When five playwrights got together last spring and formed their own producing company there was a general impression that they were plotting against their one-time producers and against the whole producer-management-entrepreneur tradition. Sitting in on the plans I didn't get that impression at all. No, we came together because we shared several strong and positive ambitions for the theatre, some of them dreamy and some of them selfish, and because we wanted to quit hoboing from one office to another and build up permanent personal and business relationships within an organization of our own.

"In this country a playwright has always been a bird of passage, selling his script where he could or where its chances looked best. Inevitably his contacts were ephemeral, and almost every new production was a voyage of discovery in unknown waters. Unless he produced his own play in daring isolation there was no office in which he could feel at home, and his business arrangements were no less transient than the run of a play. Now the best writing that was ever done for the stage was done in the seventeenth century by men who were associated with stable producing companies composed of playwrights and actors. It was done by men who invested their own money in going theatrical concerns and had a share in their management. If the five playwrights had been looking for precedents they might have found encouragement in that one, but, as I remember it, there was never any talk of precedents. Our preliminalry discussions were few and fairly brief, and concerned such practical matters as the investment required, the necessity for a business organization, and the possibilities of profit and loss.

"We wanted to work with craftsmen whose work we respected, and whose advice was always worth considering because it came out of long experience in the craftsmanship of playwriting. We wanted, in essence, to create a local habitation pleasant enough to put an end to our migratory careers, and it seemed to us that fellow playwrights,

The playwrights at a rehearsal in 1938: Robert E. Sherwood, S. N. Behrman, Sidney Howard, Elmer Rice, and Maxwell Anderson. (*Theatre Collection, New Public Library*)

with common problems, common aims, and a common enthusiasm, ought to be able to build such a structure, even in that shifting cloud of achievement and dissolution known as the American theatre.

"And, unless my guess fails, the main business asset of our company will turn out to be the quality of the advice which the five are able to give and which they show an equal ability to use wisely. We are a group of individualists, but each man among us has a sharp ear for the word in time that happens to fit his particular problem. Hearing it, he makes use of it. This cooperation among playwrights is, so far as I know, new in dramatic history. It is a unique arrangement, and should prove eminently profitable, for no producer living knows as much about scripts and theatrical effectiveness as any one of my confreres. The words of wisdom that came my way in regard to *Knickerbocker Holiday* had a concision, an aptness, a humorous understanding, and a laconic impact unequalled in my fifteen years of fitting plays to the evasive and shadowy patterns of the New York audience.

"In short, I like my brothers in arms. In a slinking way I admire them, though I shall take care not to tell them so to their faces. My chief satisfaction in our initial good fortune results from the reflection that we can now continue our adventure. For a time, at least, we have a home in the theatre; we can put on our own plays in our own way; we can work among friends who are also experts with identical interests.

"And one more satisfaction. In the past, when a playwright has survived a production and finds himself, the morning after, in the corner of some hotel room, bleeding from many wounds and wondering why a critic is never able to think of anything more subtle than assassination to indicate displeasure, he has usually put the theatre behind him as far as possible. He likes nobody in it at such a moment, including himself, and he'd rather not write another play, thank you, lest it might be produced. Well, I've just had a play produced, and I'm cut to ribbons, but for the first time I don't care."

CHAPTER

IV

Business by Correspondence

By May of 1939 the playwright members had scattered to far corners, but there was no abatement of interest in Company affairs. Consequently, we became a sort of Committee of Correspondence; letters, telegrams, and cables flew back and forth. Dramatists enjoy writing, and there was plenty to write about. I was soon drawn into it myself.

Elmer had decided to dramatize a story by Alphonse Daudet entitled "The Siege of Berlin." I warn all young playwrights that securing the dramatic rights to anything written by a French author is a project resembling a Napoleonic campaign; superhuman patience and perseverance are required. Obstacles appear which only the French imagination can conjure up. Elmer went through such a campaign, sent drafts of his dramatization to all of us, and then set out with his wife for a trip to Europe.

Max betook himself to Hollywood, where a popular director of the day, Leo McCarey, was trying to get him to write a political movie; McCarey had heard that Max's political play, *Both Your Houses*, had won the Pulitzer Prize. Whether he had ever read or seen the play is more doubtful; Hollywood folk usually worked from one-page summaries, sometimes even of eight-hundred-page novels. But Max's mind was really on a new play idea, and he whipped off a first draft of it in short order.

Sherwood was in England, becoming more and more concerned

with the war clouds, but intensely interested in all Company problems. Behrman was there, too, planning an English production of *No Time for Comedy*.

Sidney Howard was mostly at his farm in Tyringham, Massachusetts. He had completed the script of a play which came to be called *Madam, Will You Walk*. It struck out on a line new for Sidney; he created a demonic character, Brightlee, an interesting concept but still a bit hazy to Sidney himself after several drafts.

The correspondence on these plays—and on such nonartistic matters as Shubert booking contracts, reports to stockholders, and so forth—was constant. Looking back, I am amazed at how much was covered in this way. A part of the correspondence for a part of just one month is illuminating.

Rice to Wharton

May 24, 1939

Dear John:

This is to amplify the cable which I have just sent you. This morning, I received a wire from Muni to the effect that he is

Rex Harrison and Diana Wynyard in the London production of *No Time for Comedy*. Although Harrison, as a young actor, played many leads in English light comedies, Broadway later considered him a "serious type." We were amazed when the Theatre Guild advertised him as "Sexy Rexy."
(*Angus McBean photo Harvard Theatre Collection*)

"unable" to do the play [*The Siege of Berlin*]. That may mean (1) that he has other plans, (2) that he does not like the part or (3) that he does not like the play. He says he is writing, but, of course, the letter won't reach me for some time. . . .

. . . I think it would be foolish to attempt to do the play, unless I can find the actor who can play the lead. It is a virtuoso part and calls, I believe, for a top-notch player. The only ones that I have been able to think of, are Charles Laughton and Pierre Fresnay. But I want other opinions about them, any information that you may have about their availability and also suggestions of other names.

More important still, I want the frank opinions of yourself, Max, Sidney, Sam, Harold, Vic, and Bill about the play itself. (I'll get word from Bob direct, as I had a script sent to him.) I'd like to make my position very clear to you. In spite of any technical rights that I may have to do with the play, if it comes within the budgetary limitation (which, of course, it does), I most emphatically do not want to do it, unless the consensus is that it is worth doing. . . .

I really mean this. I'm too old a hand at this game and have had too many flops, to want to go through with a dubious job, just for the sake of getting another play on. So please ask everyone to give me an absolutely frank opinion of the play and of the advisability of doing it. I don't mean that it must be regarded as a masterpiece (it definitely isn't that) but unless most of you think that it is at least up to our standard and has a reasonable chance of box-office success, I'd much rather scrap it and get on to something else. . . .

I'll probably have some word from you in reply to my cable, by the time I get to Paris. But, of course, I couldn't put all of this into a cable and as this should reach you about the 2nd or 3rd of June, I'd appreciate a wire to Paris, summarizing the reactions to the script and advising me what to do.

I am very glad that we took a chance and came to Greece. It is all even more exciting than I had expected it to be. We are doing a lot of pretty strenuous sight-seeing, and besides are having an active and interesting social time with Greek authors and theatre people and with the American diplomatic representatives and

Elmer Rice, a complex character, hard to describe. But one thing was clear: no one ever had greater loyalty to his friends and to his own high ideals.

archaeologists (who are doing an astounding job on the excavation of the Athenian Agora.) We were lucky enough, too, to see the new finds at Delphi. But I am not going to bore you with rhapsodies about Greece. Anyhow, by the end of next week, we shall be pretty tired, and for that reason and because Yugoslavia is a hell of a place to get in and out of, we have decided not to go there, but to fly right back to France. We leave here on June 3rd, and as I said shall be in Paris on the 4th or 5th.

Since the general tension seems to have relaxed somewhat, I shall probably stick to my original plan, and remain in Europe until the latter part of July. But, of course, the situation changes from day to day, and if things begin to look ominous again, we may decide to leave in a hurry. The Greeks are not too happy about the general outlook, with Italian concentrations on three sides. They haven't the slightest chance of resistance, and Athens itself has practically no defensive preparations against an attack by sea or air. The government has a definitely fascist tinge, but all the people I have talked to are violently pro-American. The trouble is that they are geographically dominated by Italy and economically by Germany, due to the incredible stupidity of the democracies in not building up satisfactory trade relations. However, a lot of people seem to think that there will be no new crisis until the fall, and many (including Lincoln MacVeagh, our minister) are of the opinion that Mussolini is none too happy with his German partner, and is not anxious to get too deeply involved with him. Of course, it's all guess-work, and by the time you get this, the march of events may have made my comments look silly.

I'm delighted about the success of Sam's play and wish I had more news about it and about *Lincoln*, as well as about what the boys are getting ready for next season. I'm very enthusiastic about Sidney's play, though not at all sure of its box-office values. Well, we had a grand first season (barring my little fiasco) and I think we can all feel that we have made an excellent start. Incidentally, I suppose you know that we are all most grateful to you. We could never have done it without your help and advice. . . .

I hope that you are entirely well again and that you have a good long vacation somewhere. Best regards to Carly and to yourself.

Yours,

Elmer

SHERWOOD TO WHARTON

May 25, 1939

Dear John:

I had just cabled you about the English option on *Abe* when your letter arrived asking my opinion on the Shubert booking question. I think I told Vic that I have no intelligent opinion on that, being ready to accept yours and his because I simply don't know what it's all about. But—all other things being equal—I should certainly prefer not to be tied to the Shuberts, which is probably the unanimous opinion.

As to the report to stockholders draft . . . I feel that you have been too modest on behalf of the company—that we should do a bit more crowing about our record during the first year, not only for our financial success but for our industry, our business management, and the prestige which we have created with the public and the theatrical profession. In fact, I think I'll type out some suggested revisions and enclose them with this. Please don't think that I'm criticising your literary composition; it's just that I'd like to lay it on a little more thickly for Guinzberg, Harriman and the rest. By the way, Bob Lovett was on the boat with us and said that this was the only really sensible investment Averell has made in years. . . .

The theatre here is slightly improved in business, but still in an awfully bad way, and while I think that *Abe* with Ray in it would stand a good chance in London, I see no earthly point in considering any other production of it. It is worth remembering that, in the event of war, every theatre and cinema in London will be instantly closed, and the same probably applies to Birmingham and all other centers. The government will do its utmost to prevent any congregations of people anywhere, especially in the evenings, for obvious reasons. People seem to feel a lot more hopeful now, but they know that every brick thrown through a window in Danzig may be the signal for the bombers to take off.

Give my best to all.

Yours,

Bob

WHARTON TO SHERWOOD

May 26, 1939

Dear Bob:

. . . Before writing this letter I cabled you for a telephone appointment and I imagine by the time you receive this letter we shall have talked together about Elmer's play and about Richard Gaines [to follow Massey in *Abe Lincoln*]. Elmer's play was a terrific disappointment to me, for the reasons you mention as well as others, and I am certain a production of it in its present form would be more disastrous to Elmer than to us. . . .

Sincerely,

John

The first draft of Max's play, *Key Largo*, arrived about this time.

WHARTON TO ANDERSON

May 31, 1939

Dear Max:

I read *Key Largo* over the holiday weekend and hasten to congratulate you. I think it is one of the finest things you have ever written. . . .

I agree with your own comment that more comedy should be inserted, but I am sure you will have no trouble with this. I have only one other question, but I shall defer writing you on this until I have had a chance to talk to Sidney and find out whether he was puzzled by the one scene which was not clear to me. . . .

I hope that you will cut your motion picture assignment as short as possible, because I think we should get this play on as early as possible in the fall and the sooner you get back the sooner we can really get down to business.

Sincerely,

John

ANDERSON TO WHARTON

June 5, 1939

DEAR JOHN YOUR LETTER WAS THE FIRST WORD ABOUT MY PLAY AND MAKES A NEW MAN OF ME HEARD FROM SIDNEY TODAY ALSO FAVORABLY SIZE OF THEATRE SOMEWHAT DEPENDENT ON ACTORS BUT I FAVOR SMALL HOUSE MUNI IN HONOLULU RETURNING JUNE FOURTEENTH LONGMIRE MAY BE TOO TALL TO PLAY OPPOSITE POSSIBLE LEADING MAN PLEASE ASK VICTOR TO SEE HOMOLKA ABOUT DALCALA PART

MAX

ANDERSON TO HOWARD

June 6, 1939

DEAR SIDNEY YOUR WIRE AND JOHNS LETTER TOOK A WEIGHT OFF MY SOUL BECAUSE I WONDERED STOP THE PLAY CAN BE IMPROVED A LOT AND IM WORKING ON IT ANY SUGGESTIONS YOU HAVE WILL BE MORE THAN WELCOME BEST TO YOU AND LUCK WITH YOUR CASTING

MAX

WHARTON TO ANDERSON

June 3, 1939

Dear Max:

I had a long talk with Kurt Weill and Sidney Howard yesterday about your play. You may recall that in my previous letter I told you there was one scene which puzzled me. I find that Sidney and Kurt were unable to give me any answer, and the same is true of one other person who has read the play.

It is hard to explain my difficulty in a letter, but I will try to do it. The scene is the one in the final act where King makes Murillo point his gun at him while King points his and which eventually results in the death of both. The question which I put was why does King go through this performance. Nobody seemed able to give an answer. My fear about the scene is that while it may prove very exciting dramatically, I think it may also obscure what you are trying to say at the final climax of the play. [Max never did clarify his intentions.] . . .

Incidentally, no one seems to feel that Burgess Meredith would be right for the play. Everyone seems to think Paul Muni would be the best, if he can look young enough; if he is not obtainable, everyone feels that someone more forceful than Meredith would be better and Sidney feels that to use Meredith would inevitably mean drawing comparisons with *Winterset*, whereas this play is much too good to have to rely on any kind of comparison. Sidney also thinks that Margaret Webster would be infinitely preferable to Guthrie in directing it.

I have read the new version of Sidney's play and I am still worried about the third act. I think it lacks dramatic excitement and have so informed Sidney. He is somewhat worried about the play and I think any constructive suggestions of good cheer which you could send him would be appreciated enormously.

Sincerely,

John

P.S.   John Garfield has been suggested as someone who might be excellent in your play. I think Jimmy Cagney would be the prize and I think it would be worth your while to look him up; I have heard that his contract is expiring this summer.

J.F.W.

SHERWOOD TO WHARTON

June 6, 1939

Dear John,

   . . . I am deeply sorry to have to agree completely with the general verdict on Elmer's play. It's deadly dull. At one or two moments, some fine writing lifts it out of its essential lethargy, but it sinks right back again, because the basic situation is so excruciatingly unimportant. I consider it utterly hopeless, and shall tell Elmer so. Any work rewriting would be a total waste of time.

   Max Gordon has been cabling me frantically to get to Hollywood five weeks before the start of production [of the motion picture of *Abe Lincoln*]. This I flatly refuse to do. I think that Max and John Cromwell have a bad attack of Hollywood jitters and want me there just to increase the size of their conferences. I can make all reasonable revisions in the script in a week or two, not to mention the work to be done during shooting—but if they want revisions that would take longer than that they can get someone else to do them, and I'll stay out of the picture entirely. This is a simple play and should be a simple picture and there's no excuse for all sorts of complications on the script.

   I expect to sail from here about July 12th and will pause briefly in New York on the way West to see how *Abe* is doing after Massey's departure. If you have been able to persuade Walter Huston to do it, I think there's a chance that the New York run might be prolonged into the fall. Walter could carry right on at the Plymouth, and then Ray would go out on the road. We might send the whole New York supporting cast out with Ray, or split up the principals between the two companies—keeping, say, Billie Longmire in New York in case we have another and better part for her in some future production. However, this is all wild speculation. My guess is that Walter won't do it. [He wouldn't.]

   I'm getting a little shaky about my next play. It's constantly on my mind, but there seems some obstacle in the way of its

Robert and Madeline Sherwood. In those simpler days travel by ship was universal.
(*Collection of Mrs. Robert E. Sherwood*)

complete crystallization. I don't know just what the obstacle is, but past experience tells me there's some element lacking and until I get that the play can't be written. I worried about *Idiot's Delight* for two years before it occurred to me that the leading male character should not be just a solitary vaudevillian but should be touring with six blondes. After that, the whole thing was easy. Unfortunately, I can't use blondes in this one. . . .

Yours,

Bob

In my legal career I learned from painful experience that putting anything unpleasant in a letter is a dangerous action. Judging from the following letter, the playwright-members had also discovered this fact and put off facing it. I really didn't believe Elmer wanted "the brutal truth"; my esteem for him fairly jumped when, later, I found that he did want it and could take it.

RICE TO WHARTON

June 7, 1939

Dear John:

I am just back in Paris, and find that as yet there is no letter from anyone, commenting on my play. One may have come on the *Clipper,* but that was a day late, and the mail won't be in until tomorrow; and as I want to get this off on the plane tonight, I can't wait. So if a letter from one of you is actually en route before you get this, you can probably ignore most of this.

I am really very anxious to get some reactions to the play. Muni wrote me a very nice letter, saying that he saw the possibilities of the part, but didn't react emotionally to it, and therefore, felt that he shouldn't do it. But I suspect that he was just being tactful and really didn't like the play much. What I want from our outfit is not tact, but the brutal truth. . . .

Presumably Sam has arrived in Europe and I suppose I'll hear from him shortly. I've had no further word from Bob either, about my play or about his own plans. I'll certainly try to see both Bob and Sam before I sail. For the time being, I'm going to stay in Paris. We had a very strenuous time in Greece (though a thoroughly delightful one) and the trip back was fatiguing, too. So I'm going to sit here a while to get rested and to gather my thoughts. I expect my daughter here in about three weeks and then we'll probably go to some resort in Normandy or Brittany. I'm planning to sail for home about July 20th. (I might even fly if the service is working and not too costly.) . . .

Excuse the haste of this. I'm writing against time. Best regards.

Yours,

Elmer

ANDERSON TO WHARTON

June 7, 1939

Dear John:

Since you and Sidney wrote at about the same time and your letters asked almost the same questions, I'm enclosing a copy of a letter I'm sending him today. My thanks are sincere for both praise and criticism. It will be a much better play before I'm through with it. I hope to make it the best I've ever written, though it's not now.

Whether or not I go on with this job out here, I shall probably stay a while at the ocean to think about Kurt's musical. He's driving out now, and we can spend some time over it in the evenings. McCarey's story is one which neither he nor I can be sure we want to proceed with—it's dangerously political—but it may look better tomorrow. Or maybe we'll drop it.

I hope Victor has been able to see Homolka for I can't think of a better choice for the father.

As ever

Max

P.S. I think Victor should see this.

ANDERSON TO HOWARD

June 7, 1939

Dear Sidney:

Thanks for the letter, which pretty closely parallels my second thoughts on *Key Largo* and clarifies what I have left to do, or a beginning on it. Just to indicate what I've been thinking I list the changes I have in mind. [The letter then lists seven specific changes.] . . .

You are certainly right about Burgess—and I had the same fears. Being out here has one advantage—I shall be able to see Muni and can attempt to cast the part elsewhere if he's not interested. As for Longmire [who played Ann Rutledge in *Abe Lincoln*], I wrote the part with Zita Johann in mind, and have practically promised it to her, so I don't like to switch now. I'm not sure I'd be gaining anyway, except in youth. I'm inclined to think Zita has more stops to her instrument than Longmire has—though none too many at that.

John mentions Cagney and Garfield. I had thought of Garfield, but I don't like his diction. Cagney is a possibility. As for Margaret Webster's direction, I don't know her work. And I have no way of finding out about it before we start.

John also says that you are still not quite certain of your last act. I haven't seen the play since the first revision, but I can reiterate a couple of points which I hope you haven't forgotten. One is that the audience should be conscious all the while that Brightlee is a demon who is affecting those about him. It seemed to me you were letting them guess a little. Also I hope you end with a lover's knot, maybe rather bizarre, but quite convincing. And maybe Brightlee should discover compassion at the end. Since he ought to know everything. I'm very happy about that play—even at this distance in time and geography, and only hope it's well cast. It will depend on its actors as much as mine does, and the best are none too good.

The criticisms have helped a lot—especially since you and John have somewhat illuminated each other's remarks.

Love to you and Polly.

Sincerely,

Max

SHERWOOD TO SAMROCK

This letter was written after *Abe Lincoln in Illinois* had been awarded the Pulitzer Prize.

June 12, 1939

Dear Vic:

Enclosed is the Pulitzer check. If I kept it around here much longer it would be no good. Please make out a check for $600. to the Authors' League Fund and send it to Luise Sillcox. This is a donation. The remaining $400.00 can be left to my credit.

I haven't time to write to John Wharton to catch this boat,

Great Enton, the Sherwoods' house in England, was the scene of annual "Drama Festivals." Here, Bob portrays Shakespeare; Madeline is the Dark Lady of the Sonnets prodding him to get busy and write another play.
(*Collection of Mrs. Robert E. Sherwood*)

but I enclose herewith some stuff which I think should also go into the report to stockholders if he has not already sent it out. Please get this to John.

We had some big meetings here last week with Sam Behrman and Guthrie McClintic, the latter giving a reading aloud of Max's play. I think most of it is absolutely superb, but there are some elements the introduction of which I can not understand. Guthrie is also very enthusiastic about it—but from the way he read it, I'm glad he's not going to act it.

They were considering Rex Harrison as a replacement for Olivier [in *No Time for Comedy*], but I was vehement in the opinion that if they could get Maurice Evans they should certainly do so. I suggested laying off for July and August and reopening September with Evans. That would be like a new opening night and the play would have a wonderful new impetus. I think that Kit is certain to play it all season in New York and on tour and it will do tremendous business.

As for *Abe* this summer, I believe it will fold quickly after Massey's departure, but I still think it's right for us to make the effort to keep it open and the actors working. Be sure that Ray's contract is straightened out—I mean, the provisions for the future.

I am terrified at the possibility that Sid Howard might get Jack Barrymore. I cabled Sid to that effect, and suggested Basil Sydney or Leslie Banks as possibilities. The former had been suggested by Guthrie, and I think Sydney is a far better actor than he's given credit for. I also think Banks would be an absolutely safe bet.

I have written Elmer saying that in my opinion *The Siege of Berlin* is hopeless and that he'd be wasting his time trying to do anything with it. This was a mighty disagreeable task.

This country is wild with enthusiasm over the reception of the King and Queen, and tonight the picture theatres are running the films taken in New York the day before yesterday. They were flown over by the *Yankee Clipper*. Many English people have been stuffed with so much falsehood about the attitude of the U.S. that they feared Their Majesties were going to get the bird from the American pubic and are all the more startled by the cheers. I could hear the cheers on our cook's radio (we don't own one).

Best to Bill and Miss Mitchell and all at the office. Feeling fine.

Bob

RICE TO WHARTON

June 13, 1939

Dear John:

I have just received your letter of the 3rd, and am dashing this off, in order to catch tomorrow's sailing of the *Queen Mary*. What you have to say about the play confirms my suspicions of how you all felt about it. I do wish, though, that everybody had followed Sidney's excellent formula and written me a frank opinion. Apart from you, I haven't had a line from anyone. But that's relatively unimportant, at the moment. What is important, as far as the organization is concerned, is that I have definitely decided to abandon the play. . . . So I'll try to get busy on something else. I have an idea that interests me, but I am not far enough along with it yet, to be able to see it all clearly. But I expect to keep at it, and maybe by the time I get back, it will have begun to take shape. In any case, it certainly won't be ready for an early production. . . .

Naturally, I am very anxious to be as helpful as I can, in getting things started for next season, and you can tell Sidney that he can count upon me, from the moment I get back, for any

Do you remember? The first transatlantic commercial flights were in a Pan American hydroplane. Flights to the west began at Marseilles and ended at Port Washington, Long Island. Flying time was thirty-one and a half hours.
(*Pan-American Airways*)

assistance I can give him (though I am sure he is fully capable of handling his production himself).

I have read Max's play, but have not written to him yet, because I want to read it again and think about it some more, before attempting to comment on it. My first impression was a very mixed one. I had great enthusiasm for a lot of it, particularly the first half, but it didn't seem to me to carry through. Why, I don't yet know, and as I say, I must reread it and ponder over it.

I feel very let down after the Grecian trip, which was exceedingly strenuous, but one of the unforgettable high-spots of a long career of travel. That's why I haven't been able to settle down to serious work yet. We'll probably leave Paris for Cabourg or some other Normandy resort, about the 25th, and there I hope to be able to work.

It's too bad that business isn't holding up better. I never expected *No Time for Comedy* to be good for more than ten weeks or so, but I did hope that *Lincoln* would hold its pace right through the summer. I do think that unless the punishment is too great, we should try to keep it running, even after Massey leaves. I should think that with the saving on his salary, we could break on about $7,000. and even if we went under that, we could afford to take losses for a few weeks, for the sake of prestige. But I may be all wrong about it. Everybody writes me enthusiastically about the Fair, so it's easy to see why nobody is going to the theatre.

I'll be seeing you, I hope, in about six weeks—or will you be away? If you feel it is imperative for me to be back sooner, don't hesitate to say so. Best regards.

Yours,
Elmer

All of which was only a part of less than three weeks in the life of the Company. Obviously, we were all excited, and, except for Elmer's aborted effort, very happy.

As June rolled into July, our sense of happiness grew. We had no premonition that the Company was about to suffer the first of a series of blows which brought to my mind, again and again, the phrase "slings and arrows of outrageous fortune." In August Sidney Howard was killed in a terrible accident. Thus, our first season was the only one in which the Company had five actively working playwrights.

CHAPTER
V

Sidney Howard

The Man

"And the lonesome traveller derives a sort of comfort and society from the presence of vegetable life."

Howard died before he had finished one play for the Company, crushed to death by a tractor on his farm. He had cranked it from in front while it was still in gear. The unfinished play and the memorial award created in his name were both important to the Company's development.

My first contact with Howard came in 1925 through my representation of the young producing firm Brady & Wiman. (Brady was the son of Pop Brady.) They had retained him to dramatize a book and had paid him the usual nonreturnable advance of $500, equivalent to perhaps $3,000 today. After considerable work he wrote them that he couldn't see how to make a worthwhile play out of it, *and* he returned the advance. "That's like Howard," said Brady, "he's a fine fellow in every way."

Later, they produced his play *Lucky Sam McCarver*. It was not well received; some critics thought it confused. Howard had asked that the program include, under the title, the quotation at the head of this chapter, which led Alexander Woollcott to end his review as follows:

The acting, then, did not altogether clarify the dimly seen people in *Lucky Sam McCarver*. But it was all happily straightened out by the program. For, under the title, Mr. Howard inserted a somewhat sedulously cryptic quotation from an unacknowledged source—this year's seed catalogue, perhaps. The quotation read, "And the lonesome traveller derives a sort of comfort and society from the presence of vegetable life."

And that, as they say, is that.

But it wasn't *just* that. I am convinced that Howard had spells of secret depression in which he saw himself as the lonesome traveller, and he fled to his farm for surcease. Elmer Rice, who knew him far better than I did, was also convinced of this and carried the idea still further. Rice, despite his dislike of psychiatry, once told me that he thought Howard had a subconscious suicidal strain which had brought about his death.

If so, his outward behavior belied it. True, he had had an unhappy marriage to a star, Clare Eames, and an unhappier divorce proceeding. Sherwood told me something of this and added that Howard had written a dreadful play to justify himself; a fact which I remembered when one of our members did the same thing. But his second marriage, to Polly Damrosch, of the famous musical family, had turned out well; he obviously loved his wife and she adored him—too much so for the good of his final play. I remember his telling me a charming story about her insistence on visiting a nudist colony which admitted gawkers for a price. He was contemptuous of the idea, but felt he could not let her go alone among a lot of lascivious Peeping Toms. "And my God, John," he said, "I found I was practically the only man in the crowd, with the women staring at me as if I were some strange, unpleasant creature."

Next to Sherwood, we looked to Howard for leadership. He also had a keen eye for talent; he always made himself available to a young author seeking help. He predicted correctly that *Abe Lincoln in Illinois* would win the Pulitzer Prize. He declared, again correctly, that the selection of Victor Samrock as General Manager was "the best piece of casting this company will ever do." There are few people of whom I became fond so quickly.

In two letters written from Hollywood in February 1938, he had analyzed, in a manner superior even to Sherwood's, the problems which might—and did—come up.

February 16, 1938

Dear John:

I am still here and likely to stay for another fortnight. Where

formerly I was bootlegging Goldwyn time on Selznick I am now bootlegging Selznick time on Goldwyn. I shall be glad when I am down to doing one job again.

I have read through the draft of the agreement carefully and I am prepared to sign it as it stands. I am, however, holding up my signature while I query a point or so.

I query the idea of suggestion that the $25,000 budget need not include the out-of-town tryout. Obviously it could not do so. It does seem to me, however, that the agreement might do well to add a separate head to the effect that the policy of the corporation is to utilize the services of its directors in lieu of the out-of-town tryout and that the out-of-town tryout, when and if necessary, must be discussed and approved by the Board of Directors and should place the play in the special class of those which exceed the budget.

The paragraph at the top of Page 7 seems dangerous to me unless it is somehow qualified to the effect that it shall be the policy of the members to write plays which do not require unavailable stars or outside managements. There are only two or three stars unavailable to us who are of any real box office importance, but all of us are too prone to the habit of thinking of them first. I wish that the agreement could discourage us from plays for Cornell and encourage the habit of thinking of plays which the organization can handle without extreme measures.

There is a slight question of phraseology in Section 11. "Each of the playwrights agree to be available *to* New York" would please me better than "in New York City."

I believe that the date August 1st is a little early for those not immediately concerned with the first production. Theoretically we would know and have expressed ourselves on the first script of the season to be produced and the author of the first script would probably not require our critical services as a whole before the third week of rehearsal. Later, the last sentence of the same section seems to me a bit too easy. Even though I might be writing a play of my own at a time that a play of Sherwood's is

Sidney Howard, a born leader, with a curious quality of dominance that defies description. But it worked. David Selznick, notoriously tardy, was never late to a Howard appointment. Perhaps the fact that he was paying Howard $4,000 a week had something to do with it.

(*Cosmo-Sileo*)

in rehearsal, it is mere self-indulgence on my part to say that I cannot interrupt my work to say what I think about his.

I am sorry to hear from the Selznick office that you will not be here this week.

Affection.

Sidney

February 28, 1938

Dear John:

I just cannot make it East for a while yet. We all get strapped now and then and I am here to get myself out of a hole and if I do not concentrate on getting out I will never be able either to pay my way into our enterprise or to deliver a play for production next season. I could of course fly East for a day but the flying weather is bad at this end of the line and in addition to that—though it is dreary to plead health—I have been having a hell of a sinus session and really want to avoid the ordeal of two nights on a plane.

I wish that I could be on hand for the meeting because I see symptoms of the same have-your-cake-and-eat-it-too which wrecked the predecessor of this enterprise. I do not see how our plan can work if any of us feels really free to produce plays elsewhere except under very special circumstances and with the permission of the group as a whole. To illustrate, let me ask a question: suppose I am able to write only one play in a season and feel that it will be better acted by Helen Hayes, who might not be available to us, than by Ruth Gordon, who would be. I take my play to Gilbert Miller, who produces it with Miss Hayes and it is a great success. Am I then entitled to my cut on plays by the other four? Has our organization any chance of succeeding if the actors, managers and public are not trained to understand that they cannot see our plays except under our management?

O'Neill has a contract with the Theatre Guild in which he agrees to submit, and they agree to produce, any play he writes. For good and sufficient consideration O'Neill must have given up hope of casting Katharine Cornell. Our organization is agreeing to produce any play that we write and each of us has, furthermore, a share in the organization's profits on the plays by our colleagues. If the Guild or Gilbert Miller can still produce our plays, our organization can only look futile and ineffectual. I do not say that we may not ask and be granted an exception but I do feel that the organization should have at least a right to attempt to cast any play written by any one of its members to the satis-

faction of its author. I feel this so strongly that I do not believe
that the enterprise is worth going any further with unless it is a
condition which we are all willing to recognize. If we are successful, actors and outside managers will come to us. We cannot
be successful if we continue our normal habits of going to them.

Another angle to be considered is my position if I write two
plays in one season. One of them I give to our organization, the
other I give to the Guild for the Lunts. The first is a failure, the
second a pronounced success. What can I feel toward our
partners in our organization except guilt that I have gypped them
out of a very handsome profit? The answer will be: But the
Lunts made the profit for me. Well, my answer to that again is
that we have got to screw our courage up to developing people
for ourselves and to doing without Lunts and Cornells until the
Lunts and Cornells are willing to appear under our management.
After all, there are only a very few stars who are not available to
us.

Again, I am sorry and ashamed to be begging off from this
crucial meeting and should not be doing so if I were not even
flatter than usual. I, too, am working on a one-set comedy. It will
be a happy relief to let Sherwood spend a little of the money
Elmer and I are saving. I shall be more sunk than I know how to
say if this scheme does run aground again.

Affection.

Sidney

We held an informal meeting immediately after receiving the news
of Sidney's death. I have seldom seen a group of men so shaken.
Behrman was unashamedly weeping; the rest of us would gladly have
released our own emotions the same way. We made plans for attend-
ing the funeral and broke up.

The funeral was in the country and was a true old-fashioned New
England affair. We were asked to be pallbearers, and it proved to be
more than an honor in name only. We carried a heavy casket up a
long hill to a grave in a beautiful spot. After the burial we went to the
Howard house, where, again in New England tradition, food and
drinks for a party had been prepared. It suddenly turned into a very
pleasant gathering. Polly said to me, "The only thing wrong is that I
can't believe Sidney isn't here enjoying it."

Madam, Will You Walk

We then turned our attention to the production of the play to which
he had given the above cryptic title. The problems drew the Com-

pany together more closely than ever. Everyone pitched in and tried to do whatever he could.

Sherwood volunteered to put aside his own work and do the necessary work on the script. Everyone was delighted, including Mrs. Howard. But soon—we learned about widows from her. Despite the fact that Sidney himself had declared that the play needed one more solid complete rewrite, she objected to every change Sherwood suggested. Obviously the objections sprang from her adoration and admiration of Sidney; we felt that they wouldn't last. We were wrong.

The next problem was the selection of a director. Margaret Webster was then enjoying a successful career in America; we offered her the job and she accepted. We met with her to discuss the play; the meeting evoked in me dark forebodings. It seemed to me that neither the playwrights nor Miss Webster were clear on what the play was driving at, yet they were unconcernedly and unhesitatingly going ahead. I began to realize that even the best of playwrights could rely too easily and too heavily on a director's current reputation, and vice versa.

The biggest problem was to find an actor for the leading role of Brightlee. Brightlee was obviously meant to be a supernatural character, but just what he was meant to represent was by no means clear. It *was* clear that the role needed a star, but we were all puzzled as to what kind of star.

I then made a brilliant suggestion which unfortunately turned out to be a disaster. George M. Cohan was approached and, because of his faith in Sherwood, accepted. Shortly thereafter my forebodings grew darker. Mr. Cohan confided to me that he thought it was "one hell of a difficult role for a flag-waving song-and-dance man to attempt"; it was clear that he, too, had no idea of what the character was meant to represent.

A final unpleasant straw in the wind appeared at the dress rehearsal. Brightlee was meant to have a startling, dramatic entrance; he was supposed to be invisible as he entered the room (chairs and tables moved about) and then suddenly to become visible, in some striking way, to the frightened occupants of the room. But all that happened was that Cohan calmly walked out from behind a high-backed chair.

Present at the rehearsal was an old vaudevillian of the days when stage tricks were at their height. At the end he bore down on us and pointed an accusing finger at the four playwrights. "Sherwood, Rice, Anderson, Behrman," he said solemnly, "You call yourself distinguished playwrights! And you can't think of a better entrance than walking out from behind a chair!" And he stamped out of the theatre.

George M. Cohan, Anderson, Sherwood, and Rice backstage before the debacle of *Madam, Will You Walk*.
(*Theatre Collection, New York Public Library*)

Secretly, I agreed with him. Why couldn't one of us have thought of something as creative as the enchanting scene in *The Wizard of Oz* where the dismembered scarecrow is put together again? But I said nothing.

Our dark forebodings proved not to have been dark enough. The play which had confused playwrights, director, star, and cast obviously confused the audience still more. That was expected. But then Mr. Cohan delivered the final insult to Sidney's memory. At the end of the play he pulled an American flag from his pocket, waved it in the air, and *danced* off the stage as the curtain went down. The flag-waving song-and-dance man finally had his say; *no one* liked it. Much to everybody's relief, he withdrew from the play.

But such was the Company's devotion to Howard, we did not give up. We continued to work together to find another star, confident that Mrs. Howard would finally give Sherwood a freer hand, which might indeed have been the case. We interested Sir Cedric Hardwicke, who gave the play deep consideration. But finally a meeting with Sir Cedric and Mrs. Howard was arranged, and it became plain that there was still too much confusion. The decision was made to drop the play for all time.

However, it did not stay dropped—a tribute to Howard's ingenuity and dialogue even in an unfinished state. Years later Hume Cronyn obtained permission to revise the play for himself and his wife, Jessica Tandy. Cronyn chopped out a lot of superfluous verbiage and rearranged scenes as he saw fit. The play then opened the Phoenix Theatre and launched that organization on its illustrious career.

The Sidney Howard Memorial Award

Elmer Rice was the man who suggested that we should do honor to Sidney's memory by establishing an annual award. Everyone readily agreed to the idea, but there was no instant agreement on what it should be given for. The subject was discussed at a number of meetings; finally, it was decided that it should be given each year to some young playwright whose first play had been a smash hit on Broadway. The amount of the award was fixed at $1,500.

An announcement to the press was drafted and all the members began fussing over the wording; moreover, there were arguments as to whether the Company members should make the selection or some outside committee. The delay proved to be a good thing, for something began to dawn on us that should have been apparent from the start; it was a rare year indeed that a new playwright had a smash hit with his first play. True, there had been dramatists who had won the Pulitzer Prize on their first productions, but we wanted to give the award *every* year. The terms were thereupon amended to read as follows:

> The award, to be made on or about April 1 of each year, is designed to encourage the development of new playwriting talent. Eligible authors will be those who, without previous substantial success as playwrights, have one or more plays produced in New York during the current season. Authors of plays

produced after March 15 will be eligible for the following season's award.

Directors of the Playwrights' Company will compose the award committee. They reserve the right, however, to consult other qualified judges, or—under unusual circumstances—to appoint a committee to select the author whose work is deemed most meritorious.

The prize money will be contributed to the Author's League Fund in any season in which no new talent seems to merit the award.

(These rules were never followed strictly.)

It was a new toy and very exciting to all of us. The 1939–40 season fortunately presented us with a made-to-order selection; a young friend of Sidney's named Robert Ardrey won his first acclaim with *Thunder Rock*. He was given the award, and he wrote the directors the following charming letter of thanks.

April 15, 1940

Gentlemen:

This letter of thanks is going to be too damn long. I ought to dust off something quick and understated, but you see, I can't.

It's easy enough, in a way, to express my gratitude to you. You're alive, you're working, you're feeling things, and you undoubtedly know how I feel. Had any of you, when you were younger, received the vote of confidence which I have just received—well, dope it out for yourselves. You know how I feel. You know what I mean when I say, thanks.

What's hard to express is my gratitude to Sidney.

You see, Sidney and I were never what you could call close friends. We never had the chance to get that way. But through the few short years that were the end of his career, and the beginning of mine, his shadow kept falling across my way. I want you to know how it was.

It began with my first play, *Star Spangled*. That was how I met him. There was something about my play that reminded him of *They Knew What They Wanted*. I worshipped his play as one of the finest in the American theatre. And I guess *Star Spangled* made him think—not only of his own play—but of writing it, and how things were with him in those early days. He got attached to my writing.

I remember having lunch with him a couple of days after *Star Spangled* opened. I was suffering under the load of my first set of

Robert Ardrey.

bad notices—I'm more accustomed to them now, but you know how you feel with the first batch. Sidney said: "I'm not the one to tell you not to mind. I know how it is. When you walk down the street in a crowd, you feel like you ought to warn them away from you, and holler, "Unclean! Unclean!" But after a few years you'll find out about notices. They always blame you for something you never did; and then you have a success, you'll find they praised you for something you never said. It comes out even." He was thinking, I believe, about *Yellow Jack* and *Dodsworth*. Well, it was my first play, and his great *They Knew What They Wanted* that brought us together. And he was the first to console me. And encourage me to go on.

Later on, in 1937, when I hit bottom financially and there was a question whether I could go on writing any longer, it was Sidney that suggested I get a Guggenheim fellowship, and it was Sidney that went to the director of the foundation and talked me up. On the year of grace that the Fellowship provided me, I got *Casey Jones* produced, and *How to Get Tough About It* written and produced.

When those two failed, practically simultaneously, it was

Sidney who again came to the rescue. I was up against the usual financial crisis. My Fellowship was just about finished. I'd been living hand to mouth for a good many years, I wanted to get married—you know the formula. Sidney was working at Goldwyn's. Some of my friends were urging Goldwyn to hire me. He was rightfully doubtful. They said, "Ask Sidney."

The result of his asking Sidney being that I got married, thank God, lived two years off the Goldwyn loot, wrote *Death of an Indian* (on the shelf), and *Thunder Rock*.

Last summer, up in Connecticut, I was living about fifty miles from Sidney's place. I was working on the last act of *Thunder Rock*. I read in the paper about Sidney. I quit writing for several days. I think it's the only time I ever had to quit writing. I did a couple of short stories finally for my own distraction and at last got back to work.

And now the end of the story, of Sidney and myself. For the past month I have been out here doing the screenplay of *They Knew What They Wanted*. Saturday, when you wired me, I was up in the northern part of the state, in the Napa Valley, wandering around among Sidney's people. I found your wire when I returned.

I wanted you to know how it was, how Sidney's shadow kept falling across my path. I wanted you to know how it was, how my gratitude must be directed less to you, and more to Sidney. And why it's so hard to say.

Sincerely,
Robert Ardrey

It is true that Ardrey was not encouraged enough by the award to devote all his time to writing plays. He was lured to California by film offers and, after a successful career there, distinguished himself as an ethologist. Two of his books, *African Genesis* and *The Territorial Imperative*, were and still are widely read. But he never wrote another successful play.

Despite the modified terms, we found it wasn't easy to agree on a play each year. We skipped 1940–41 and 1941–42 and in the 1942–43 season the $1,500 was given, in lieu of the award, to an Off-Broadway production sponsored by Erwin Piscator entitled *Winter Soldiers*, by Dan James.

In the 1943–44 season the war still overshadowed everything and the award was not given. In the 1944–45 season interest revived. The choice was the simplest yet; Tennessee Williams burst on the scene with *The Glass Menagerie*. 1945–46 also presented little difficulty;

Luther Adler and Frances Farmer in *Thunder Rock*. She was another outstandingly beautiful actress whose life had a tragic ending. Her book, *Will There Really Be a Morning?*, is a truly harrowing story. (*Vandamm*)

Garson Kanin wrote *Born Yesterday* and Arthur Laurents wrote *Home of the Brave*. The award was divided between them.

The 1946–47 season brought real trouble. There was nothing quite so startling as *The Glass Menagerie;* such plays as might qualify needed a close look. And then it became abundantly clear that something vital had been completely overlooked when the award was established; the playwrights were not interested in going to see plays by budding authors—indeed, one or two had begun to lose interest in going to the theatre at all. I saw trouble coming; I was right.

But I brushed it aside and concentrated on the award. There was one play, written by a friend and client, which I thought deserved it and I tried vainly to get the others to go to it. As I recall it, one or maybe two did so and were not very much impressed, although they gave tentative votes for it, pending Sherwood's opinion. Sherwood wouldn't go, but he offered to read it if I could get a script. With some difficulty I got one; he read it and reported that he was in some doubt but on the whole couldn't see any bright future for the author. He voted no, and no playwright ever received a Sidney Howard Memorial Award from that time on.

The rejected play was entitled *All My Sons;* the author was Arthur Miller.

Sherwood once admitted to me that when he picked up a paper with a review of an important play, he could not, to his shame, repress a subconscious desire to find the review unfavorable. Perhaps some such psychological fact explains the resistence to *All My Sons,* which embarrassed us further by winning the New York Drama Critics' Circle Award. In any event, there was no further interest in trying to pick individual promising playwrights.

But Sidney Howard matters did not die easy deaths. In 1950 a group of young authors, including Robert Anderson, who was later to become a Company member, asked the Dramatists Guild to support a plan to encourage and help young playwrights. The matter was referred to a committee headed by that extraordinary quadruple-threat actor-author-director-producer Howard Lindsay, whom we all knew and admired. Lindsay and his close friend and co-worker Russel Crouse favored the idea, but $3,000 was needed to launch it, and neither they nor the Dramatists Guild was prepared to give such

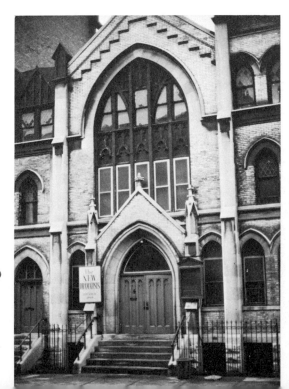

The house that Sid built.
(*Collection of*
The New Dramatists Committee)

a sum. The Dramatists Guild, at that period, could be quite eloquent about the need to help new authors, but when any project required money, it quickly pleaded poverty and asked producers to supply the cash needed. Lindsay hit on the notion of applying to the Company, which was both author and producer.

Samrock and I were looking for a way to get the Sidney Howard Memorial Award out of our hair. We jumped at the idea of using it to support this plan. The others readily agreed, and The New Dramatists Committee was born. It has outlasted not only Lindsay and Crouse, but also the Playwrights Company. Today it has a roster of amazing talent who were helped at one time or another. They are listed on a plaque in a whole *building* which the Committee raised funds to buy. It seems as permanent as theatre itself.

I feel quite sure that no other author who left one unfinished play ever helped to launch two organizations comparable to the Phoenix Theatre and The New Dramatists Committee.

CHAPTER

VI

A Little Trouble Now
and Then

Long before I met Max Anderson he had acquired a reputation for being an indefatigable worker. Be passion dead, unborn, or hot, he wrote—and wrote, and wrote, some say every day of his life. Until he joined the Company he frequently attended only the first reading of his play in production; he then returned home and began work on another play.

He had a wonderfully inquisitive mind; he was always seeking new subjects for plays and new slants on old subjects. He was the most versatile of the five, both in choice of material and style of writing. *Saturday's Children* is a realistic study of the problems of youthful marriage, with what was then considered realistic dialogue. *High Tor* is largely fantasy, with some delightful blank verse. When he dramatized Alan Paton's book, *Cry the Beloved Country*, he adapted the dialogue to Paton's somewhat cryptic style. (When the play was revived in 1972, some youthful critics who had never read Paton's book, denigrated Anderson's writing because of the style.) He delighted in historical drama: *Mary of Scotland, Elizabeth the Queen, Anne of the Thousand Days, Joan of Lorraine, Valley Forge.* For some reason he found English historical characters better material than American; he admitted complete failure to bring George Washington to life in *Valley Forge.*

In 1952 I asked Hugh Beaumont, who was, at the time, the dominant producer of the English stage, why he never brought over

Mary of Scotland or *Elizabeth the Queen.* He replied that Anderson's concept of English character would be laughed off the boards in London. Twenty years later, Beaumont produced a play on Mary which, except for the performance of Eileen Atkins as Elizabeth, differed in concept only by making everything seem dull. This was followed by an English TV show and a film on the same subject; I had similar feelings about both, only more so. If some famous pair—perhaps Burton and Taylor, or Finney and Maggie Smith—were to put on *Elizabeth the Queen* in London, I would bet heavily on its success.

Max was a deeply serious thinker, but he also had a quiet, contagious sense of humor. At one meeting someone reported a rumor that the Lunts and Katharine Cornell were going to do a play together. Max had written for both Miss Cornell and the Lunts, and he knew their demands as stars. He first simply assumed an expression of complete disbelief, then said, with a chuckle, "Can we get the picture rights to the rehearsals?"

In 1939 he became interested in a profound subject—the origin and workings of honor, a subject which had fascinated the famous novelist Joseph Conrad all his life. Max decided to show what happened to a man who did a clearly dishonorable thing, then ran away and tried to redeem himself. He chose Spain during the Civil War and a gang-ridden spot on a key off the coast of Florida as the scenes. He interested Paul Muni, then at the top of his career, in playing the star role. Guthrie McClintic, also then in the top-flight category, agreed to direct it. The title, *Key Largo,* was enticing. As the letters in Chapter IV clearly show, we were all excited and as confident of success as any theatre professionals can ever be.

The play begins with a prologue laid in Spain. A Loyalist brigade has been ordered to make a stand that will surely annihilate them; the order has come at a time when the whole Loyalist cause has become hopeless. King McCloud (played by Muni) has been their leader; now he asks what sense there is in getting themselves killed for no purpose. The question, of course, raises a deeper question; what is it that will make a human being feel that he *must* act in a way that will almost surely destroy himself. Max gives his answer in one of the most moving speeches he ever wrote. A brigade private (played by José Ferrer) replies to King:

> Yes, but if I die
> Then I know men will never give in;
> Then I'll know there's something in the race
> Of men, because even I had it, that hates injustice

The prologue of *Key Largo*, a play about honor, and how a man may be able to retrieve it once he's lost it. James Gregory, Alfred Etcheverry, Charles Ellis, José Ferrer, and Paul Muni.
(*Vandamm*)

> More than it wants to live.—Because even I had it—
> and I'm no hero. . . .
>   If I went with you
> I'd never know whether the race was turning
> down again, to the dinosaurs—this way
> I keep my faith. In myself and what men are.
> And in what we may be.

What Max is implying here is the existence of an instinct to preserve and improve the *species*, an instinct so strong that at times it can override the desire for individual self-preservation. Oddly enough, many years later the same Robert Ardrey who received the first Howard Award, by then a leading ethologist, put forward the same thesis, using the animal world to illustrate it. In his now famous book. *African Genesis*, he describes the murderous raids in the dark by a leopard on a tribe of baboons. Then, one day, the leopard arrives early, in daylight. Two baboons fall on him from a tree branch and bite through his jugular vein while being clawed to death. The story has become a classic.

To go back to the play.

King McCloud is not convinced; he deserts. The play then picks him up in Florida where he is trying to square his desertion with his conscience. When the play got to Florida, however, a strange thing happened; it became a "little play." In Spain, King's honor represented a universal human problem, and the warring forces also were world forces. In Florida, King became an insignificant little man. All the characters became little people. (The fact that Max created two minor, unneeded parts for out-of-work friends was anything but helpful.) Despite some excellent writing and some tense scenes, the importance was gone.

Fortunately, audiences did not altogether see what had happened to *Key Largo*. The play ran for 106 performances in New York and 13 weeks on the road, a hit by the standards of those days. While it did

Paul Muni and Uta Hagen in *Key Largo*. Miss Hagen, an actress of superb technical skill, later became an acting teacher. Modern audiences remember her best as the vehement wife in Edward Albee's *Who's Afraid of Virginia Woolf?*
(*Vandamm*)

not entirely fulfill Max's intentions it remains one of the few plays that presents the question of honor in other than superficial romantic terms. In the world of the seventies, when so many people seem to be at a loss as to *why* they should do anything, *Key Largo* is worth some thoughtful study.

What disappointed me most was McClintic's direction. For a long time I had been puzzled by his fame in this field because of two things. First, he would not permit anyone but the author to be present at rehearsals; to me this indicated a lack of self-confidence. Second, Robert Ardrey told me that when McClintic produced and directed his play, *How to Get Tough About It*, he (Ardrey) was astounded by McClintic's inability to give any clear directions to the cast. The actors developed their own characterizations without help. When McClintic finally agreed to let all of us come to a rehearsal of *Key Largo*, I quickly saw what Ardrey meant. He gestured and mumbled without effect for much of the time. But there was still another nuance—they never end in the theatre—he *could* bring out the best in women stars. Katharine Cornell and Dame Judith Anderson have always extolled his direction. Unfortunately for Max, *Key Largo* is a man's play.

I recall one minor contretemps which illustrates McClintic's routine thinking. In the last act a very important speech is delivered by a blind man. McClintic took the position that blind people never used gestures and the actor was placed backstage on the side and droned out the words. The result was so bad that it was put at the top of the agenda for the next Company meeting, and here group pressure again proved its worth. McClintic gave in to the pressure of four playwrights; the scene was restaged and it worked.

But the play remained a near-miss.

For the 1939–40 season Elmer Rice had written a charming play about young people in New York, *Two on an Island*. It was a fair success, although it did not exactly shake up the Broadway theatre. But it did shake up Elmer's life. Halfway through rehearsals it became clear to the rest of us that Elmer was becoming very creative in staging scenes and inserting lines that would enhance the role of the leading actress. Samrock and Fields early divined that he had fallen madly in love. It ended with his obtaining a divorce from his wife Hazel and marrying the actress, Betty Field. All of us believed that Hazel, as well as Elmer and Betty, would be better off, but the divorce obviously gave Elmer a sense of guilt which he never entirely got rid of.

As I got to know Elmer better, I was amazed by the contradictions in his character. I came to be fonder of Elmer than any other of the five, except Bob, but he could do strange and disappointing things. He firmly believed himself a stalwart champion of the rights of the "little people," and most of the time he was just that. He would spend days auditioning unknown actors just to give them a chance. But when one of his plays was involved, he forgot about such chivalry. While *Two on an Island* was on its way to New York, a young producer was trying to make his way with another comedy about young people. It wasn't a very good comedy, but when Elmer heard about its theme, he called me in great agitation, asking me to change his opening date so as to be sure his play came in first. This put me in a rather embarrassing position, because my wife was a silent partner in the other play. Fortunately for me, the young producer set his opening date well after Elmer's so there was no trouble at home. But I do not recommend such conflicts of interest as means of making a marriage richer and fuller.

The most important event of our 1939–40 season—our production of another Sherwood play with the Lunts—began with a minor mystery. It took shape at the Company meeting held December 7, 1939. Sherwood announced that he was working on a revision of his play *Acropolis*; we later learned that he was telling others the same thing. Still later we learned that it just simply wasn't true; why he went about saying it has never been clear to me.

Acropolis was the only Sherwood play given a presentation in England and not in America. I had read it and was fascinated by its possibilities. The characters of Pericles, Aphasia, and Phidias were brimful of interest; so much so that the theme got lost in three different points of view presented by three different but intensely interesting people. I seized every opportunity to discuss the play with Bob, which must have bored him immensely, and which made me feel like a fool when the truth came out that he had no intention of revising it. I suspect this had something to do with my initial reaction to the play he *was* writing, *There Shall Be No Night*, originally titled *Revelation*.

I also became subconsciously annoyed on another plane. He had talked about getting the Lunts for *Acropolis*. I felt sure that this would stir up trouble in two ways. The Theatre Guild insisted that

Betty Field when Elmer fell in love with her. She was an indefatigable worker, insisting that her agent constantly find her jobs somewhere: Broadway, Hollywood, summer stock, winter stock. And she became more and more skillful right up to her untimely death. (*Voss*)

the Lunts had agreed to do a road tour in its production of *The Taming of the Shrew;* a real brouhaha was brewing. Moreover, we had a contract to play only Shubert theatres, in return for which we were given exceedingly favorable terms. But the Lunts had become enchanted with the Alvin Theatre, a non-Shubert house, and would demand that the play be booked there. I knew Mr. Shubert would insist they play a Shubert house in a Company production and go to law about it if they refused. Therefore, I had an instantaneous, short-lived joy when Bob stopped at my home, told me he had written an entirely new play, and gave me his very first draft to read. Short-lived joy it was; he added that it had two parts that *only* the Lunts could play. I was most unhappy.

As I sat down to read it, I suddenly began to wonder why on earth he had concocted the *Acropolis* story. I couldn't figure it out then and I can't today. But the deception, plus my worries about what a

The Lunts, the greatest husband and wife acting team of the mid-twentieth century. Mr. Lunt was also a great director. Mrs. Lunt, Lynn Fontanne, is a modern example of a woman of whom it can truly be said that age does not wither her, nor custom stale her infinite variety. (*Theatre Collection, New York Public Library*)

play with the Lunts might bring about, did not incline me to a favorable view of the play. As I read, I kept going back to the puzzle of why he had told us the false story of *Acropolis*.

The story of *There Shall Be No Night* revolves around a Finnish physician, Dr. Volkonnen, who finds himself impelled to enlist in the hopeless war against the Russian invasion and is killed in action. John Mason Brown, Sherwood's authorized biographer, seems to think the false *Acropolis* story had to do with some tremendous soul-searching on the part of Sherwood; that he was finding it necessary to abandon his totally pacifist position and admit that there were times when a country must fight. The second volume of the biography (brought out after Brown's death) is titled *The Ordeal of a Playwright*. He may well have been suffering a personal ordeal, but this does not explain his need to keep it a secret. He *was* troubled by the question of whether the United States should plunge into war with Germany at this time, but so were the rest of us. He could have found no more sympathetic companions with whom to discuss the matter. Moreover, the theme of *There Shall Be No Night*, in my opinion, goes far beyond the questions of peace and war, although this did not become clear to me until after he wrote *The Rugged Path*.

In any event, subconscious and conscious thoughts aside, I did not like the draft Bob had given me. It was not my first mistake of that kind, nor will it be my last if I keep on reading manuscripts. I can say in self-defense that this draft had a pretty confused first act; there was a lot of irrelevant talk about Pavlov's dogs which disappeared even before the first rehearsal. One thing did impress me enormously: the final curtain where the heroine was showing how she had learned to load a gun. This was eliminated as a curtain scene, although it was retained in the play. No, I can't say much for my artistic advice where *There Shall Be No Night* is concerned. (Of course, every producer with any partners has had similar experiences. Lawrence Langner once offered to retain me if I thought I could legally stop his partner Teresa Helburn from having the Theatre Guild produce a musical—*Oklahoma!*)

Group thinking scored another victory. The other members were immensely excited by the draft and urged Bob to proceed. He did so, and the result received an enthusiastic response from the Lunts. Production went forward at a breakneck speed; tryout performances in Providence began shortly after the first draft was submitted to the Lunts; the play opened in New York on April 29. It ran in New York for 181 performances and gave Sherwood his third Pulitzer Prize.

My record on the business side of *There Shall Be No Night* was a

First reading of *There Shall Be No Night*. A first reading of a play is a mysterious thing. A gloomy theatre, stacked scenery, everyone in street clothes; but by the end you can often accurately rate the play's chances of success, and, usually, you can also tell where the weak spots are. (*Vandamm*)

little better. The brouhaha with the Theatre Guild had developed, and Mr. Shubert had duly entered the conversation, as I expected he would. We settled with the Theatre Guild by making them co-producers without power, which also solved the Shubert problem, since our contract clearly did not cover co-productions. Because our contract with the Shuberts was enormously favorable to a hit show, our settlement with the Theatre Guild cost the Company a very pretty penny. But I was relieved and felt myself lucky to have learned so cheaply a lesson: even the top playwright of the day will give in to the demands of a star he wants to get, whatever the financial cost.

Owing to illness, I attended neither rehearsals nor the Providence or Boston tryouts. As soon as I was well enough to travel I went to Baltimore. Kurt Weill accompanied me; by this time we had become great friends. He was later to become a Company member; at the time we had not thought of electing a composer. Kurt was a kindly, thoughtful man, distinguishable by boyish charm and a round, boyish face; he was quite short; we called him our mascot. He was not only a brilliant composer but also an extremely knowledgeable man of the theatre, a fact which was not generally recognized. It is odd that of the members of the Company, a musician was the only one to have a successful posthumous career; *The Threepenny Opera* ran for six seasons, years after his death.

On the way to Baltimore, Kurt enthusiastically described Sherwood's new final curtain. It did not sound exciting: an old man playing the piano while Miss Fontanne silently shifted her gaze from one empty chair to another. But I knew enough about Sherwood's sense of theatricality and also the skill of the Lunts—together or separately—to wait and see, which was wise, for it proved one of the most moving curtains ever seen. Sherwood was singularly able to gauge the reaction of audiences to off-beat scenes; in *The Rugged Path* he put in a scene where everyone is ordered to abandon a ship. It was full of technical orders given over a loudspeaker, which were meaningless to 90 percent of the audience. Yet the scene held the audience beautifully. I asked Bob if he had expected the scene to be *that* successful; he answered simply, yes.

After the performance of *There Shall Be No Night* in Baltimore, I went backstage with Bob and congratulated the Lunts on their performances, also assuring them that the play as a whole had all the earmarks of a sure hit. Sherwood told me later that the Lunts were greatly pleased and *relieved* to learn that I thought so highly of both play and performances. I was really startled. The Lunts and I barely knew each other; I could hardly believe that my opinion could mean much to them; I was greatly puffed up that such was the case. In retrospect, I greatly doubt that such *was* the case. I suspect they really cared no more about my opinion than they would have cared about the stage doorman's; they were, to put it simply, polite and politic people. It has also occurred to me that Sherwood may have embellished their reaction to my praise; he had an unfailing instinct as to how to cheer up a convalescent.

Eventually, I came to know Alfred Lunt quite well; he did come to care about my opinion; at least he listened intently. The fact that I extolled the Lunts' abilities everywhere undoubtedly helped the relationship. Most of us fall for flattery; *sincere* eulogy will cause even the iciest heart to thaw a little. And my praise of the Lunts was sincere.

All successful actors and actresses have one or more of certain qualities: technical skill (they know how to move, how to gesture, how to shout and whisper), good looks, personality that creates an immediate empathy with the audience. (Howard Lindsay was wont to say that the last was all that counted; if audiences cared about the actor, nothing else mattered.) The Lunts had *all* of those qualities *and something more.* Playing together they could, by some mysterious

Lynn Fontanne, Montgomery Clift, and Alfred Lunt in *There Shall Be No Night*.
(*Vandamm*)

magic, bring a scene to life in a way that no one ever quite understood. Lynn Fontanne suggested the ending to Scene III of *There Shall Be No Night*, which involves the fact that the coffee Mrs. Volkonnen has made has cooled off. Sherwood agreed at once because he knew that the Lunts would somehow make a discussion of coffee the climax of a moving reconciliation of husband and wife. It did.

The career of *There Shall Be No Night* had some curious aspects. It was attacked in this country as being undisguised warmongering. This did not worry any of us very much. But then the day came when the United States and Russia became allies against Hitler; obviously, further production of a play about a Russian invasion of Finland was impossible. However, Bob contrived in some way to revise the play into a story of Italians attacking Greeks. I never saw nor read this version; it sounds terrible. All the characters are distinctly Nordic. But I believe such a version was played in London during the war.

Some version was played in London and had a most unpleasant kickback through a coincidence that no one would accept if used in fiction. One day my partner, who supervised Sherwood's tax work asked me why Bob excluded English royalties from his income tax returns. It seems that Mrs. Sherwood had been advised by someone that these need not be reported and she had so informed my partner. He stood in great awe of the Sherwoods and had accepted her statement without further investigation; it was, unfortunately, 100 percent incorrect. But the way the omission had come to light was the fascinating part.

An Internal Revenue agent who was a most devoted admirer of Bob had been assigned to audit Sherwood's returns; he pored over every detail. Suddenly he expressed astonishment that no royalties from the English production of *There Shall Be No Night* were included. How did he know about any such production? He had been a member of the American army in England and had seen the play there, having obtained leave expressly for the purpose. That an American soldier should have seen the play and then become a revenue agent and then have Sherwood's returns assigned to him was unlikely enough. But to have him such an admirer that he recognized the omission, with the result that his admiration would cost Bob a substantial sum of taxes, all seemed just a little bit too ironic to be true. Unfortunately, it *was* true.

One cannot help wondering what the impact of this play would be if revived today. The Soviet Union would surely not be pleased; would anyone in America care about the Soviet reaction? I think not. But I fear that the superficial reaction of a reader today would be that it was *only* war-mongering. Indeed, in 1972, a young couple with a theatre background expressed to me the opinion that it was "chauvinistic jingoism." I was startled; then I realized that neither of them had been born when this play was written; they had no conception of what the United States was like in 1940, and consequently could not understand its impact. I am sure older people would feel differently. But, in any event, I don't see how it could be successfully done without the Lunts.

CHAPTER
VII

Mixing Pleasure with Business

Because of our outside stockholders, we were meticulous in complying with legal formalities. We also kept careful financial records. For the latter we retained the leading theatrical accounting firm of Pinto, Winokur & Pagano, a firm name which amused a great many people when they first heard it. John van Druten, who always tried to put a curious word in his titles (*The Voice of the Turtle, The Distaff Side*) declared this firm had gone him two better; they had three curious names. It does roll off the tongue in a curious way; the only theatrical firm name to equal it, to my mind, is Briggle-Willig, Inc.

We always held annual meetings to which all stockholders were invited; none ever came. We had a duly elected president and other officers, but the president had no more power than anyone else. At first we simply rotated the office each year. Sam Behrman became president without knowing it; during his first term we paid back some of our capital, which required sending out some technical notices full of legalistic jargon. At a party two outside stockholders asked him the meaning of one of these notices. Sam derided the documents, disclaiming any understanding, and was bewildered when shown that they were signed in his name. (I had probably told him about it without forcing him to read the papers.)

Soon after incorporation we set up a schedule of *weekly* directors' meetings. These turned out to be extremely important, not because of any legal necessity, but because they welded the group together in a way that made the Company greater than the sum of the individuals who were parts of it. True, we took up all business matters at such meetings, but we also discussed any and all subjects which anyone cared to put forward, ranging from rather profound discussions of war and peace to the latest gossip of the day.

In the beginning the meetings were held either in my office or at the home of Sherwood or Rice, who both lived in the city. Sherwood had a beautiful apartment, neat as a pin, in a swank building on the East River. I believe it had a small garden leading to a private dock. Mrs. Sherwood enjoyed sitting and reading there, which, for some reason, amused Behrman greatly. (It *was* an incongruity that she studied shorthand there.) Rice's apartment was on the West Side and was absolutely cluttered with paintings, which, on close inspection, turned out to be early abstract art from the brush of far-famed artists. He had recognized, at an early date, the genius of Kandinsky, Klee, Modigliani, Leger, Miró. On his death in 1967, his collection brought $400,000, probably fifty times what it had cost him.

Later, we located permanent offices at 630 Fifth Avenue, with space for the press department, private offices for Samrock and for our general secretary, Lucy Mitchell, and one largish room for meet-

A typical meeting.
(*The Newspaper PM*)

ings, single auditions, and general use. Gradually, we all acquired the habit of dropping in there when in the neighborhood. It became sort of a clubroom as well as a corporate office. Also, Sherwood did a great deal of work there on his book *Roosevelt and Hopkins*, which won him a fourth Pulitzer Prize.

The major subjects of discussion were, of course, the plays. Group discussion meant that all jealousy had to be eliminated, and this came to pass quickly and effectively. Every playwright clearly and honestly wanted—wanted desperately—to see his colleagues' plays succeed. We were all really depressed when one failed.

We invariably met on the morning following a play's New York opening. Bill Fields, our press representative, would get early editions of the afternoon papers and we would pass both morning and afternoon reviews around. If the play was a hit, the whole meeting was fairly short and very gay. The important gatherings were the ones on the day following a failure.

On the morning after a flop, an individual playwright is in much the position of a political candidate who suffers an unexpected crushing defeat at the polls; for weeks he has been working at high speed with all sorts of supporters; each day has been too short even to permit him to answer all the phone calls. Suddenly, there are no excited co-workers; the phone doesn't ring. He sits alone wondering what went wrong, what is he to do in the future.

A playwright, after a bad opening, no matter how brave a front he puts up, is outraged by the reviews, sick at heart, and unduly depressed. I had always made a *particular* point of calling any client—author or producer—on the day after a disaster. I never succeeded in cheering anyone up one iota, but they appreciated my trying to do so. Hence, I urged "morning-after-flop" meetings of the company, and they did help.

Discussions of plays before production are quite different from postopening congratulations or commiserations. As I have already said, most authors are extremely touchy about any criticism of a new script. It was a standard joke among producers that if you asked a playwright to cut out some long and boring speech, he would invariably reply that the whole play had been written for that one speech. A director of the Theatre Guild once told me that Max presented a special problem; if you succeeded in convincing him that a scene was too long because of extraneous matter, he would eliminate the irrelevancies, but also insert new matter that made the scene longer than before.

Although the members of the Company did not try to tell each other that some one speech was all-important and although they did listen to, and carefully consider, suggestions, they still were not easily persuaded to make any drastic changes. This did not surprise me; what did surprise me was their belief that they *could* persuade each other. Rice was particularly naive. He once reported to me that, at a meeting from which I was absent, they had explained to Max why a certain scene was wrong and he, Elmer, had even marked the speeches to be cut, yet Max wouldn't take any action.

The meetings that really tried men's souls and tempers were those where a member had submitted a play which everyone else felt not to be worthy of production. Elmer was the first to have this experience with *The Siege of Berlin*. To this day I shall never understand what Elmer saw in the story or in his dramatization. It was an anecdote about a senile Frenchman at the time of the Franco-Prussian war. He was confined to his house; he thought the reports of the Germans' siege of Paris were reports of a siege of Berlin by the French army. There was no drama that anyone could see; merely a lot of sound and fury signifying nothing but unmitigated boredom.

Elmer was a pre-World War I playwright who dashed things off at top speed, and they frequently showed it to an embarrassing degree; if, for example, he wanted to get a character off the stage, he would use the most incredibly crude devices; a man might take out a cigar and then say he had to go out to get a box of matches when there were characters on stage smoking cigarettes and obviously equipped with plenty of matches. Elmer would, however, cheerfully agree to correct such scenes, but his revisions could be almost as embarrassing as the discarded device.

Of his rejected plays the one that sticks in my mind most clearly was one written after his divorce from his first wife and his marriage to Betty Field. He sent scripts around at a time when I was unusually busy and so I was delayed in reading mine. I usually read every script immediately; I knew authors (of any kind) yearned for quick reports. Max called me on the telephone, asked if I had read it, and when I said I was just about to do so, begged me to call him as soon as I finished it, as he was bewildered. Naturally surprised, I inquired what the play was about. "That's just it," replied Max, "*it isn't about anything*." I think this remains the most damning comment on a script that I have ever heard.

Max was wrong on that point. The play was a symbolic defense of Elmer's action in divorcing Hazel and marrying Betty. But Max was right in thinking it a very, very, very bad play. The meeting to discuss it can only be termed "awful." No one wanted to bring up Elmer's marital affairs, but if you didn't bring that up, Max was right; the play wasn't about anything, and the attempt of first-rate minds to

carry on a meaningful discussion about something they found meaningless would have been ludicrous—indeed, it *was* ludicrous. I suspect
everyone rushed to a bar as soon as the meeting was over. I know
I did.

Happily, such meetings in the early days were rare. Most meetings
were fascinating and great fun. There were no hierarchical distinc-
tions. Technically, Samrock and Fields, both of whom attended all
meetings, were employees and not directors, but no one ever thought
it made any real difference. They were both—perhaps Samrock more
than Fields—members of the group.

The merriest member of the group was unquestionably Sam Behrman. He was a perpetual fountain of wit, comment, and anecdote.
His agent at the time was Harold Freedman, who was without doubt
the top playwrights' agent of the day; he and his wife, Mae, were also
Sam's close friends. Freedman was famous for being close-mouthed,
which was admirable; however, it led him into lowering his voice until
he was frequently almost inaudible. Behrman came into a meeting one
day fairly bubbling with news of Harold. He declared that Harold
had invited him to his home, taken him into the living room, drawn all
the blinds, and taken Sam to the middle of the room. He began to
speak, but suddenly, said Behrman, he rushed over and locked the
door. Returning, he whispered, "Mae is going to have a baby."

Not long thereafter, Sam brought *me* up short. I was in bad shape
over a number of problems irrelevant here; one effect was that I had
begun to restrain inner anger by talking in unemotional tones that
were fainter than I realized. At one meeting Sam cupped his ear
behind his hand and said, "You know, John is a *quiet* Harold
Freedman."

Behrman cared little for any group discussion of business. He loved
his colleagues as social friends, but he really did not want to produce
his own plays and eventually said so. The business end bored him. I
recall a meeting where Sidney Howard proposed that we should
produce our plays during the coming season at a $2 top instead of the
$3 top which was the custom in those simpler, noninflationary days.
Samrock and I were aghast; we tried to point out that most of our
plays could barely pay their weekly running costs at such a scale.
(Eventually, we proved it.) But Sidney had supporters in Max and
Elmer, and even Bob was inclined to go along. The debate became
heated. Suddenly Sam, who had been silent, broke in to say that he
had another appointment and must go. As he left, he handed Samrock
a slip of paper. When the meeting broke up, Victor asked me to wait
a minute and showed me the paper. On it was written, "Fuck Two
Dollar Top."

Victor Samrock.
(*Friedman-Abeles*)

They were as devoted to the Company as were the playwrights themselves.

William Fields.
(*Theatre Collection,
New York Public Library*)

During our second season we had long and arduous discussions about our relations with the Shuberts, and the possibility of our buying a theatre. I sent out a menorandum on the subject and quickly received a reply from Sam.

May 7, 1940

My Dear John,

I have just been reading with absorbing interest your memorandum on the theatre situation. May I point out that there are some inaccuracies in this memorandum? You convey that the impression I gave at the last meeting that you are unalterably opposed to the purchase of an interest in a theatre is a misleading one. The memorandum itself, if read with persistence, will show that the difference between your being unalterably opposed to a proposition and being just opposed to it is infinitesimal. However, my objection to your memorandum is more serious than this.

You say that there seems to be a general agreement among the four playwrights that they would prefer not to continue with the Shuberts. As far as I am concerned—this is a mis-statement. When have I objected to dealing with the Shuberts? I am very happy with them. My relations with the Shuberts are unmarred by any unpleasantness. I find them universally courteous and capable. Next to Rozencrantz and Guildenstern there is no one that I would rather deal with than the Shuberts. They are charming.

I can well understand the difficulties your clients encounter when they deal with other theatre owners than the Shuberts. I must tell you, as man to man, that I actually *enjoy* doing business with the Shuberts.

I can pass over the next paragraphs of your memorandum as they make it very clear except possibly to Mr. Sherwood and Mr. Anderson why it is undesirable to own a theatre. Bob's interest in the Lyceum is, I think, platonic and won't last. It need cause us no permanent concern but Max's interest in the Adelphi is positively morbid and may make it necessary for us to send him on a holiday. Of course, Elmer's favoring both the Belasco and the Hudson is only a manifestation of his general promiscuity.

In summary I agree with you entirely that before any decision is to be made about the purchase of a theatre, we should first find

Sam Behrman, "a fellow of infinite jest, of most excellent fancy."
(*Graphic House*)

one. Should you care to discuss any of these points with me, I will be glad to meet you in my private office at 630 Fifth Avenue.

S.N.B.

At one point Sam's good nature gave the Company a much needed lift. It was the fall of the year 1943. We were all depressed by the war; our depression began to extend to other things. Max was in a bad mood; he took it out frequently by berating Roosevelt's monetary policies, which I supported; Elmer was unhappy over lack of substantial success. We missed Bob, who was almost continually in Washington as an $8,000-a-year consultant. Moreover he was not his usual cheerful self, having had a large sum of money embezzled by a dishonest financial advisor.

Interest in meetings had dropped. We needed an antidote of pure tomfoolery. Sam supplied it. In an attempt to spur interest, I suggested that the rest of us organize a campaign to defeat Behrman's reelection as president.

Behrman was overjoyed to hear of his opposition. He informed us that he would present an oral and a written campaign statement at the next meeting. The following is an excerpt from the minutes of the meeting:

> Mr. Wharton stated that the first business to come before the meeting was the election of officers for the coming year.
>
> Mr. Behrman thereupon stated that he wished to make both an oral and a written statement in regard to his candidacy. He stated orally that an irate stockholder, Mrs. Robert E. Sherwood, had written him a critical letter, which he read to the meeting amidst great applause. He further stated that he had answered this letter and demolished Mrs. Sherwood's arguments, but it was noticed that although he quoted some of his more pungent phrases, he did not ask that either Mrs. Sherwood's letter or his reply letter be placed on the minutes. He did, however, hand to the directors a written statement which was ordered spread upon the minutes and reads as follows:

October 14, 1943

> Members of the Playwrights Company
> Gentlemen:
>   I am aware that there is a powerful movement on foot in the Company not to re-elect me. If I followed my own desires, I should have retired to my acres in Connecticut (acquired through a life-long adherence to the principles of sound money). It is a hard office. Its guerdon is bitter and unreasonable criti-

cism. Only the other day, I received a letter from an irate stockholder, protesting that she could not understand my annual financial statement. She said this as though that inability was a reflection not on her, but on me!

As I say, gentlemen, I would willingly retire if I saw a possible successor; but I do not, and therefore I am forced to write this letter. It will be frank, even brutal. I shall name names. I shall neither coddle, nor flatter you. I see no other way.

Were it not that I am appealing for the suffrages of a quartet of economic illiterates, I should not have to conduct this campaign. I should simply say: "Gentlemen: Please consult the figures. Look at the net worth when I assumed office, and look at it now!" That would be all I would have to say. But I am only too painfully aware that the principles of sound money, on which I have conducted the affairs of the Company, are alien to your normal habits of thought. I am therefore forced to a pitiless analysis of each of you, who may be my potential sucessor.

Mr. Robert Emmet Sherwood

Mr. Sherwood, whose literary gifts are as brilliant as his economic sense is tenuous, earns $8,000. a year! Moreover, he does this voluntarily!! His wife, a brilliant and witty woman, who deserves the best, is now living in reduced circumstances near the docks and trying painfully to acquire the rudiments of shorthand. I solemnly prophesy, gentlemen, that if you elect Mr. Sherwood to the Presidency, you will all, a year hence, be studying shorthand. And let me warn you, gentlemen: you are no longer in the first flush of youth! I am informed that, after a certain age, shorthand is not easy to come by. Mr. Sherwood, through the exercise of his literary gifts, has in the past acquired considerable means, which he dissipated through his blind reliance on an unworthy reputation. When I inquired of him one day, in horror, how he had allowed such a man to go on, year after year, without a check-up, he answered at once—not, indeed, like a flash, but in his own good time: "I tell you, Mr. President, he was so boring that I avoided him." Will you put your affairs during these critical times in the hands of a man who puts excitement above solvency? I can scarcely believe it! Which do you prefer—a solid income with me, or shorthand with Mr. Sherwood?

Mr. Elmer Rice

Mr. Rice once lost a small fortune (because he had no larger!) on the ownership of the Belasco Theatre. With a passion for sending good money after bad, which often animates such visionary characters, he at one time insisted that we also buy theatres. Your memories are short, gentlemen; doubtless, you do not remember this perilous time in the history of the Company, when it was swept by a wave of maniacal theatre buying. I well remember a meeting during which Mr. Rice held forth on this subject. I well remember Mr. Maxwell Anderson (of whom more later) sitting there, carried away by Mr. Rice's eloquence. If you will recall, gentlemen, I—alone, and unaided—stemmed this dangerous tide. Had it been allowed to go on unchecked, we would now be completely owned, body and soul, by several theatres (may I remind you, also, that I saved the country-at-large several years ago, when it was swept by a craze for populism?). Fiscally speaking, Mr. Rice is the kind of man who does not appear to know the difference between recouping after a loss, or increasing it. Strange to reflect that a man may write STREET SCENE and have no notion whatever of elementary arithmetic!

MR. MAXWELL ANDERSON

Mr. Anderson has been known to state in public that he did not believe in authors having any money. Mr. Anderson has often put this belief into practice. Sometimes, through the exercise of his literary faculty, which he cannot control, he comes into considerable quantities of sound money. But this always startles and embarrasses him. Were it not for the recurrent seizures to which he is subject, of his other gift, I dislike to think where Mr. Anderson would be. Again, gentlemen, let me prophesy: elect Mr. Anderson to the Presidency, and you will all be very likely, within one year, to be living in a lean-to on Walden Pond. There are very severe Winters there, gentlemen!

MR. JOHN F. WHARTON

I do not know a more charming, or agreeable companion than Mr. Wharton. He is widely read, cultured, and charming to be with. Nevertheless, in all my conversations with him, I have never gotten from him the faintest intimation that he could either add or subtract. Moreover, he has a penchant for outmoded economic nostrums. Once, sitting with him in a drawing room on a train, his expression assumed that dreamy, faraway look which his friends know, and he said to me: "Mr. President, do you know, I think the most underestimated character in American history was William Jennings Bryan. He is due for a revaluation. We have not yet heard, I assure you, Mr. President, the last of 16 to 1." Now, gentlemen, I ask you flatly, do you want to give yourselves over to Bryanism? Do you want to get your next dividends (so-called) in debased silver currency? Elect Mr. Wharton!

Gentlemen, I have been forced to speak bluntly, but I assure you it is not from personal ambition. I have been a hard taskmaster. I understand your impatience, your desire for a new face, but I implore you: don't get the new face on the currency —don't pay our stockholders with fiat money minted in New City! If you must replace me, gentlemen, let Pinto, Winokur & Pagano replace me. Yes, gentlemen, let us be governed by a triumvirate. At least they do not expect an integer to be a metaphor, nor a decimal point a dot on the "i" of inefficiency!

Respectfully yours,
S. N. (sound money) Behrman

After discussion of the aforesaid statement, Mr. Wharton moved the re-election of Mr. Behrman by acclamation. Mr. Anderson stated that he thoroughly disapproved Mr. Behrman's fiscal policy but on the basis of his literary ability he would second the motion. Mr. Rice gave up any effort to resist, and the election was carried.

Every member had a fund of anecdotes. One of Elmer's is still a classic on the subject of governmental buck-passing. When working for the Federal Theatre he proposed a course of action which would require a slightly unusual amount of money. His superior stated that Elmer could only get this approved by seeing the Treasurer of the United States, a gentleman, incidentally, with the odd name of A. A. Adee. Mr. Adee was in Washington; Elmer was in New York; Elmer appealed to his own superior's superior. He got the same answer; he must see Mr. Adee. After being told the same thing by still others, he gave in and said, "Very well, I'll go to Washington. How do I arrange to see Mr. Adee?" The reply was startling: "Mr. Adee never sees *anybody!*"

Almost invariably there was some item of current interest to lend a lighter touch to the business meetings.

In the fall of 1940 we scheduled a meeting for two o'clock. Some of us went to lunch at a popular restaurant nearby. We were astonished to see Sherwood obviously hosting a luncheon for Clare Boothe Luce—a successful dramatist but a conservative among conservative Republicans in her social viewpoint. She was a woman with supreme self-confidence; she believed she could get anything she wanted. (After her divorce from her first husband she confided to a friend that any attractive woman could marry a man who was old, rich, and powerful; *sh*e intended to find and marry someone young, rich, and powerful.) We shuddered at the thought that Bob might be persuaded to propose her for membership in the Company. When we assembled, the first order of business was to question Bob about the purpose of the luncheon.

Bob laughed. "You won't believe this," he said. "She spent the

The child actress Joyce Fair who grew up to be Clare Boothe Luce, writer, dramatist, Ambassador to Italy. I still remember a line in her play *The Women*. A cook and a housemaid are discussing the master's futile attempt to make his wife understand his feelings toward her and "the other woman." Says the cook, "The first man who can think up a good explanation how he can be in love with his wife *and* another woman is going to win that prize they're always giving out in Europe."
(*White*)
(*International News Photo*)

whole luncheon trying to persuade me [typical long Sherwood pause] to come out for Wendell Willkie against FDR." We all howled and sighed sighs of relief.

Bob also, at a later date, told us a story about the producer Max Gordon which I have never forgotten. Gordon, one of the most successful commercial producers of the times, was a theatre man to his fingertips. What endeared him—and still does—to everyone in the theatre was his unrestrained joy about every good thing, and his passionate rage over any bad thing, that affected the theatre. It was hard for him to understand even-temperedness; he once told Ilka Chase that he guessed I was all right but I seemed to be "the cold, Yankee type."

Gordon was never cold. In 1939 he became almost a legendary figure by reason of his boiling reaction to the failure of his musical *Very Warm for May*. It was the last score Jerome Kern ever wrote; Gordon loved Kern and the show. But the critics were unkind; they wrote reviews calculated to keep people away, and people stayed away. For months—no, years—Gordon would seize any opportunity to tell anyone how unfair the critics were; he may have been tiresome, but Broadway loved him for it.

He took one fling at film producing, which is how Bob became close to him. By a roundabout deal he became the producer of the film version of *Abe Lincoln in Illinois*. Sherwood developed a great personal fondness for him; no one could resist the infectiousness of the Gordon passion for the theatre. When the film was finished, Sherwood arranged for President Roosevelt to request a showing at the White House. "We stood in line waiting for FDR to enter," Bob reported, "I was next to Max and his wife and I heard her say, 'Now, dear, *please* don't try to tell the president what the critics did to *Very Warm for May*.' Max did restrain himself, but I think I detected a visible effort on his part to do so."

Of all the incidents at meetings, the one that still stands out most vividly is the remembrance of Sherwood suddenly letting his hair down to an astonishing extent. There was some desultory talk about people's fantasies; Bob suddenly volunteered to tell a fantasy that came to him again and again. "It's the last half of the ninth inning. We are three runs behind. The bases are full, but there are two men out. Sherwood comes to bat, and what does he do? [Pause, while we all wondered.] He hits a home run!"

Bob left the office shortly after finishing this story. We all looked at each other quizzically. Finally, Sam Behrman said something to the effect that *he* couldn't have told such a thing about himself. I never heard anyone mention the incident again.

Max and Millie Gordon in Washington for the premiere of the film of *Abe*. Definitely *not* the cold Yankee type.
(*Theatre Collection, New York Public Library*)

CHAPTER

VIII

Somewhat More Than
a Little Trouble

Sidney Howard's death was the first great blow to the Company. It reduced the number of working playwrights from five to four. Sherwood's absorption into the war against Hitler was the second blow. It reduced the number to three. However, Bob's interest in the Company never flagged; he made himself available to the fullest possible extent. But his continual calls to Washington hurt the internal workings of the group.

His extracurricular work during the 1940–41 season did add enormously to our external prestige. Today, when every American schoolchild is taught the truth about Hitler's massacres and general brutality, it is hard to remember that our own country, before Pearl Harbor, was sharply divided in its attitude toward the Nazis. An organization calling itself America First, backed by wealthy pillars of the then current Establishment, opposed any kind of military preparedness and was quite ready to do business with Hitler. The most dynamic opposition to America Firsters was the Committee to Defend America by Aiding the Allies. Sherwood was one of the leaders of this group.

He became nationally known through a newspaper advertisement which he wrote, headed "Stop Hitler Now." This was published in over one thousand newspapers throughout the country. The Company supported him in this to the best of its ability; we helped to raise money; Sam Behrman worked all one night helping Bob revise the

STOP HITLER NOW!

WE AMERICANS have naturally wished to keep out of this war —to take no steps which might lead us in. But—

We now know that every step the French and British fall back brings war and world revolution closer to US—our country, our institutions, our homes, our hopes for peace.

Hitler is striking with all the terrible force at his command. His is a desperate gamble, and the stakes are nothing less than domination of the whole human race.

If Hitler wins in Europe—if the strength of the British and French armies and navies is forever broken—the United States will find itself alone in a barbaric world—a world ruled by Nazis, with "spheres of influence" assigned to their totalitarian allies. However different the dictatorships may be, racially, they all agree on one primary objective: *"Democracy must be wiped from the face of the earth."*

The world will be placed on a permanent war footing. Our country will have to pile armaments upon armaments to maintain even the illusion of security. We shall have no other business, no other aim in life, but primitive self-defense. We shall exist only under martial law—or the law of the jungle. Our economic structure will have to be adjusted to that of our gangster competitors. We shall have to change ourselves from easy-going individuals into a "dynamic race."

"Government of the people, by the people, for the people"—if Hitler wins, this will be the discarded ideal of a decayed civilization.

Is this "Alarmism"? Then so is the challenging scream of an air-raid siren, warning civilians that death is coming from the skies. We have ample cause for deepest alarm. It should impel us, not to hysteria, but to resolute action.

It is obvious that there is no immediate danger of direct invasion of the United States. Hitler doesn't strike directly when he doesn't have to. He edges up on his major victims, approaching through the territory of small and defenseless neighbors.

We have twenty-one neighbors in this hemisphere, in addition to the colonial possessions of Britain, France, Holland and Denmark. We must not forget that however wide the Atlantic and Pacific oceans may be, the Canadian and Mexican borders are no barriers to invasion.

The Monroe Doctrine is not an automatic safety catch, securing the entrance to our hemisphere from all intruders. We have to enforce it—all the way from Greenland and Alaska to Cape Horn. Furthermore, we have to guard night and day against the manifold enemies from within. We can not ignore the fact that Trojan horses are grazing in all the fertile fields of North and South America. The Western Hemisphere contains the richest territory for exploitation on earth today. And the international gangsters want it. They have already started the process of taking it. For many years the agents of the Nazis have been effectively at work in

THE FIFTH COLUMN

is led in this as in other countries by Nazis and Communists and their fellow travellers who are well trained in the dissemination of poisonous propaganda. Their object is to destroy national unity, to keep the United States in a state of confusion over all world issues so that we will be weak and helpless when our time comes. All Americans should beware the prevailing Nazi-Communist propaganda which attempts to capitalize our desire for peace by opposing all our moves toward national defense—sabotaging all aid to the Allies—preaching that Hitler has already won and we must meekly appease him.

Latin America, gaining ground by persuasion, bribery, intimidation. They have been fighting a trade war and a political war; and what we have lately seen in Norway and Holland and Belgium proves to us that these agents are ready to fight a military war when the orders come through from home.

"Divide—and conquer!" has been the Nazi watchword in the insidious invasion of all countries. The preliminary work of division has been carried out here with devastating success.

We can and should and will devote ourselves to a vast program of defense. But we must not try to fool ourselves into thinking that security can be bought. It will be achieved only by unity of purpose among ourselves, by the spirit of sacrifice that we can summon from our own hearts and minds. Overwhelming destiny will not be stopped "with the help of God and a few Marines".

This is a job for *all* of us! It will take years for us to build the necessary machines and to train the men who will run them. Will the Nazis considerately wait until we are ready to fight them?

Anyone who argues that they will wait is either an imbecile or a traitor.

How long shall we wait before making it known to Hitler and the masters of all the slave states that we are vitally concerned in the outcome of this war—that we would consider a victory for them an unmitigated calamity for civilization?

Whatever our feelings about the tragic mistakes of statesmanship in England and France we know now that the free people of those nations are willing to fight with inspiring heroism to defend their freedom. We know now that such men will die rather than surrender. But the stoutest hearts can not survive forever in the face of superior numbers and infinitely superior weapons.

There is nothing shameful in our desire to stay out of war, to save our youth from the dive bombers and the flame throwing tanks in the unutterable hell of modern warfare.

But is there not an evidence of suicidal insanity in our failure to help those who now stand between us and the creators of this hell?

WE CAN HELP—IF WE WILL ACT NOW

—before it is forever too late.

We can help by sending planes, guns, munitions, food. We can help to end the fear that American boys will fight and die in another Flanders, closer to home.

The members of our government are your servants. In an emergency as serious as this, they require the expression of your will. They must know that the American people are not afraid to cast off the hypocritical mask of neutrality, which deceives no one, including ourselves.

Send a postcard, a letter, or a telegram, at once—to the President of the United States, to your Senators and your Congressmen—urging that the *real* defense of our country must begin NOW—with aid to the Allies!

The United States of America is still the most powerful nation on earth—and the United States of America is YOU!

COMMITTEE TO DEFEND AMERICA BY AIDING THE ALLIES

(Composed of representative Americans from all sections. Sub-committees are already in existence in eighty-five cities and towns.)

National Chairman—WILLIAM ALLEN WHITE, Editor, *The Emporia (Kansas) Gazette*

NEW YORK OFFICE: 8 WEST 40TH STREET

THIS ADVERTISEMENT, appearing in newspapers from coast to coast, has been paid for with funds contributed by a number of patriotic American citizens who believe in all seriousness and sincerity that the safety of our country, the whole future of our national faith, is gravely threatened by the world revolution of Hitlerism. The names and addresses of all those who contributed to the publication of this advertisement are being filed with the State Department, Washington, D. C.

IN A DICTATORSHIP, THE GOVERNMENT TELLS THE PEOPLE WHAT TO DO. BUT—THIS IS A DEMOCRACY— WE CAN TELL THE GOVERNMENT WHAT TO DO. EXERCISE YOUR RIGHT AS A FREE CITIZEN. TELL YOUR PRESIDENT—YOUR SENATORS—YOUR CONGRESSMEN—THAT YOU WANT THEM TO HELP THE ALLIES TO STOP HITLER NOW!

I first saw a draft of this about five o'clock on a June afternoon. So great was its impact that I put a copy in my pocket and set out to raise the money to run it in the *New York Times*. By seven o'clock, I had almost reached my goal.

final copy. Of course, both the "Stop Hitler Now" campaign and the presentation of *There Shall Be No Night* drew plenty of fire from fanatics on the other side. But theatre people were pretty solidly on Bob's side and gave him ungrudging admiration.

The Company, naturally, came in for a bit of reflected glory, which proved to be a very good thing for us. It was the first of two things which tended to cover up the fact that the Company had its first really bad season, financially and artistically.

The second thing was the fact that almost all of the leading dramatists had their troubles in the 1940–41 season. Seventeen of the most expert theatrical craftsmen—such as Philip Barry, Ferenc Molnar, Rodgers and Hart—unveiled productions which were disasters. Anderson's *Journey to Jerusalem* and Behrman's *The Talley Method* were hardly noticed in the general debacle. Rice's *Flight to the West* was not a disaster; on the contrary, it was a minor success. But some of our members thoroughly disliked it.

Sherwood was most unhappy about the first draft of Elmer's play. One result of this was an incident which gave me my greatest moment of feeling important to the Company. This draft showed the usual signs of haste that so often appeared in Elmer's plays; there *were* inconsistencies and some unbelievably trite clichés. We discussed the draft at a meeting which I had to leave before it was over. When I reached home there was a call from Samrock begging me to come back at once.

Sam Behrman described to me what had happened. Sherwood could on occasion burst out with a vehement criticism of something he didn't like. Such outbursts were rare; I only remember hearing one—years later, at the tryout of *The Fourposter*. It seems that Bob suddenly unleashed such barbs at Elmer's script, to such an extent that Elmer made a quick, angry exit from the room. Sherwood, said Sam, was then horror-stricken at what he had done and, turning to Victor, said despairingly, "Send for Wharton."

I remember returning to the meeting, flattered to discover Bob thought I was the only person who could fix things up, but bewildered by my inability to think what to do. To this day I cannot recall what, *if anything*, I actually did do. Quite possibly, Elmer took Bob's criticisms to heart—Elmer was the kind of man who could do just that—found them valuable, and dismissed the whole incident. Subsequent drafts were improvements.

I asked Bob what his objections were, and received a reply which raised a point to which I had never really given full consideration. Sherwood declared that the trouble with the script came down to one

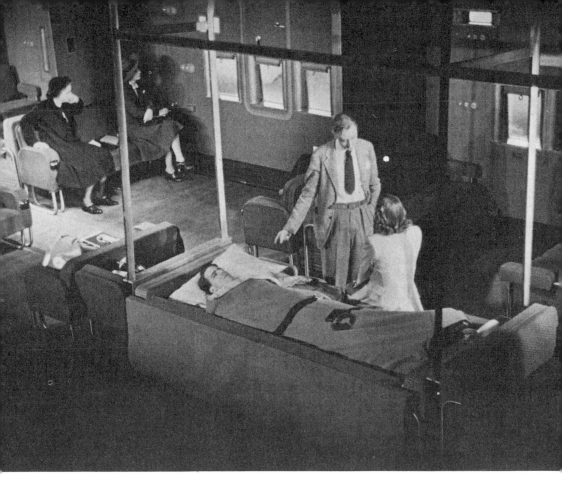

Scene from *Flight to the West*. Jo Mielziner's superb representation of the inside of a clipper. (See page 64 for exterior.)
(*Graphic House*)

thing: the "quality" of the writing—or, rather, the lack of quality. This is another mystery of playwriting, and, in fact, of all writing.

Quality in writing is as difficult to define as "importance." I am inclined to think it is completely impossible to teach. As Maggie Wylie said about charm, "If you have it, nothing else matters; if you haven't got it, it doesn't much matter what you do have." It is hard to explain the presence or absence of charm; the same thing is true of the quality of writing.

Howard Lindsay once gave me a tangential slant on the problem. He was always ready and willing to read scripts by fledgling authors and this often resulted in a puzzling situation. "If I express doubts about the play," he said, "they ask me if their plot structure is wrong, are the characterizations false, is the dialogue untrue, are the climaxes in the wrong place, and such-like things. The problem is that all those things are often in apple-pie order. The trouble is just that *the play isn't any damn good!*" I think he was saying that these scripts lacked "quality."

Journey to Jerusalem lasted only two weeks, but in an odd way it helped to solidify Company relations. At that time a statute forbade presentation on stage of "The Deity" and no one was clear whether this phrase applied to the boy Jesus, who was the central figure in the play. The matter was discussed at several meetings; Max finally decided that his own name, backed by the Company's prestige, would carry him through; there was a feeling of standing together. I thought of those meetings in 1971 when I attended *Godspell* and *Jesus Christ Superstar* (the above-mentioned law had been repealed). Such productions would have left Broadway aghast in 1940.

The big disaster for us, which I felt (correctly) boded no good for either the present or future was Behrman's new play, *The Talley Method*. This plot revolved around a Dr. Talley, a highly intellectual-

Threesome in *Journey to Jerusalem:* Arlene Francis as the Virgin Mary, Horace Braham as Joseph, and Sidney Lumet as Jesus. Lumet, then sixteen, had an ethereal quality on stage. Miss Francis was, and is, one of the radio and TV "greats," as well as a stage actress. She was anything but ethereal. When Sherwood heard of Rice's choice, he remarked to me, "Well, *that's* 'casting against type' if anyone should ask you."
(*Fred Fehl*)

ized man of about fifty who tries to run everybody's life on what were then called "scientific principles." (At one time the play was called *The Mechanical Heart*.) Despite his nonprogressive attitude, he has enough likeability to win the love of a beautiful but wholly emotional younger woman. His two children object to his trying to run their lives and solicit the lady's help. A charming, witty foreigner appears and throws everything into such confusion that eventually the lady decides to wait, the children go their own way, and the doctor is forced to admit flaws in his "method."

The underlying theme, to my way of thinking, was an attack on, or at least a questioning of, the then current adulation of science. It was couched in comedic terms, a difficult job for such a theme. We had great trouble in casting it, and in finding a proper director. We tried to get Katharine Cornell, who had been so successful in *No Time for Comedy*, but she (wisely) said no; it was not a suitable role for her. Finally, we persuaded Ina Claire to play one more Behrman heroine, and then made a ten-strike in getting a brilliant actor, John Halliday, for the role of the doctor.

We discussed half a dozen directors at length, but suddenly Sam pitched on to the idea of Herman Shumlin. Shumlin had had a spectacularly successful ten years as both a producer and a director. Most of his successes were dramas; but he had directed Behrman's *Wine of Choice* in 1938; however, I was suspicious when I learned that it had run only five weeks. He was to go on, after 1940, to even greater dramatic successes, but everything worked against him in *The Talley Method*. He was, and still is, an intense personality; he had outbursts which made Sherwood's seem like calm and collected reasoning; the problems of this play must have evoked many such explosions.

Miss Claire was toying with the idea of retiring; she did not play again for five years, and in only two more plays. She always had trouble in learning her lines and this trouble was accentuated by the constant rewriting of this particular script. It was difficult to discuss anything with her, because she could talk faster and longer than any man; it was hard to get a word in edgewise. She was the antithesis of what Shumlin sought in a star.

Halliday was something else again; everyone was delighted with his work. Then a blow fell. On Christmas Day, 1940, I received a call that Halliday had been stricken with pneumonia. I hastened to a meeting, as did every other member—Christmas notwithstanding—a further demonstration of Company solidarity—and by taking immediate steps to pursue every possibility we secured the immensely popular Philip Merivale for the role. It seemed too good to be true,

Ina Claire, Herman Shumlin, and John Halliday during a rehearsal of *The Talley Method*, prior to Halliday's illness. Shumlin was, most of the time, authoritative but soft-spoken. However, he could explode, often suddenly, with a diatribe worthy to be linked with the Philippics of Demosthenes.
(*Vandamm*)

but somehow it didn't work. All sorts of friction developed. Behrman became increasingly unhappy.

Shumlin, I suspect, was most interested in trying to bring out the serious values of the play. Sam was interested in the comedy. I recall one incident when Victor Samrock tried to discuss a certain scene with Behrman. "They don't laugh as much as they did before I rewrote it," was Sam's only comment. In any event, by the time the play reached Cleveland, Sam and Herman were at such odds that Sam phoned New York pleading for help.

Elmer volunteered. He took the night train to Cleveland and went to Behrman's hotel room the next morning. It took him only three minutes to sense that the situation had become impossible. As he described it later, Sam was sitting crouched disconsolately in a corner, while Herman, a cigar in his mouth, was striding up and down reiterating fiercely, "The trouble is that there isn't enough love in the world." Certainly, there was not enough in that hotel room at the moment (although I am sure Elmer's version was exaggerated), and somehow it was worked out that Shumlin should retire and Rice take over.

But it was too late to save the play. Everything Sam wanted was tried. The title was changed to *The Mechanical Heart* and then changed back again. The production moved into the Henry Miller Theatre in New York, began dress rehearsals, and Sam decided he needed another week out of town; we postponed the New York opening and trudged to Philadelphia, all to no avail. The play had its official opening in February. It was apparent that it was not a hit. A depressed Behrman took off immediately for Hollywood. Later, in the spring, I received a typical cheery letter from him:

April 22, 1941

Dear John:

I have been meaning to write to you for some time but I have been getting to the studio at eight-thirty in the morning and sometimes leaving at the same hour in the evening. Your first letter, about the award [the Sidney Howard Award], I answered to Victor by telegram the next day. [Irwin] Shaw seemed to me

Ina Claire and Philip Merivale in *The Talley Method*. Both Miss Claire and Mr. Merivale were loaded with charm, but somehow they could not bring Sam's play to life—one of the strange, inexplicable facts of theatre life that dramatists have to face. (*Vandamm*)

a justifiable recipient but I see that the others did not agree. Your second letter I am answering now. You see, I am a methodical man!

I appreciate and take in your words about the sad career of *The Talley Method*. I am sure there is much truth in what you say. The experience was unsavory; I am putting it behind me.

I thought that by this time I should be on my way back to New York. But I came out here to work on an "original" for Garbo; and I think you know what that means. As there is no basis for the story it can be constantly torn down by everybody. I wrote ninety pages and then Cukor didn't like it. I began all over again on my own, with a line of my own. Cukor now likes it and I am about half way through. Miss G. would not give an extension and they are now paying her whatever she gets weekly. On the one hand they put great pressure; on the other they chat through numberless conferences as if the picture were going to be done in the next generation. I doubt very much whether I shall get back before the fifteenth of June at the earliest. More likely the first of July.

I miss you and the "company" very much. How is Bob feeling? I read the attacks on him in the *Times* by the Pinchots et al. Have you done any more work on your book? How is Max's play? I wish I could get a copy. By the way, Elizabeth Bergner is very anxious (desperate in fact) to get a play for next season. Would that interest any member of the company? And, what would be most agreeable of all, is there a chance of your coming out here in the next months? Shall I look for somebody for you to represent? I see lots of vague characters around here and I get strongly the feeling that they would have more definition in their characters if you represented them.

Please give my best to Max and Elmer and to Vic and Bill. The news is horrible. It's not easy to sit here spinning these improbable yarns while the facts of life are what they are. Miss G. gets better and better. I'll save them [*sic*] for you.

> Ever yours,
>
> Sam

I had an ominous feeling that his attitude toward the Company was going downhill again.

The general Company mood in the spring of 1941 was optimistic. *There Shall Be No Night* was still playing successfully on the road. Anderson reported that he had a new play in mind; Rice had been asked by Producer Jed Harris to dramatize a book, *Tucker's People*, and Harris seemed agreeable to a co-production. We hoped Sam would soon finish his Hollywood stint. We paid a dividend; motion picture financing was offered for a new Rice play; it was rejected. But the wellsprings of our optimism began very shortly to show signs of drying up.

It became clearer and clearer that Sherwood was not likely soon to begin work on a new play. Behrman showed no sign of dramatic creation, either. Jed Harris, as usual, began to be difficult.

So many stones have been thrown at Jed Harris that I do not wish to pick up another. Rather, I wish to say I found him to have one quality which I believe to be universal. A simple incident revealed this.

Lawrence Langner of the Theatre Guild asked me to lunch with Jed and some fourth person whom I cannot remember; Langner wanted to interest Jed in a revival of *The Country Wife*. After Harris had insulted each of the three of us in turn, I decided to see whether praise of one of his *unsuccessful* projects would soften him. I told him, quite honestly, that I thought his dismal flop, *Spread Eagle*, was actually a brilliant production; what had happened to the authors? Would he be doing another play by them? It worked. After delivering a eulogy of the play and himself, he was polite to me for the rest of the meal.

But we weren't able to work out anything on *Tucker's People*. Negotiations dragged on until the author of the book sold the film rights. This ended the possibility of a stage production; the financial risk became too great.

Hence, we suddenly discovered that we had nothing in sight for the foreseeable future. We didn't realize it then, but the truth was that the Company was in a precarious situation and would have to struggle to stay alive. Max Anderson came to the rescue. He wrote the only play we produced during the 1941–42 season, brought us our first play by a nonmember, and wrote an outstanding success in the 1942–43 season.

CHAPTER

IX

Anderson to the Rescue

Max supplied our only presentation in the 1941–42 season, and that was a co-production with the Theatre Guild. It was a play about the war in Europe, titled *Candle in the Wind*. Helen Hayes accepted the star role. The play's conception of the Nazis was such that Max must have looked back on it with embarrassment, but Miss Hayes was at her radiant best; audiences loved her, cared about the character she portrayed, and—happily for the business side—went to see her in droves. She carried *Candle in the Wind* through to a moderate success.

I had been enchanted, years before, by her performance as the dream daughter in *Dear Brutus* and had avidly followed her career, but I never worked with her until *Candle*. I quickly saw why producers and directors considered her to be the dream star. She was never late to rehearsals, always knew lines (even newly rewritten ones), never fussed, never upset other members of the cast. And—I repeat—she sold tickets.

She had a mind of her own, however, and did not hesitate to use it, although she was unfailingly charming and polite; no temper tantrums. In 1943 she agreed to play the star role in *Harriet*, which Gilbert Miller was producing and directing. Miller had had enormous success staging American productions of foreign plays, but directing an established foreign success is something quite different from taking on the direction of a brand new American play. Miss Hayes, so the

Maxwell Anderson, Alfred Lunt, and Helen Hayes studying a set design for *Candle in the Wind.*
(*Vandamm*)

story goes, was patient and silent for a week, then suddenly said, in her sweetest tones, "Now, now, Gilbert, this simply won't do. We have got to have *a director*." Miller meekly accepted her ukase; she selected Elia Kazan; his professional standing, already high, was further enhanced by her choice.

Alfred Lunt directed *Candle in the Wind*; it was during those days that I really got to know and appreciate him. I knew that he could direct Miss Fontanne and himself; I quickly saw that he was equally skillful with a completely strange cast. I recall only one troublesome item in the rehearsals of *Candle*. One part was given to an actor who, while he had personality, had no technical training, and this drove Lunt into a mild frenzy. He burst out to me one day, "John, that man doesn't even know how to lift his ass off one chair and put it down on another." But eventually Lunt got a performance out of him.

In the meantime, Max had arranged for the rest of us to meet, and read a new play by, an extraordinary playwright, Sidney Kingsley.

Helen Hayes in *Candle in the Wind*. She radiated that kind of charm which, "if you have it, you don't need to have anything else," but she had plenty of technical skill, too.
(*Vandamm*)

Extraordinary because his very first Broadway play, *Men in White*, had won the Pulitzer Prize, and he had followed this up with another, and even more popular, hit, *Dead End*. Both of these were "important plays"; I know of no other serious playwright who achieved such immediate success. (Even Arthur Miller had one total flop to begin with.) As I look back, I wonder why we did not invite Kingsley to become a member and fill the vacancy caused by Howard's death.

Perhaps Max *had* broached the subject to him, and had found him unenthusiastic. Certainly he struck most of us as unduly self-centered at the time. He would talk *endlessly* about the problems of working out his new script, utterly oblivious to the fact that his listener might have something else to do. I think he irritated all of us. Later, when I came to know him better, I found him extremely likable and stimulating as a friend. I also acted as counsel to his production of *Night Life* and found him equally likable as a client. I regret that he did not become a member; surely it would have helped the Company, and Kingsley, too. *Night Life*, which failed by a hairsbreadth, would, I think, have been a success if our members had lived to produce it.

It took Kingsley more than a year to lick the first draft of his new play, *The Patriots*, into a shape that he felt producible. Even then there was still some hesitation on the part of some of the playwright-members, and Samrock and I worried over the cost. Then another extraordinary theatrical figure entered the picture, Rowland Stebbins. Mr. Stebbins had, in 1930, appeared out of the blue and agreed to produce a play which all the leading managements had shied away from, *The Green Pastures*, by Marc Connolly. It was an enormous success and must have made a fortune for Stebbins. He had no more doubts about *The Patriots* than he had had about *The Green Pastures;* he readily took a half interest. The play won the New York Drama Critics' Circle Award.

Despite the success of *The Patriots*, I always felt that it never quite achieved what Kingsley wanted, largely because he was torn between two themes. He was fascinated by the idea that Thomas Jefferson was in love with the ghost of his dead wife; he also wanted to show that the creation of our nation was the work of comparatively young men, with one older leader, George Washington. Neither idea came through clearly enough. If the play could be revised today (1974) to

Sidney Kingsley. After thirty years I cannot recall why we did not persuade him to join the Company. Both *The Patriots* and *Darkness at Noon*, which the Company co-produced, won awards; his social philosophy was much like the members'; he had producing talent and eventually produced his own plays. What kept us from getting together? (*Vandamm*)

House Jameson, Cecil Humphreys, and Raymond Edward Johnson as Hamilton, Washington and Jefferson in a scene from *The Patriots*. In this scene Kingsley brought to life the dominance of Washington over his brilliant contemporaries with such force that Rice remarked, on seeing it, "It makes you understand why Washington is called the father of his country." (*Graphic House*)

stress the latter point, it might well be an illuminating success. The older generation, which today shakes its collective head sadly over the demands of inexperienced youth, would be reminded that Jefferson was thirty-three when he wrote the Declaration of Independence and Hamilton was younger than that at the time of the Constitutional Convention. Our young people, contrariwise, should be inspired by what their counterparts accomplished two hundred years ago.

My chief recollection of the production centers around the casting problems. Kingsley knew more about radio than the rest of us and had a list of radio actors whom he auditioned. *All* of them gave surprisingly good readings, although they had not seen the script before the audition. There was a reason. In those days an actor or actress performing on radio was frequently given the script shortly before the program went on the air. The performer had to learn how to size it up and give it life immediately. Hence the skillful auditions. But, alas, all too frequently that was the limit of the actor's potentiality; during four weeks of rehearsal his portrayal never changed. Unfortunately, some of the acting in *The Patriots* showed this all too clearly. But it was another hit for the Company.

However, Max's greatest contribution to this phase of the Company's activities was a play he had first released for production by regional companies throughout the country, doubtful of whether he would ever bring it to Broadway; he was, at the time, in a downbeat mood. This was *The Eve of St. Mark*, a simple moving story of the impact of war on simple people doomed to live out their lives, as Thoreau put it, in quiet desperation. We urged Max to give it a Broadway production; he finally agreed to do so. It was directed by a young man named Lem Ward, who immediately won the confidence not only of Max but also of every member of the Company who worked with him.

The play opened in New York in October 1942, some ten months after Pearl Harbor. The output of other serious dramatists during that period had been shockingly disappointing. Most of them had either ignored the war or had written really fatuous plays touching on it. One play, *The Wookey*, imported from England, actually denigrated the importance of the war; Rice suggested (to the somewhat pained surprise of the rest of us) that the Company should join as co-producer in its presentation. We declined.

In this climate, *The Eve of St. Mark* was a triumph. Brooks Atkinson, the famous *New York Times* critic, opened his review by saying "Maxwell Anderson has restored to the theatre its self-respect." The reaction everywhere was favorable, deservedly so. And in November, Max had perhaps the greatest isolated financial triumph of his career. The rest of us learned about it in an amusing way; the following is a transcript of the minutes of the meeting held on November 14, 1942. (One dollar then had purchasing power of perhaps four or five today.)

Mr. Anderson stated that he had three announcements to make.

Maxwell Anderson and Lem Ward.
(*Graphic House*)

He reported that Mr. Rowland Stebbins had agreed to take a one-half interest in the Kingsley play and that in conformity with the decision heretofore reached by the Board it was now definite that a joint production of the play by Mr. Stebbins and the company would be made as soon as possible.

He further reported that he was about to accept an offer from Twentieth Century-Fox Film Company to purchase the motion picture rights to *The Eve of St. Mark* for $300,000.

He further reported that he had written each member of the company a letter in regard to Lem Ward and that he would like some discussion in this matter in the near future.

Mr. Behrman asked that there be placed in the minutes a statement that he felt that never again in Mr. Anderson's career would he be able to achieve such an anti-climax as he had achieved by putting the announcement about the picture sale second instead of third of his three announcements.

But life is unfair. This sale had disastrous effects on Max.

In 1942 it was undecided whether the sale of motion picture rights to a play resulted in ordinary income to the author or was taxable only under the rules relating to "capital gains." If the latter was the

Mary Rolfe and Aline MacMahon in *The Eve of St. Mark*. As I look back, I am more than ever astonished that the man who could portray kings and queens so skillfully could also move an audience by scenes of simple country folk.
(*Vandamm*)

case, the tax would, in most instances, be less—in Max's case it would be very much less. Max's lawyer, Howard Reinheimer, undoubtedly advised Max to report the sale as a capital gain, but to stash away safely, in a savings account, the sum that would be payable if the proceeds were taxed as ordinary income. Max reported the sale as capital gain; he did *not* stash away the required sum. When the government finally ruled that the proceeds were ordinary income, he could not pay the difference and he spent the rest of his life struggling with the ensuing financial problem.

In the meantime, Behrman had finished a new play, *The Pirate*. Like *Tucker's People*, it had no connection with the war; indeed, it had no social overtones of any kind. It was an adaptation of a play written by a Continental playwright some twenty years before and Alfred Lunt had played in it at a local Wisconsin theatre. Apparently, he had always kept it in mind and now thought it would make an excellent romp for his wife and himself, after Shakespeare and *There Shall Be No Night*. Of course, it needed thorough revision. He mentioned it to someone at the Theatre Guild, who approached Behrman. This immediately caused trouble; we all said that if Behrman deserted the Company at this juncture and wrote for the Theatre Guild, the loss of Company prestige would be enormous. But Sam wanted to do the play. We finally straightened out matters by arranging a co-production, but I began to suspect, rightly, that it was a shadow before some coming event that wouldn't be so easy to settle.

Sam went out to the Lunts' home in Genesee Depot, Wisconsin, to confer on the play, and on his return entertained us all with a highly embellished description of their attempt to be real farmers—obviously, to Sam, they were anything but that. He declared that Miss Fontanne had forbidden him to go look at their herd of cattle until he removed a red sweater which she feared would enrage the bull. However, the herd, according to Sam, consisted of four or five miserable animals in some peculiar state of depression marked by their standing unhappily with their heads sunk close to the ground. They never even looked at him. To this day I have never felt sure that the Lunts owned *any* cattle; I have discreetly refrained from any discussions of farming with either of them.

The Pirate was a moderate hit. Hence, in the spring of 1943, the company was represented by *The Pirate*, *The Patriots*, and *The Eve of St. Mark*—all of this accomplished despite the holes left by Sidney Howard's death and Sherwood's absorption in the war effort. We were all pretty pleased with ourselves, rightly. We looked forward with anticipation and, yes, cockiness, to the coming season.

But life is not only unfair. It has a way of tripping one up so as to justify the old adage that pride goeth before a fall. And our coming fall was to rival Humpty Dumpty's.

Whether or not the Lunts had a herd of cattle, they *did* have geese.
(*Theatre Collection, New York Public Library*)

The Lunts in *The Pirate*. In outlandish costume, or in Shakespearean costume, or in modern dress, the Lunts worked their magic equally well.
(*Vandamm*)

Hard Times

As unexpected as Sidney Howard's death came the death of a man who was not a member, but whose death was also an incalculable loss to us. The man was Lem Ward; he had directed *The Eve of St. Mark*. Max had developed absolute faith in him, the rest of us were almost equally impressed. Unquestionably, he would have been invited to become a member; he probably would have accepted and have been a tower of strength. Even if he had declined, he would have kept Max from some serious errors, and his availability might well have prevented Behrman's defection. None of us had any doubt then, and I have no doubts now, that he would have achieved a position equal to Elia Kazan or Harold Clurman as a director of serious plays.

Prior to Lem's untimely death, we had opened the season with a play by Elmer, *A New Life*. Betty Field, by then Mrs. Rice, played the lead and astonished many people by playing a scene in which she was delivered of a baby. (Pretty tame by the standards of the 1970s, but it caused many raised eyebrows in 1943.) The play received an excellent reception out of town, and Elmer was pleased, but the rest of us—particularly Behrman—had our doubts. The play was about a charming, middle-class girl who had married a soldier on his way to the front without realizing just how rich his family was. At the opening of the play, her husband has been reported dead. When she meets his parents she dislikes them and when the baby is born, she becomes determined not to let them have anything to do with the

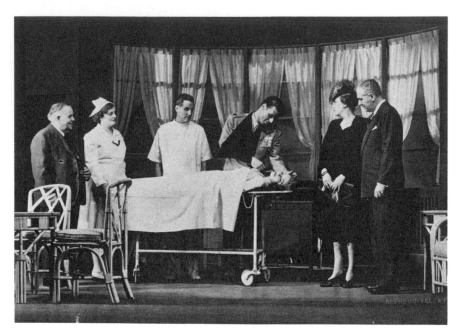

Arthur Griffin, Frederica Going, Blaine Cordner, George Lambert, Betty Field, Merle Maddern, and Walter N. Greaza in *A New Life*.
(*Alfredo Valente*)

child's upbringing. Behrman privately scoffed at the whole idea of a girl resenting the discovery that she had married into a wealthy family, but it seemed to the rest of us a possible (although improbable) situation which, by great skill, could be developed into an interesting problem. *Our* trouble was that the script did not show evidence of such skill.

There was a reason. Elmer apparently had a deep subconscious hatred of the inherited rich—or, indeed, any very rich person. He admitted he could not portray such people adequately. But somehow—no one could understand why—he could not see that the whole play depended on a skillful portrayal of rich people. The parents came out as such one-dimensional ogres that the New York critics derided the whole play. Miss Field's charm kept it going for nine weeks, but it was distinctly a failure.

However, Max had written another war play, *Storm Operation*, for which we all had high hopes. But when Lem Ward died, Max selected as a director a young man who had directed a second company of *The Eve of St. Mark*. He asked no one about this decision; he simply announced it, in a rather belligerent way. Max must have known that copying someone else's direction is a very different thing from staging a new script and that to entrust an expensive production to such a man was a highly risky thing to do. (He was soon to learn just how risky.) But he was in an aggressive mood and would not listen to Elmer, Sam, or me; Sherwood, unfortunately, was in Washington.

As for myself, an innocent mistake rendered me *persona non grata*. In the original script a young corporal from the Middle West was a leading character with a very comedic role. He fell in love with an Arab girl. When someone suggested that he marry her and take her home with him, he was startled by the realities of the situation, and had the line, "Gosh, take an *Aye*-rab girl into Detroit?" I naively asked Max why he had inserted a comedy line at this particular point; he angrily informed me that it was *not* a comedy line but a very serious, moving one. I said no more, but, unhappily for me, when the

Myron McCormick, Sara Anderson, and Cy Howard in *Storm Operation*. The "Aye-rab" girl was the unwitting cause of a temporary rift between Max and me.
(*Graphic House*)

play opened out of town, the audience, which had been chuckling at the corporal's remarks, burst into roars of laughter when he delivered this line. That finished the line, but it also finished me, as I knew it would; I had *prayed* that I'd be wrong and that the audience wouldn't laugh; *then* Max could have shown contempt for me and have forgotten the whole thing. But I had been proved right, and it was days before he would really talk to me again.

However, that was a small item in one of the greatest out-of-town opening night debacles I ever witnessed. The young director not only was inexperienced; he was naive. Never having worked with top calibre actors, he assumed that he didn't have to do much more than see that they knew their lines; they would do the rest on their own. What each one did do, of course, was to try to make his or her part the showiest and the whole thing quickly became a shambles.

The sensible thing would have been to close and cut our losses and Max's frustration, but he had faith in the play and wanted to go on; the Company had the money; we all pitched in and tried to rescue the play.

There were problems of script, direction, and casting. The last had not occurred to us before the opening, although a friend had warned me of it. My wife had formed the producing firm of Wharton-Gabel with a young man named Martin Gabel. He was not only a stage actor, but also the star of a radio show; he had an extremely wide acquaintance with, and knowledge of, young actors and actresses. He had remarked to me that he had read in the papers who had been cast in this play and he was surprised, because he thought so many of them were "dull actors."

I had never before considered the problem of the "dull actor." Some actors had personality and some didn't, but the idea was new to me that some actually *projected dullness*. But it's true. It is a curious, inexplicable faculty, and it is fatal. A play may survive a cast of so-called wallpaper actors, who seem to disappear into the set's wallpaper for lack of personality. But dullness can be a positive force. Too many of the actors in *Storm Operation* had it.

We did our best. We found a new director. Myron McCormick, a young actor with undoubted personality (he later scored heavily in *South Pacific* where the cast included such overshadowing stars as Mary Martin and Ezio Pinza) was persuaded to take the leading role. Other changes in cast and script were made. All to no avail; we opened in New York in January 1944 and closed in three weeks.

A more serious situation was in the making. Behrman finished the script of a new play which had all the earmarks of success, and which became one; it was *Jacobowsky and the Colonel*, based on a work by

Franz Werfel. But he announced that the Theatre Guild had first claim on the play; Werfel and he had been involved with the Guild before our Company was formed. The Guild exercised its claim and refused to consider co-production. Their attitude wasn't surprising. Their Board had felt that the formation of The Playwrights Producing Company had been a slap in their faces. They knew that some of our members felt that they had muscled into *There Shall Be No Night* and *Candle in the Wind;* this stirred up antagonistic reactions and they had no objection to causing the Company some embarrassment.

Embarrassing it was. Our press agent, Bill Fields, was no end upset. He had been doing his best to maintain the Company's stature in the face of two failures, and he felt that the news of the Guild doing a Behrman play would be a smasher. But the real smasher was yet to come; it involved Sam's next script.

Behrman always did more rewriting than any of the others; incidentally, it was a slow and painful process with him, unlike Rice's reactions; if Rice adopted another member's suggestion, he would rewrite a whole scene in one evening. Sam once declared that if reincarnation were true, he would like to be born again as Elmer Rice. But his first draft of the new play, *Dunnigan's Daughter,* had a sound structure, and we were delighted that, at least in a tangential way, he was striving to say something worthwhile about the reaction to the war.

When Sam had a draft that he was ready to show to possible directors, John van Druten had just established himself as a top director. Behrman decided that he would be an ideal director for the new play. Behrman was correct. My wife and I knew van Druten well and had no doubt that he would understand the kind of people Sam wrote about and that he would know how to give Behrman's lines the right readings. We sent the script to van Druten, but he returned it with a letter in which he asserted that this was simply the same plot and same characters that Behrman had been using for several years. He was not interested.

At the time I was reading a book by a smart-aleck but amusing writer, Jack Woodford, entitled *Plotting: How to Have a Brain Child*. At one point Woodford states that young writers frequently are afraid to show their work to a successful author for fear he will steal the plot. Such fears are groundless, asserts Woodford; if the author is successful, it means that he *already has a plot*, one that he hopes to use in various forms for the rest of his life. I couldn't help wondering whether van Druten was right and that Behrman did have only one plot. (T. S. Eliot once said, "We (writers) have only one thing to say, but must keep on finding new forms of saying it.")

But that didn't help the situation. As soon as Sam learned that he could not get van Druten, he went after another popular director, Elia Kazan.

Success in the entertainment field frequently produces an initial euphoria which makes a man (or woman) difficult to deal with—more so than is the case in any other field. Perhaps it is because the change from nobody to SOMEBODY can be so swift. After one success, a director who may have been seeking assignments unsuccessfully finds himself deluged with offers to do new plays, fix plays in trouble, help with rewriting—any and all kinds of work that a director can do. A man would have to be more than human for all this not to have some effect; if he really has the right stuff, it usually wears off or, at least, to use a current phrase, "winds down." Kazan, at this time, was suffering from euphoria; the winding down process had not started. (Eventually it did; he became a great friend.)

He was represented by H. William Fitelson, Esq., who was also counsel to the Theatre Guild. Fitelson was a personal friend of mine, whom I admired in many ways, but he was one of the toughest, roughest adversaries and negotiators I have ever known. On behalf of Kazan, he concocted a letter which was the first direct insult—indeed, the only one—the Company ever received. It stated that Mr. Kazan would be glad to direct Mr. Behrman's play, but he did not consider the Company a competent producing organization and therefore would not undertake the assignment unless the Theatre Guild was made the producer.

Sherwood was in town. We called a quick meeting, and everyone was outraged and agreed that Fitelson's letter was insufferable. (Fitelson himself was surprised at this reaction, and quite angry about it; he considered the letter a simple statement of terms.) But it quickly became clear to me that Sam wanted Kazan more than he wanted the Company. He soon made this indubitably clear to everyone. It was suggested that a co-production be worked out; Sam declared he wanted one man as producer. Sherwood thereupon offered to free himself from his political work and be that man; Sam then took the position that he wanted that man to be someone like Lawrence Langner of the Theatre Guild, because he could berate Langner for incompetence, which he couldn't do with Bob. This was obvious nonsense; Sam admired Langner and eventually spoke at a memorial service for him and delivered a eulogy, which Langner certainly deserved. The situation was then *crystal* clear: Sam really did not want to produce his plays; he wanted out. Reluctantly we released the play; Sam resigned from the Company. But we all continued to love him and later I tried to get him to rejoin; he considered the invitation carefully but finally decided against it.

I believe it was a terrible mistake on Sam's part. It certainly was a mistake as far as *Dunnigan's Daughter* was concerned. He began rewriting the play again and again; it finally opened to unenthusiastic notices and was a flop for both Behrman and Kazan. I never saw the final production and do not to this day know whether Sam stuck to "his plot." It is a fact, however, that Behrman never had another success with an *original* play. I cannot help believing that the story would have been different if he had stayed with the Company.

Kazan, too, must have been badly shaken up. I suspect that this led him to resent the Company, and he shortly caused us more trouble.

Anderson showed us a script of a new play titled *Truckline Café.* It bewildered us. Max had always had a keen sense of dramatic conflict; in this script he had abandoned any use of conflict. The play was laid in a café where truck drivers, and other people, stopped for a bite. As each character came in he would recall some past event and *tell* about it; of actual action or conflict there was almost none. We all advised Max not to go on with it. But Kazan, who had formed a producing partnership with another top director-producer, Harold Clurman, got hold of the script and told Max they would present the play. They did, however, agree to a co-production—putting their own names first; but it was a sticky situation and did not make life within the Company any happier.

The play was destined for failure from its out-of-town opening in Baltimore. As I look back, its only strong point was a new young actor named Marlon Brando. I sat with Samrock. After the curtain fell, we stopped for a cup of coffee while on our way to the usual postopening meeting. Victor stared mournfully at his cup when it arrived. "You know," he said, "I bet even the coffee was bad at the Truckline Café!"

To make things worse, after the play received bad notices, the co-producers put out a defensive advertisement and encouraged Max to put an advertisement in the papers attacking the critics. The rest of us got together and decided we had to support Max, so the Company placed an advertisement backing him up. I have rarely seen a document with such a strong subconscious ring of untruth. None of the three advertisements had any good effect on the box office.

However, Max's own advertisement was a remarkable document. It began with a dignified statement of why Max believed the theatre to be an important factor in civilization—all expressed very movingly—and then suddenly launched an attack on the critics which surpasses, in its violence, anything else on that subject I have ever seen in print. But I can testify that if anyone wants to be a playwright, and dreams of fame as such, he will have a day when his feelings will coincide with those expressed by Max.

This was the advertisement:

To the Theatre Public:

It never comes gracefully from a playwright to defend his own work, and I find it difficult because I feel a very real humility toward the art I practice and toward the great men who have written for the theatre. I have not always succeeded either with myself or the public, but I have never written a play in which I did not try to say something honest about the strange, tragic, humorous, incredible life of men on this planet—men who know so little of what they are, who are only beginning to read a meaning in the darkness that surrounds them, and in the even more impenetrable darkness within themselves.

In *Truckline Café* I attempt to suggest the confusion in men's minds and lives—as they try to find a way to live after the fantastic dislocation the war brought to nearly all of us. Certainly I meant nothing cheap by it, and nothing easy. I am driven to believe that the men who reviewed it are either unaware of our current problems or disinclined or unable to think about them. Thinking about them is not easy. No certain answers are possible. But I have presented the picture as I see it and given the only approach to an answer that I know.

The public is far better qualified to judge plays than the men who write reviews for the dailies. It is an insult to our threatre that there should be so many incompetents and irresponsibles among them. There are still a few critics who know their job and respect it, but of late years all plays are passed on largely by a sort of Jukes family of journalism who bring to the theatre nothing but their own hopelessness, recklessness and despair. For a great theatre it is necessary to have not only great playwrights, great audiences, but great critics too.

Maxwell Anderson

Marlon Brando in *Truckline Café*. The unknown young actor who gave a spark of life to Max's play later dominated theatre and film audiences the world over. Yet Elia Kazan, who directed Brando in *A Streetcar Named Desire*, insisted that he often felt sure he was making no impression on him, because of his peculiar ability to make one feel he was psychically unreachable.
(*Fred Fehl*)

While all this was happening we were cheered by the fact that Sherwood emerged from Washington with a new script, *The Rugged Path*, in which he had interested Spencer Tracy, then at the top of his movie popularity. We were all certain that this would pull us out of our troubles. And it did start off brightly.

Both Sherwood and Tracy wanted Garson Kanin to direct it. Kanin was in the army in a division making motion pictures. Sherwood told us that he was working to get him released for the length of time needed to direct the play. Since Sherwood was then on intimate terms with President Roosevelt, no one was greatly worried. But I did chance to remark that I had been told that to get things done surely and quickly in the army you needed a regular army general's help. Bob smiled and said, "You're right. I've heard that, too. We have General Marshall working on it."

I suspect Kanin is the only army captain who, during a war, ever had the President of the United States and his Chief of Staff cooperating to make sure of a short leave of absence for him.

Spencer Tracy, Grace Murphy (Sherwood's secretary), Garson Kanin, and Sherwood in conference before the great worries began. (*Graphic House*)

Kanin and Tracy duly arrived; the play went into rehearsal; the opening was set for Providence, Rhode Island, where one of Bob's previous successes had tried out. A few things still stand out clearly in my memory.

It was a big barn of a theatre, quite unsuited to a drama, but Spencer Tracy's name had filled it. At intermission the audience began reversing the usual trend; they marched *down* the aisles, instead of up and out. The reason was simple: Katharine Hepburn was sitting in the front row. How the Providence audience knew this remains a mystery; *I* was unaware of it until Bob told me. But they knew; they marched; they stared; they marched on. Because of the size of the audience this went on through the entire intermission. I felt that it was not calculated to increase interest in the soul-searching of the character Tracy was portraying.

But this was minor. What was major was the inexplicable aura of failure that began to settle over the play. Except for the one scene where the men abandoned ship, the aura increased. It is a phenomenon known all too well to theatre professionals. I tried to dismiss it, but in my soul I knew something was very, very wrong. I think the others went through the same let-down, but none of us at first admitted it.

The trouble was that Sherwood was now using "his plot" for the third time. As in *Abe Lincoln* and *There Shall Be No Night*, the protagonist of *The Rugged Path* is a man leading a full life who becomes obsessed with the belief that he must give more of himself to a worthy public cause. He gives up his simple, successful career, plunges into politics or war, and suffers a martyr's fate. Only this time we saw that this plot wasn't working any better than Sam's plot worked for him in *Dunnigan's Daughter*.

Sherwood knew something was amiss; he never fooled himself. But this time he couldn't find the way to fix it. Tracy became worried; there was talk of closing out of town. Indeed, Miss Hepburn, whom I had known for years, made a comment one day which astonished me. She said, "John, I think it will take a lot of courage to open in New York, and Spencer hasn't got that kind of courage."

But he did open, and his name and reputation did fill the theatre for a short time; then the audiences began slowly to dwindle. Tracy chose not to believe it; he was the King of Hollywood at the time; he demanded sell-outs. Samrock and Fields began to apply Disraeli's doctrine that most people like flattery, and when it comes to royalty you can lay it on with a trowel. They constantly found items of praise in the press and they did not scruple to prepare box office statements showing full houses.

Katharine Hepburn. She had beauty and exuberant charm—and, when I first knew her, some idiosyncrasies. If you phoned her, you would hear her being summoned to talk to you; she would pick up the phone, omit any "Hello, John" or "How are you?" and begin talking as if you were already in the middle of a discussion. I once thought of telling her of a plumber working in my house whom I summoned to the phone to take a call from his boss. He picked up the mouthpiece and declaimed, "Start the conversation."
(*Theatre Collection, New York Public Library*)

To no avail. It became clear to everyone that the play was a failure, and it closed after eighty-one performances. We were all crushed. I recalled Bob's baseball fantasy; this made me recall a poem made famous in my youth by a great comedian, De Wolf Hopper: "Casey at the Bat."

The poem describes how the baseball fans of a little town called Mudville see their team slowly going down to defeat; in the last inning they pray that their star, Casey, will get one more chance to bat. He does—with two out but with two on base—a hit could tie—a home run could win the game after all. The fans are exhilarated, willing to wager even money! But the last stanza reads as follows:

> Oh, somewhere in this favored land the sun is shining bright,
> Somewhere the band is playing and somewhere hearts are light.
> And somewhere men are laughing, and somewhere children shout,
> But there is no joy in Mudville; mighty Casey has struck out.

With three straight failures, including Sherwood's, and with only three playwrights left, it surely looked like a Humpty-Dumpty fall. But somehow or other, what all the king's horses and men couldn't do, we did do. We put Humpty-Dumpty together again, although not too securely. This time it was Elmer who started the rebound.

Spencer Tracy in *The Rugged Path*. His personality came over the foot-lights with the same force as from the screen, but the play did not catch fire. By the second act Tracy was "working too hard," a peculiar phe-nomenon that destroys an actor's impact, although the audience doesn't know why. Another inexplicable hazard for a dramatist.
(*Graphic House*)

CHAPTER
XI

Ups and Downs—More
Down Than Up

During the 1940s there was a popular ditty titled "Sing Me a Song of Social Significance." The phrase "Social Significance" caught on and was used to describe "important plays." When our members' thoughts were concentrated on their best plays, they would sometimes express the wish that they could write some purely commercial successes, without a trace of social significance. Elmer Rice got his wish with *Dream Girl*.

This play was written solely as a vehicle for Betty Field. I have been told that she herself suggested the uproarious prostitute dream sequence. Whether she did or didn't, the play was a superb vehicle for her; at first Elmer thought that no one else could play it. It took quite a bit of argument by his colleagues to get him to hire and rehearse an understudy. Actually, it was a vital step, for Miss Field at that time had a strange, almost weird, habit of contracting influenza (then called grippe) when at her radiant acting best.

Sure enough, after the play opened to good reviews in New York, Victor phoned me to say that the first week's business was fine. Then

Betty Field in *Dream Girl*. This scene was considered very up-to-date in the 1940s; we thought "we'd gone about as far as we could go."
(*Vandamm*)

he added dolefully, "And Betty has the grippe." The understudy carried us through until Betty's return, and I hereby salute Miss Helen Marcy. *Dream Girl* proved to be one of the Company's longest running plays.

A Well-Paid Lawyer

The play was my first experience with the actual workings of an innovation that came to be known as the Wharton-Wilk plan. The Dramatists Guild, when it came into power in 1926, had decided to put an end to the nefarious practice of impecunious producers forcing impecunious or fledgling authors to sell film rights in advance and using the money to produce the show. If such a play turned into a smash hit, the dramatist had sold these rights for a mess of potage.

Betty Field and Helen Marcy in *Dream Girl*. Miss Marcy was also Betty's understudy.
(*Vandamm*)

The Guild stopped this by insisting on a contract provision that if film rights were sold, no production could be had until a year had elapsed. But a great many dramatists wanted to sell film rights in advance. My plan was designed to permit this without the mess-of-potage risk.

It was not an invention of such scope as to make Mr. Edison or Leonardo da Vinci jealous. It simply provided for a minimum down payment by the picture company, plus further payments based on the weekly grosses of the play. This protected the author completely; a long-run play could and did pay handsomely. But the Dramatists Guild submitted the plan to a group of "elder statesmen" who were typical No-no-no people. The objections they raised were infuriating; I could see why others who may have had similar ideas had not bothered to present them. I finally gave up in frustration. My law partners asked sadly why I wasted my time on such profitless affairs.

However, Jacob Wilk, the eastern representative of Warner Bros. Pictures, Inc., had seen the plan and he did not give up. He patiently and consistently met with the objectors and strove to show them the errors of their way of thinking. He finally succeeded to the extent of the Guild's permitting a trial of the plan. It was such an immediate success that within a few years most people had forgotten that there was a time before it existed. Today only a few people remember that it was ever called the Wharton-Wilk plan.

The Company playwright members were at first very suspicious of the plan, but they finally decided to risk one venture. Accordingly, I took the script of *Dream Girl* to John Byram of Paramount Pictures and explained what we wanted. He read the script and at once saw its possibilities; he agreed to satisfactory terms for the sale; he also arranged for Paramount to back the production.

Rice had no agent. He insisted, generously, that I receive a full agent's commission on all receipts from the sale. The whole negotiation hardly consumed two hours of my time; the sale yielded a sum which made my commission eventually add up to more than $20,000. At various times in my legal career I have been retained by members of some of the wealthiest families in America—Whitneys, Fields, Rockefellers, du Ponts; none of them ever paid me $10,000 an hour.

A Deflated Lawyer

Actually, as far as subsequent New York audiences were concerned, Elmer was right in feeling that Miss Field was a necessity. When she returned, in good health, business was superb, but she became ill again and business began to drop off when people were not sure she would be playing. Eventually, Elmer took her to the Caribbean, having arranged for Haila Stoddard, a charming and talented actress, to take over. Business slumped, but not too much. Then Miss Stoddard decided to leave.

I was on vacation at the time Miss Stoddard gave notice. When I returned I found, to my surprise, that June Havoc was playing the lead. To my further surprise, I learned that Elmer had not bothered to return and direct Miss Havoc. Moreover, no playwright member of the Company had bothered to go see her; it was the only time in the Company's history that an actress was treated rudely. I decided

June Havoc and Richard Widmark in *Dream Girl*, playing the hilarious scene depicting "the dream girl's" conception of a prostitute. (*Hugelmeyer*)

that I was the best substitute available and hastened to arrange with Bill Fields for my attendance.

I was not very happy at the theatre. Miss Havoc, for all her personality—or because of it—gave such a different characterization from Betty that the whole play needed redirection. During intermission I wandered moodily about, planning what to say to her. An acquaintance approached me and asked what was on my mind; when he heard I was to go backstage to meet Miss Havoc, he interrupted to say he envied me. "But look out," he warned, as the bell rang for the next act, "she's a man-eater and can dredge up such overpowering sex, charm, and emotion that no man can resist her."

Well, thought I, at least *that* gives a filip to my mission; what man could fail to be excited about meeting such a lady!

Alas, within three minutes after Bill introduced us, certain things became painfully apparent. Miss Havoc certainly *was* magnetic, and obviously had the earmarks of a "man-eater," but clearly she was a fastidious gourmet in selecting the type of man to eat. *I* was not such a type. She was polite and restrained; she clearly regarded me as a machine sent by the Company to perform a mechanical function. I performed it and left.

As I left, an old phrase of a nineteenth-century humorist, Elbert Hubbard, suddenly rose out of my subconscious. He used the phrase to express his idea of complete and utter lack of emotional interest of any kind: "the mental attitude of a monkey toward a hen." Somehow I felt that I had been on the reverse side of such a situation.

As soon as I could, I called a meeting and reported my belief that the play needed a master's hand. But it was too late; business was declining badly; we had to close a play that should have run another six months. And I never met Miss Havoc again.

Down—Then Way Up

Money from *Dream Girl* rolled into the Company's coffers during the first half of 1946. We organized a second company with a promising young girl, Judy Parrish, in the leading role. Miss Parrish was superb; business in Chicago was excellent—by prior standards. But when the final figures came in, we made, for the first time, the discovery that costs, both of production and weekly operations, had quietly risen much faster than ticket prices. Strange economic forces which came to be called "inflation" were at work.

We were startled by the production cost and more startled by the operating figures; the play was playing to what would have been

Lucille Ball in a summer-stock production of *Dream Girl*. Summer-stock rights were, in the 1940s, leased for a specific sum per week. If business was bad, the stock theatre took the loss; the author took no risk. Miss Ball, then a film star, soon to be Lucy on TV, played to such crowds that a risky percentage deal would have yielded two or three times Elmer's risk-free flat fee. Elmer, who had curious quirks of thought, couldn't help feeling that he had somehow been cheated.
(*Fred Fehl*)

excellent Chicago grosses in 1945; in 1946 this gross was too small to achieve anything but a meager weekly profit. Eventually, illness hit again; this time it was Miss Parrish, and the second company had to close with a heavy loss.

However, Max then came up with as close to a sure-fire money-maker as the theatre can ever provide. It was a play about Joan of Arc, a character which for some reason attracts star actresses. If you ever attempt a full-length play, try your hand at a Joan biography; if you have any dialogue ability, you will at least get some distinguished

June Havoc, even more alluring than her famous stripper-sister, Gypsy Rose Lee.
(*Theatre Collection, New York Public Library*)

actresses to read it, and probably play it. Shaw's *St. Joan* has attracted at least three American stars; Anouilh's *The Lark* had Julie Harris; *Joan of Lorraine* brought Ingrid Bergman, then at the height of her film popularity, to the Broadway stage. Any knowledgeable person could predict that only her withdrawal from the play could stop it from making money. She didn't withdraw, although she did limit her engagement; it did make money. Indeed, the standing room only sign went up for every performance.

Max conceived an unusual format for this play. It is a rehearsal of a play about the Maid; between scenes the leading characters, played by Miss Bergman as the star and Sam Wanamaker as the director, sit and discuss Joan's character—and various other things such as corruption in the Broadway theatre! The discussions are, as might be expected, superior in content. The scenes in the play within the play are pretty much the "Sunday School stories" we were told about the Maid in our childhood. But Miss Bergman's charm carried off everything successfully.

I would not term Miss Bergman a "man-eater," but "man-slayer" might be appropriate. I had first met her when David Selznick had signed her to a picture contract. The head of his eastern office, Kay Brown, was taking her to a Broadway show and asked my wife and me to join her to help entertain the new star. I was not feeling well; I had heard nothing good of the selected show; however, I could not let Kay down, so we dutifully trouped to the theatre and I reserved a table somewhere for supper. As soon as we sat down the top "youngbloods" of café society, who had somehow heard about, and met, the lady, began appearing from here, there, and elsewhere. I still recall the ease with which Ingrid swept them off their feet.

She did, and still does, radiate enormous charm. I admired her immediately and came to like her enormously. She had idiosyncrasies which sound ridiculous but somehow added to her charm: I recall her love of Chinese food and sweet pickles. The fact that she was Swedish may have had some bearing. I have never met a Swedish girl I didn't like, from the glamorous Miss Bergman to a down-to-earth nurse we once had for our children. The latter, incidentally, astonished me by suddenly asking for time off to play for the Swedish National Bridge Team; I also recall that it was during her tenure that my daughters discovered I was listed in *Who's Who;* I heard the nurse telling my wife that the children had taken to their room that big red-covered book, "Woes Woe in America." Yes, I like the Swedes.

Ingrid Bergman, a good reason for being enchanted with the Swedes.
(*Theatre Collection, New York Public Library*)

The success of *Dream Girl* and the sight of Miss Bergman playing to capacity made it seem that we really had put Humpty-Dumpty together again and reset him firmly on his wall. But some unkind fate was always just around the corner throughout the Company's whole history. We were about to meet with our greatest single financial disaster, which would be followed by a wasteland in which the well-springs of creativity seemed to have dried up forever.

Then Way Down

The financial disaster followed hard on the election of Kurt Weill to membership, which had taken place in July 1946, as soon as it became clear that Behrman's resignation was irrevocable. Weill and Rice had become enthusiastic about the possibilities of *Street Scene* as a musical. Without speaking to anyone they rushed off to Rodgers and Hammerstein and asked that firm to produce the musical. Coming right after the announcement of Behrman's defection this would have set Broadway tongues a-wagging; Bill Fields was, again, aghast. It was all very embarrassing, particularly as I was assigned the distasteful task of going to Rodgers, whom I knew well, and trying to arrange at least a co-production. Rodgers and Hammerstein would have none of it. Bill, Vic, and I began beating our brains out over some new approach, when this problem was suddenly resolved.

Elmer always asserted he was a socialist, (*not* a Communist) but he had quite definite capitalistic ideas about what large royalties should be paid where one of his prize properties was involved. Rodgers was a capitalist, born and bred, and had equally definite ideas on the subject; they did not coincide with Elmer's, and Elmer called the deal off. If only we had called off, not the deal, but the production!

Paramount Pictures had financed *Dream Girl*. The money for *Joan of Lorraine* poured in over the transom. We had no doubt we could handle the financing of *Street Scene*, and we gaily entered into a co-production contract that was to come close to ruining us.

I arranged a co-production deal for *Street Scene* between the Company and Dwight Deere Wiman. It is *not* one of the accomplishments which I recall with pride and joy. Yet it looked perfect on paper. Wiman was perhaps the only Broadway producer who could appreciate fully Kurt's genius; he had a record of success in the

Ingrid Bergman in *Joan of Lorraine*. Audiences loved Joan with a Swedish accent.
(*Vandamm*)

musical field; he was, at the time, in a position which assured his cooperation in every way. He was one of the very few producers who had joined the war effort abroad; on his return, he found that the authors and composers whose work he had produced had made other connections; hence he was eager to find other people to work with.

All went well at the start. Langston Hughes was brought in to write the lyrics; Hughes was just getting launched on what was to be an internationally distinguished career; he, too, was most cooperative. He was, incidentally, the only black man with whom I ever worked closely in the theatre. He was cultivated and charming; there was no trace of embarrassment between us. But, looking back, I shudder to think that if, in that era, I had tried to invite him to my apartment, the elevator men would probably have refused to bring him up!

Trouble began when definitive casting became essential. We needed a young star, someone who could at least approximate what Mary Martin was when she entered the Broadway scene with "My Heart Belongs to Daddy." There was no such young star. It seems unbelievable, but it is true that the era of Berlin, Kern, Gershwin, Porter, Rodgers, and others brought forth only a handful of real stars; of all the girls who played the lead in *Oklahoma!* not one became a star of first magnitude. Anne Jeffreys, who finally was our choice, was proficient and lovely to look at, but she lacked that peculiar "star quality."

The same was to some extent true of the others. One character in the play is a young man evidently modeled on what Elmer conceived himself to be at that age. It was a difficult part, for Elmer was even worse at writing himself than he was at writing rich people. Kurt found a young man of whom he felt so sure that we signed him before production began. As soon as he appeared on a rehearsal stage, everyone (including Kurt) wanted to replace him. However, these were normal troubles, of the sort which everyone expected.

What was unexpected was Elmer's attitude toward the script. He began to "mother" his dramatic script in a way that put Polly Howard to shame. The others tried ceaselessly to point out that in a musicalization one used music rather than dialogue to achieve certain

Kurt Weill, an authentic genius, and a practical showman. The day after *Street Scene* had opened in Philadelphia and his songs had received minimal applause, he said to me sadly, "I can reorchestrate any of those songs so that it will surely get a big hand, but it won't be *solid* applause. So why do it?"
(*Collection of American Society of Composers and Publishers*)

Street Scene. A poignant musicalization of one of "the short and simple annals of the poor."
(*Theatre Collection, New York Public Library*)

effects. Elmer was not easily convinced; he began to recount, again and again, how certain scenes had gripped the audience in 1929. This was particularly irritating because when Elmer talked about his past he had the unfortunate skill to make a short story long. When the Company set out for the Philadelphia tryout, we were all worried more than we cared to admit.

Our worries were justified. As I sat there I had that same chill which had seized me at the tryout of *The Rugged Path*. The morning papers confirmed my fears. As my wife and I breakfasted in the hotel dining room, Victor Samrock joined us and said sadly that two theatre clichés were all too true: the play "needed a lot of work" and "there must be an easier way to make a living." Kurt joined us; he tried to defend the show, but he was obviously whistling in the dark. We were all prepared for disaster.

We were not prepared for the *extent* of the disaster. The box office demand was almost nonexistent; *feeble* would be much too optimistic a word. Forrest Haring, Wiman's general manager, found difficulty in papering the house; no one wanted to come. At an informal gathering on New Year's morning, Wiman's sister-in-law said, almost defiantly, "Well, I like the show; I'm going again and take friends with me." Haring, with creditable deadpan, asked, "Could you use a couple of . . . hundred tickets for this afternoon's matinee?"

We were booked for three weeks in Philadelphia, and it soon became apparent that we were going to lose $20,000 a week (equivalent to at least $60,000 in 1974), with risk of even greater loss in New York. The Company was in no position to handle such losses; I had the unpleasant task of going to Wiman and working out a deal that reduced the Company's risk but almost eliminated its chance of profit. It was extremely embarrassing; only Wiman's devoted friendship made it possible, and there is nothing more distressing than having to take advantage of friendship. It was particularly galling when I considered that I had thought the co-production would be a great thing for him.

The theatre is full of incredible surprises.

My wife could not attend the New York opening, so I took a girl who knew all kinds of opera—grand or comic or what-have-you—backwards and forwards. The curtain had not been up long before I realized that a lot of needed work *had* been done. My companion's attitude confirmed this; she was delighted with the score and by no means contemptuous of the book. Audience applause began to grow in volume; people around us showed that peculiar approving look; I couldn't believe my ears or eyes.

The reviews were excellent. The New York box office the next day was the exact reverse of Philadelphia. I felt foolish about the salvage deal I had made. Wiman was smiling, Kurt, Elmer, and Langston were basking in the light of good publicity. It seemed too good to be true.

And it wasn't true.

The box office and the attendance began to slip at an early date. The mass audience clearly was "not amused." Thereupon Wiman placed some unusually large advertisements. This precipitated a violent dispute between Wiman and the authors, resulting from the curious philosophy of theatre ticket sales policy.

Most theatre people then believed—and most still believe—that the only good way to sell tickets is to make people think that tickets are difficult to get, the more difficult the better. If they really *are* difficult to get, that's a showman's dream come true; and when a play is a smash hit, tickets *are* really difficult to get, because, at every performance demand exceeds supply. Lee Shubert was an outstanding advocate of this hard-to-get philosophy for a reason which few people understood: he believed that theatregoers readily accepted the pricing policy of charging as much for the last row as the first because they were eager to get in at all. (Mr. Lee also believed, I think, that the average theatregoer actually thought a last-row seat was as good as a first-row one; he argued, very forcefully, that people's capacity for self-delusion was unlimited.)

Consequently, it was the custom of hit shows to run as little post-opening newspaper advertising as possible. This was, to the sophisticated patron, proof that tickets were difficult to get. When Wiman began to run larger advertisements he was admitting that tickets were not so difficult to get; this, the authors thought, was destroying the demand. Unhappily, the reality of the situation was that the *demand was not there*; and neither the absence nor the presence of advertising had any effect; the word of mouth just wasn't good enough. We closed after 148 performances; and everyone was again as unhappy as in Philadelphia, perhaps even a little more so.

Later on I had one small consolation from learning that Wiman never ceased to love the score. Two years had gone by; my phone rang at 3:00 A.M.; it was Dwight. "I'm playing the *Street Scene* record," he said, "it's wonderful; just listen a bit."

Dwight Deere Wiman

The foregoing does not present a fair picture of Dwight Deere Wiman. In my half century's work in the theatre I met no other man who contributed so much to the theatre as he did and received so little recognition for it. Nor do I know of anyone else who started his career with so much in his favor and ended with period after period of bleak despair. The end of his life was a tragedy—for him and for me, for he was my closest friend in the Broadway world.

I met him when he was one of the group of young men involved in the Eagels-Hunter affair. We took to each other immediately, although his background and his way of life were utterly different from my own. He came from the small midwestern town of Moline, Illinois, which was then the headquarters of the great farm machine manufacturer, Deere & Company. His family had dominated the company for three generations and had amassed a family fortune. However, if anyone ever deserved the sobriquet of "poor little rich boy," it was Dwight.

For he and his older, dominating brother Charles had been orphaned at an early age; the fact was all-important to Dwight. He knew he was rich; he knew that he and his brother could one day, if they wished, control Deere & Company; but the salient fact was that he was growing up in a big house without father or mother, only a brother whom he loved but subconsciously feared. He told me that he would often say to himself, "I'm an orphan"; the phrase invariably struck terror in him. My partner, Louis Weiss, who had grown into the Sigmund Freud of Domestic Relations Law, predicted that this type of childhood would have far-reaching unhappy effects in Dwight's later life; he was right.

But when I first met Dwight in 1924 he seemed one of the happiest, most carefree young men I had ever seen. He was married to a bright, vivacious girl; they had three daughters (a fourth was born in 1926); they lived happily in a big, rambling house in Greenwich, Connecticut, then a top-drawer suburb of New York. He and his wife enjoyed Greenwich, but also took the family to Europe whenever the fancy struck them. He told me gleefully of one trip where they traveled from city to city with three small girls, two governesses, and sixty pieces of luggage. At every stop one child or another would howl at the interruption of something she was doing with her favorite doll; whether or not all the luggage would be unloaded, no one ever knew. "But," he said, "we all had a wonderful time."

I never learned just how he had acquired his background of theatre knowledge, and of all the other performing arts: opera, symphony, ballet, modern dance. He loved them all, and drew on them when he

Some interesting young people: Clara Bow, the It Girl; Fred Waller, the inventor of the Cinerama process; Frank Tuttle, later a well-known film director; and Dwight Deere Wiman, looking pretty worried about the whole thing.
(*Theatre Collection, New York Public Library*)

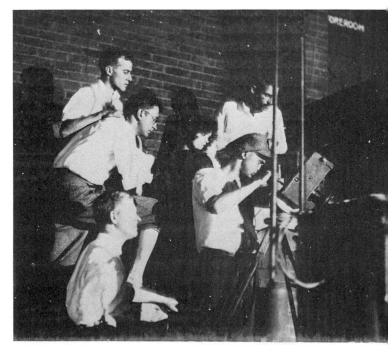

became a theatrical producer. He brought the ballet to Braodway nearly ten years before *Oklahoma!* The physical aspects of his productions reflected his knowledge of all these fields, both as to performance and design; one critic declared a Shakespearian production to be a "thing of almost overpowering Oriental beauty and magnificence." His taste in costumes was also impeccable.

He was always ready to give young people a chance, and the list of talented newcomers whom he helped would be long and illustrious. The ballerinas Nora Kaye and Alicia Alonso. both began their careers in the chorus of a Wiman show, as did the world-famous Jerome Robbins. He was an early ardent admirer of Jo Mielziner. He produced Sherwood's first two plays, also Paul Osborn's. John van Druten's early successes, after *Young Woodley*, were Wiman productions.

He entered the musical field in 1928 with *The Little Show*, which established the success of the small revue, as opposed to the Ziegfeld massive ones. Richard Rodgers and Lorenz Hart did five shows with him; the association ended when Wiman entered the war effort, shortly before Hart's death.

Despite a script by F. Scott Fitzgerald, the picture, *Grit*, was called amateurish by the critics. Wiman (in striped cap) certainly looks amateurish.
(Theatre Collection, New York Public Library)

Despite all of the foregoing, he was all too frequently described by his Broadway peers as "a talented amateur." I ascribe this to the fact that in artistic circles—and this includes the critics, too—there is a feeling that rich people *ought not* to have any artistic ability; they should simply provide the money for some poor, struggling genius to fulfill his promise. This was manifestly unfair to Wiman.

Despite my pleasure in Dwight's successes, what I look back on most fondly is our friendship. Our understanding of each other, and our loyalty to each other, was boundless, although we never mentioned such things. We became particularly close as cracks began to appear in our marriages. We would have lunch together, drink too much, and come out feeling that we had bared our souls, although it was clear that neither of us would remember the next day a single item of our conversation. The ways of friendship can be very mysterious.

I do recall one brief conversation at the bar of the famous 21 West 52nd Street restaurant; it was in the early 1940s. How we got on the subject I cannot recall, but we found ourselves commenting on a phase of the free enterprise economic system: there were always ambitious young men like ourselves coming up to challenge the men who had already made their mark. Suddenly I had an inspiration. "Dwight," I said solemnly, "let's face something. *We* are no longer the ambitious young men. We are the ones who have made it and will soon be challenged by young men whose names we don't even know!" There was enough truth in the statement to cause us to order another drink and ponder the change in our status.

Wiman was one of the very few producers who temporarily gave up producing and sought overseas work in the war. He joined the Red Cross and stayed in London for three years. After his return his whole life went to pieces. His wife divorced him; the playwrights whom he had produced had made other connections. He had only one big success: *The Country Girl*, by Clifford Odets. Worst of all, the prediction of Louis Weiss began to come true. Desperately unhappy, driven by subconscious fears, he grabbed at everything and anything which would make life more bearable. More and more, what he grabbed was alcohol. The physical results were fatal.

In 1950 he began work on two productions. He found himself in such bad physical shape that he entered an upstate sanitarium run by an old friend, Dr. Esselstyn. From there he would make trips to New York to give final approval to production arrangements made by his staff. Early in January 1951 he became unable to make such a trip; the doctor telephoned that things looked bad. I hastily took a train and arrived at the sanitarium late in the day. As I waited to see the

doctor my mind took one of those absolutely absurd turns which can crop up when one is under deep strain.

I recalled a silly conundrum of my early years: what are the three questions to which a man most eagerly wants to hear Yes as the answer? At age twenty-five, "Will you marry me?" At forty-five, "Can you repay that five grand I loaned you?" At fifty-five, "Is it curable, Doc?"

Dwight had put the last question quite differently. The doctor told me that when Dwight returned from his last trip, he had asked for a quick go-over; at its conclusion, he had said, "Essey, this is curtains, isn't it? If so, I won't fight it." Esselstyn couldn't deny the facts; it struck him that Dwight seemed almost equally dejected and relieved. "He was suffering both physically and psychically," the doctor reported to me. Shortly thereafter he went into a coma.

I went to bed with my clothes on, hoping Dwight would come out of his coma long enough to speak to me. Early in the morning, Esselstyn came in to my room and gave the bad news in a curious way. "Mr. Wiman's troubles are over."

Louis Weiss, my closest friend, had died in 1950, and the practice of law was never quite the same thereafter. Dwight's death came only a few months later, and the theatre was never again what it was to me while he was alive and active. Both events increased my attachment to the Company.

Dwight Deere Wiman.
(G. Maillard Kesslere)

CHAPTER

XII

More Ups and Downs

Street Scene opened in New York on January 9, 1947. The Company did not open another play on Broadway until December 1948. During those twenty-three months I often felt that we were living in a theatrical desert. Gray's famous *Elegy* talks about "many a flower born to blush unseen and waste its sweetness on the desert air"; there were no flowers of any sort—merely disappointments—during most of this period. Sherwood was subjected to a really cruel blow. He finished a new play, thought well of it, and wrote Victor the following cheery, excited letter:

June 7, 1947

Dear Vic:

This is to announce that I have taken time out to write that play for the Lunts and have notified them that the first draft is complete. I shall type it out when I get back to New York. It is rather unusual and may be no good whatsoever so I do not want its existence advertised until the company and the Lunts have read it. It is called *The Twilight*—a cast of eight (two of the parts bits)—two acts and only one set (but I'm afraid that will be a rather expensive one).

As to the managerial set-up: the Lunts have consistently stated they would do it without the Theatre Guild. Jack Wilson knew I was writing it and expressed the hope he would be involved with The Playwrights' Co. Of course, he would automatically have part of the Lunts' share and it would be o.k. with me to have him named as joint producer. I found him very helpful in the production of *There Shall Be No Night* and of course the Lunts are very fond of him and like to have him around. Please discuss this with John and Bill but not Sam Zolotow. [Zolotow, the *New York Times* theatrical reporter, was famous for digging out news and printing it before the facts were definite.]

If the play itself is good I'm sure the Lunts will want to do it as the two parts are certainly wonderful. There are also a boy and girl and parts for actors like Tommy Gomez and Romney Brent. The other two characters are assistant stage managers. If the Lunts do it, I imagine they would start rehearsals around the end of September. I don't much care when it's done as it's a sort of fantastic comedy without my usual topical timeliness ("Mr. Sherwood is dealing again with yesterday's headlines").

Well—I'll be seeing you very soon. I sail on the *Q.E.* June 25th, which means I'll be in New York by July 1st. Beyond that, I have no plans except incessant work on the Hopkins book. Madeline will remain here in England until the latter part of August.

Give my very best to Bill, Lucy and all at the office. Madeline joins in that, and to yourself. We are feeling fine and not stuffing ourselves with a lot of rich food. I'll have to take it easy when I get back to Shor's. The chickens are also in fine shape—happy, rosy-cheeked and laying like mad things. They remember you in their prayers and so do I when eating breakfast.

Yours,

Bob

The last two sentences in the letter refer to the fact that Victor had arranged to have made, and sent to England, proper coops for the chickens.

Off to the Lunts went the script, as soon as Bob reached New York. We were all excited about what they would say about it. It came back fairly soon with a letter from Lynn Fontanne which dug into the script's weakness like a surgeon's scalpel. Bob read the letter to us at a meeting; it is the only time I can recall seeing him hurt and angry.

He had always found Miss Fontanne difficult, although he was unstinting in his praise for her talent. He once remarked that in writing for a star team one had to keep thinking up an equal number of good lines for each—except, he added, where the Lunts are involved you concentrate on good lines for Lynn.

He also told, with some relish, about a dinner with the Lunts and the Oliviers, when the future Lord Olivier was married to Vivien Leigh. One of them said it would be wonderful if he would write a four-character play for the quartet. Bob replied that he had thought of such a play. He then described the roles for the Lunts, which everyone thought would suit them perfectly. Then he began to describe the other two roles. Before anyone could possibly grasp what the characters were like, Miss Fontanne interjected, "Oh, Larry and Vivien wouldn't be suited for those parts at all."

Bob said that he was going to do more work on the rejected script, but he never did. Until 1948 he devoted the bulk of his time to his prize-winning book *Roosevelt and Hopkins*. We weren't too happy about this, for it was, in our eyes, simply delaying the time when he would come up with another blockbuster play. We were sure he had not lost his sense of drama; had he not just written the script for the movie *The Best Years of Our Lives*, considered by many people to have been Sam Goldwyn's masterpiece? We were all very happy when Bob announced that *Roosevelt and Hopkins* was at the printers.

Bob's work on his book did have a salutary, although unaesthetic, impact on Company solidarity. Hopkins, before his death, had assembled a mass of papers, and a friend of his had gone through them and selected the items of unquestioned importance. Even these filled several filing cabinets. Bob had to have them available, so he had the cabinets moved to the Company office. The only room large enough for them was the general conference room, and there they remained, an unsightly mess, until the manuscript was finished. But the fact that Bob was in the office steadily encouraged the other playwrights to drop in and tended to strengthen the members' relationships.

Anything that kept us united was important, for we had no producible plays to discuss. Yet the meetings during these days, whether formal or informal, were surprisingly gay and happy ones as far as the playwright members were concerned. They were all confident that they *would* soon have plays; in July 1947 we voted to clear up the dividend arrearages on the preferred stock, when foresight should have told us to preserve all our cash. We talked about the possibility of doing nonmember plays; several were read and all rejected. We discussed possible new members; finally extended an invitation to the Kanins. They declined it, and we could not agree on anyone else. We talked about forming a radio company, but nothing came of it. We talked about the state of the world in general and the state of the Broadway theatre in particular. Nobody wanted to face some unpleasant facts.

Slowly but surely that unrelenting factor, money, began to make us face them. We simply could not continue to meet our overhead costs with nothing coming in except odds and ends from prior productions. But we never for a moment considered giving up. Samrock and Fields took voluntary cuts, and, when they were asked by Arthur Schwartz to handle his revue *Inside U.S.A.*, they relinquished all Company salary. Kurt Weill agreed to do a musical, *Love Life*, for Cheryl Crawford, loyally demanding that the Company be paid a percentage of the profits. Despite the fact that the talented Alan Lerner wrote the book and lyrics, there were no profits.

Finally, to everyone's relief, Max brought in a draft of his new play, *Anne of the Thousand Days*, which all of us found exciting. Elmer announced that he was readying two new plays. Shortly thereafter Garson Kanin, author of *Born Yesterday*, submitted an original play, *The Smile of the World*, and we agreed to produce it. We were getting back into business.

Garson Kanin

Kanin was, and still is, a fascinating character. By 1949 I had known him for many years and had praised him from the first. David Selznick, producer of *Gone with the Wind*, occasionally had moments of self-criticism; in one of these he reproached himself for not having paid any attention to "the Whartons' press agentry of Garson Kanin before anybody had heard of Garson Kanin." Kanin was then assisting George Abbott, the famous Broadway producer-director who helped to launch so many young people on the road to fame and fortune. (Neither Abbott nor the Whartons were "anybody" in David's mind). After my wife, who had a keen eye for unrecognized talent, had met Kanin somewhere, he had quickly become a friend of the family.

He charmed all ages. When he visited us in the country he enchanted our two little girls by inventing a game he called "Naughty Children." Gar was the naughty child; he would pretend to disobey parental orders and lie down flat on the road where autos were constantly coming and going. The children would nearly burst with excited terror as they tried to coax him back.

Having no money, he often had to take work he found undesirable. He once told me that the most undesirable—the most deadening— work he ever did was to act in a third-rate radio serial which he and two of the other actors also wrote. "You just can't imagine," he said, "how mechanical and uninspired such work can be. One night, after we finished the broadcast, we decided to sit down right away and write next week's script. When we sat down, we couldn't remember what the serial was about!"

His talent soon gained more recognition, although no one suspected then that he would eventually succeed as director, actor, dramatist, and biographer. My wife retained him to direct her first production, *Too Many Heroes*, written by Dore Schary, who was to become the studio chief of the then mighty MGM. Shortly thereafter Kanin got his first Hollywood assignment, under Samuel Goldwyn. Goldwyn was immediately impressed by Gar, calling him "Thalberg the Second," referring to the late head of production at MGM. But Goldwyn was disappointed at finding that Gar did not always follow Sam's first and foremost rule in judging a property: begin by asking "Who loves who?"

It was, therefore, not Goldwyn, but RKO, that gave Kanin the chance which resulted in a giant leap for him. He was allowed to do a low-budget, non-love-story picture, *A Man to Remember*, which astonished everyone by receiving accolades equal to any bestowed on the top Class A pictures of that season.

In this film he achieved the remarkable feat of stirring up emotion with a sequence in which only a chart appeared on the screen. The leading character is an elderly hinterland doctor. He flouts the County Medical Association by treating the children of the county with an anti-polio preventive which the association has not yet approved. As the officials meet to censure or disbar him, a polio epidemic breaks out in the state. The screen then shows a chart with boxes ruled off for each county. As new cases are reported, black dots are made in the box for the county in which the cases occur. As the boxes of the other counties got blacker and blacker, while the doctor's county showed only an occasional dot, you could almost hear the emotion swelling in the audience.

He went on to success in plays, films, books. His play, *Born Yesterday*, made Judy Holliday a star; he directed the prize-winning *The Diary of Anne Frank*. He turned to books and wrote the immensely successful *Tracy and Hepburn*. Happily, the end is not yet; we can look forward eagerly to more of the same.

In *The Smile of the World* Kanin tackled a theme which, so far as I

The Kanins, the only playwrights who were invited to join the Company and declined.
(*Graphic House*)

know, has never been successful in the Anglo-American theatre,—a story of the love between a youngish man and a considerably older woman. The subject had great interest for Kanin because his wife, Ruth Gordon, *was* considerably older than he, and I think he was determined to show that such a marriage could be a love marriage—as, indeed, his clearly was. But the fact that something has really happened doesn't necessarily make it a realistic subject for a play.

We were, of course, attracted by the skill of the writing, particularly his opening, which, based on actuality, worked well. Recently, Bill Fields had arranged for all members of the Company to be photographed by the popular photographer Yousef Karsh; Kanin had also sat for the gentleman. Karsh's method of getting his subject out of a "posing" attitude was to talk incessantly and bombard the sitter with questions about himself and his way of life. Kanin opened his play with a scene where a leading character was being photographed by such a man (admittedly suggested by Karsh); it enabled him to explain the whole situation of the play while keeping the audience chuckling.

But the play, as a whole, did not work. We fussed around with it, tried different endings, tested it on the road. Finally, we brought it to New York and one week later it was closed and forgotten. It is really staggering how quickly and completely all trace of a 100 percent failure disappears. A friend of mine once declared that there was one line in the *Rubaiyat* which convinced him that Omar Khayyam must have been a playwright as well as a poet and that he had written at least one total flop: "I came like water and like wind I go."

The Smile of the World certainly went like wind. *Anne of the Thousand Days* was a different story—and, for myself, it had one complex angle that I have never been able to figure out.

Leland, Rex, and Max

Leland Hayward was a strange, aggressive man, successful both in films and on Broadway, who never seemed to me to be very happy. He had married, divorced, and remarried his first wife; he had three subsequent marriages and a love affair which most people thought would end in marriage—all of which indicates, to me, the instability engendered by unhappiness. When he decided to try his hand at Broadway productions he retained me as his lawyer. I became very fond of him and remained fond of him even after he left my office and retained other counsel, an action which does not endear anyone to the deserted lawyer. What I remember most about his first ventures was his ambition never to have a New York failure. He closed one very interesting play out of town because he felt the tryout notices augured ill for it in New York. I remembered this during a crisis with *Anne*. He did have more financial successes than failures, but, like every other producer, his batting average dropped below 1,000 percent.

In 1948 he had a skillful technique for acquiring production rights. As soon as he heard that any popular dramatist had finished even a draft of a new play, he begged to read it, expressed unbounded enthusiasm for it and, of course, a desire to produce it, disregarding utterly any connection the playwright might have with any other producer. This at least assured him of a co-production.

Max was enchanted with Leland's reaction to the script of *Anne of the Thousand Days*. Without bothering to discuss the matter with anyone in the Company, he agreed to a co-production with Hayward. They decided to employ Jo Mielziner, incidentally agreeing to a scenic scheme which caused the rest of us to shake our heads. They also decided to seek Joyce Redman for the role of Anne and, for the most important role of Henry VIII, Rex Harrison.

Mielziner had, and deserved, an outstanding reputation for the way his sets worked. But even Homer nodded from time to time, and even Mielziner had his off-days. His first designs for *Anne* struck most of us as being just *too* complicated to work, but Hayward, accustomed to Hollywood standards, raised no question and Max followed Leland. We were right and they were wrong. I was told that one change required a stagehand to leap on a moving turntable, change a prop, and then leap off before an overhead beam cracked his skull. I do not believe this, but it illustrates the stagehands' antagonism to the first designs. In the end, the first sets were all thrown out, at considerable expense, and a new scheme by Jo adopted, which, to no one's surprise, turned out to be top-drawer in every respect.

Harrison was then a very successful actor, but still on the way up; eventually, he created a sensation as Henry Higgins in *My Fair Lady*. He had been launched on a promising Hollywood career, but, through no fault of his own, an unpleasant scandal broke about him. He had gone to the home of a starlet who was reputedly enamoured of him and found she had committed suicide. Shocked and startled no end, he made an unfortunate mistake. Instead of calling the studio publicity department, he called the police and was immediately in the headlines. Had he called the Studio, only a few people would ever

have heard of his presence at the home; in their golden days the power of the Studios to control publicity was really awesome.

Harrison, at the time, had a way of dealing with playwrights which was akin to Hayward's; perhaps he learned it from Hayward. When a dramatist sent him a play he read it promptly and, even if wholly unimpressed, sent back word that he was certainly "interested" but had other commitments which would have to be worked out. Rice, who could be extraordinarily naive, sent plays to him two different times, and waited vainly for a definitive agreement to appear, which never came, to no one's surprise but Elmer's.

Harrison did accept the part of Henry VIII; Joyce Redman agreed to play Anne Boleyn; the play went into rehearsal in the fall of 1948. Bretaigne Windust was directing. We attended a run-through before it began its Philadelphia tryout and all of us thought it looked very promising. I could not attend the Philadelphia opening because I had to be in Fort Wayne, Indiana, during the week in which the opening occurred. There was a good train (we still used trains in those days) from Fort Wayne to New York which stopped at Philadelphia at around one o'clock. I took it on Saturday and arrived at the theatre in time for the matinee performance. Bill Fields was waiting for me with some unbelievable news.

Bill assured me that Leland had decided to close the play at the end of the tryout!

This was hard to believe when Bill told it to me; it was still harder to believe after the performance, for the play, to me, clearly had the potential of a smash hit; as usual, some work was needed. Was Leland's fear of anything that didn't look sure-fire rising to the surface again? Clearly, something was amiss, for he called me at the hotel and wouldn't believe me when I praised the play highly. Nor would he believe two or three other theatre people who happened to be in Philadelphia and called him to praise the play. Max was clearly jarred by Leland's attitude; he talked of closing and rewriting the play in its entirety. That would have been the end of it.

I had reserved a room in a hotel, but I gave it up, took a late train to New York, and tried to find Sherwood. I reached him by phone early the next morning. I told him the situation and asked his permission to phone Hayward and say the Company would buy out his interest. I didn't know what this would cost; I didn't know where the Company

Rex Harrison in *Anne of the Thousand Days*. He made a striking success as the royal Henry VIII, but his greatest success was to come in the role of another Henry, surnamed Higgins, in *My Fair Lady*. (*Theatre Collection, New York Public Library*)

One of Joyce Redman's dresses for *Anne of the Thousand Days*. The designer's sketch and the finished product.
(*John Swope*)

would get the money; neither fact bothered me one bit, for I was *sure* that Hayward wouldn't dare accept the offer, and he didn't. The one thing more humiliating than bringing in a flop is to have sold out your interest in a play that later proves to be a hit.

He worked out an arrangement with Max whereby the tryout was extended long enough for Max to do some rewriting which Leland thought imperative. He brought in a new director to replace Windust: Henry Potter. When this had been done, Kurt and I went down to see the effect. Kurt's opinion was brief and to the point: "They've slicked it up, but not enough to ruin it." When Leland heard of Kurt's opinion, he asked me, in polite but troubled tones, "John, is it bad for a play to be slick?" I devoutly wished that Sherwood were present to give him the explanation Bob had given me at the time of *Abe Lincoln in Illinois*.

The play came to New York, received an excellent reception, ran for 286 performances in New York and ten weeks on tour. When it closed it did not "go like wind"; it was well remembered, so well that nearly twenty years later someone bought the film rights and made an outstanding picture, with Richard Burton as the star.

However, for myself, it became the basis for a puzzling and unpleasant situation.

A Sholom Aleichem Story

Max suddenly exhibited a definitely unfriendly attitude to me. By this time Max's mercurial character was well known and it was taken for granted that this would pass very quickly. But it didn't. Moreover, Max began to tell people that Leland had been a tower of strength, a rock of Gibraltar; a magazine article appeared which told how Leland had *bravely* closed the play for three weeks in order to give Max a chance to retrieve a doomed script. Bill Fields, who had worked hand in glove with me in Philadelphia to keep the show going, was amazed; he went to Max and Mab (Max's wife) and tried to at least get the story straight. He had no success. But I've always rather treasured this letter:

December 16, 1948

Dear John:

I see in *Variety* where Leland Hayward presented Hank Potter with a gold watch for having stepped in and saved *Anne*. This set me to musing about how Hank wouldn't have got that watch—nor Max wouldn't have had his hit—had you not been in Philadelphia on that Saturday, for, as you'll recall, when we entered the room at the Warwick we were greeted with these words from Hayward: "Windy, Max and I have decided to close the show at the end of the second week in Philadelphia, etc."

Bretaigne Windust, Leland Hayward, Victor Samrock, and Jo Mielziner—projecting worry in a way no actors could match. One glance told you that trouble was brewing.
(*John Swope*)

. . . Perhaps Leland will give me a solid gold watch, although if I have any choice in the matter, I could suggest a gift that would please me more.

Wearily,

Bill

Max's attitude continued through his next show, then gradually began to change for the better again. He may have lost more than he knew by all this. When, in 1951, he first conceived the idea of a play about Socrates, he sought suggestions for an unusual actor to play the role. He wanted someone, if possible, who was not typical Anglo-American. I suggested that he see the current Rodgers and Hammerstein hit, for many people were predicting that the lead actor would become a really great star; as yet, he was at the stage where a star part in a Maxwell Anderson show might well be attractive. Max merely smiled contemptuously and made some remark about not caring for Rodgers and Hammerstein productions. Of course, Yul Brynner might have refused the part, but if he had accepted it, *Barefoot in Athens* would certainly have had a longer run than twenty-nine performances.

I have never ascertained the cause of Max's temporary dislike of me. It did come to an end; eventually, we became very friendly again. At the time I was having some violent stress in my private life; I suspect Max was having the same. Perhaps I was difficult, too; perhaps Max needed some place, some man, as a receptacle for overstrained resentments. There is one other possible explanation, which did not occur to me until my seventy-fifth birthday, years later, and came to my mind as a result of a story told by Arthur Miller.

On the occasion of my seventy-fifth birthday—it was after Max's death—my wife, Betty, arranged an unusual and delightful party at the Booth Theatre. At her request, various friends said a few words; among them was Arthur Miller, who surprised everyone by giving a hilarious talk. In the course of it—for some reason which I cannot recall, he was not talking about me at the moment—he told the following story, which he said originated with Sholom Aleichem.

A man arrived home from work one evening with bruises and scars from an obviously recent attack. His frightened wife asked what in the world had happened.

"Well," said he, "it's very strange. I met Bill and Joe; we began to walk home together; they began to quarrel with me, and the next thing I knew they were beating me up."

"But *why*," asked his wife, now bewildered as well as frightened, "*why* should they do that?"

He replied, "I think I can understand Bill's behavior. After all, when his father went broke, I gave Bill the money to go through college, and after that I gave him enough more so that he could start his own business. But Joe! In my whole life I never did anything for Joe!"

CHAPTER
XIII

Prestige without Profits

Anne of the Thousand Days was a great artistic success, but it did not replenish our dwindling funds. However, we chose to put our minds on other things. 1948 was the tenth year of our enterprise, and we were happy to recount to each other—and to anyone else who would listen—our accomplishments over the ten-year span. Quite a few people were ready to listen; the press printed interviews on the subject, all favorable, and we lived pretty much in an aura of success. Certainly, at the time, no producing firm was more prestigious.

In all honesty, this was not an earth-shaking accomplishment. Broadway in 1948 was a small pond in the nation's economy, and parts of the pond were pretty dirty puddles. One could be a sizable and respectable frog without too much effort.

The dramatists had freed themselves from any dictation by producers; indeed, the wheel had almost turned full circle. But the dominant factor in the industry was now the theatre owner, and the dominant theatre owner was the Shubert organization. The Shuberts were still pretty tough customers.

During the 1930s' depression some producers were able to exact extremely favorable terms from theatre owners; the Shubert organization went through bankruptcy but was bought in by Lee and J.J.; when the war brought back prosperity, they decided to give up producing on their own and try to get contracts as favorable as possible to the theatre owner. Before the depression the theatre owner frequently took 35 or even 40 percent of the gross box office receipts as rent; in the early thirties the powerful producers cut theatre owners, including the Shuberts, to 20 percent. By 1948 the Shuberts were again getting at least 30 percent and were striving for, and sometimes again getting, the old 35 percent. They tried to stiffen other clauses. They could do this because they were close to a full-fledged monopoly; fortunately, there were a few independent owners; this competition kept the terms within reason. But they never missed a chance to try to outsmart a producer.

Once, when I was on vacation, a young producer retained a partner in my firm to negotiate a contract for the lease of a Shubert theatre. He showed my partner the printed form which had been handed to him by Mr. Lee; my partner found it outrageously unfair. He accompanied the young client to Lee Shubert's office and began to argue clause after clause. Mr. Lee looked at him strangely and suddenly asked him the name of his firm. "Oh," Mr. Lee said, "the Wharton office! Why didn't you say so? Here's the form we give to *his* clients." He pulled out a completely different and much more favorable document and tore up the other.

They permitted their bookers to take bribes for giving a producer a good theatre as opposed to a second-drawer one. Even if an honest producer got a first-class theatre, he might discover that he had been chiseled as if by a fine Italian hand. Herman Levin once booked a Shubert house under a contract which gave him exceptionally favorable terms in any week in which the gross box office receipts reached a certain figure. He was pretty pleased with himself for having obtained such terms; more so when the show, *Call Me Mister*, got smash notices. The Shuberts thereupon announced that there was a question about the fire laws and removed enough seats to make it impossible to reach the figure which gave the favorable terms.

As the power of the theatre unions grew, the Shuberts more and more took over the negotiations of union contracts. They could do this because the producers, to their shame, could not get together and raise enough money to retain a man to negotiate for *them*. (They finally did do this.) As a result, the Shuberts could and did trade onerous terms to producers for more favorable ones to theatre owners.

However, the real rotten apple in the Broadway barrel was not put there by the Shuberts, although they made no effort to remove it. This was "Ice."

Very few people understand what Ice is; even those who think they do often confuse it with speculative profit. Ice *is* linked to speculation, but it is something quite different. The term probably derives from Incidental Campaign Expenses, a heading which politicians once used to cover up money spent to bribe voters. Another explanation holds that ice is something which melts away. Ice involves what is technically called "commercial bribery."

Speculation is the purchase of something solely because the buyer hopes that it can be resold at a profit. If you buy a stock with the intention of holding it indefinitely and simply adding the dividends to your other income, you are called an investor. If you buy a stock solely because you've been told that something will shortly send the price up, and you intend to sell as soon as that happens, you are called a speculator. Of course, your tip may prove to be untrue; the stock may go down in price. Speculation always involves a risk of quick loss as well as the hope of a quick profit.

Most Americans who can afford it indulge in speculation to a greater or lesser extent. The stock market is thronged with speculators, but it is not the only such market. People speculate in markets for wheat, corn, and other necessities of life. Land booms are simply speculation gone mad. In Holland there was once a great speculation in tulip bulbs, which sent prices to ridiculous heights. Speculation can be very foolish, and costly to the amateur. But hardly anyone in America considers speculation to be immoral—something that should be forbidden by law.

Except for speculation in one object: a theatre ticket!

How this poor little piece of pasteboard produced such a revulsion is hard to explain. The first attempts to legislate against ticket speculation were laughed out of court; one judge pertinently asked, "What is so holy about a theatre ticket?" But the revulsion continued; the do-gooders finally had their way, and normally sane judges gave solemn approval to all sorts of impossible regulatory laws.

These laws require that theatre tickets must have printed on them the price for which they can be purchased at the box office; no one can buy a ticket for resale unless licensed to do so; such licensees, called "brokers" (a misleading term, they are only retail stores), can mark up the tickets only by an amount prescribed by the State Legislature (most of whose members know nothing about the theatre). Thus, if the legislature permits a $1.50 markup, a ticket with a printed price of $10 may be sold by a broker for $11.50, and that is the *legal* top.

But a theatre has just so many seats and no more, and when a theatre with, say, 600 orchestra seats is housing a new smash hit there may well be two or three thousand people a night who would like to get orchestra tickets. Among these are many who are ready, able, and willing to pay $25 (or more) per ticket. So, what happens? As always, when there is a big enough demand, someone appears who furnishes a supply. In this case the suppliers are *speculators who are willing to break the law;* they may or may not also be licensed brokers; in any event, they want the $25 price for a $10 ticket instead of the maximum $11.50 prescribed by law.

But how do they get the tickets? That is where the Ice comes in. The speculator pays a bribe of, say, $5 per ticket to the box office man (now called a "treasurer"). *That $5 is Ice.* After paying it the speculator has a profit of $10.50—*if* he does get $25 for the ticket; he may misjudge the market and be unable to sell the ticket at all (called "eating the ticket"). There is a risk in every speculation. There is no financial risk to the Ice-taker.

Five dollars doesn't sound like much. But if $5 can be collected on half the orchestra—300 seats—that is $1,500 a performance, and six evening performances will yield $9,000 a week. Multiply that by ten or twenty theatres and it not only sounds like, it *is,* big money. Actually, the amount of the bribe varies from show to show, from ticket to ticket, and may vary from night to night. Some shows may not have enough demand to warrant Ice payments except at week-ends; some may not warrant any payment. The best seats can command more Ice than poorer seats, and so on.

Who gets the Ice? This is also a big variable. If the theatre owner and the producer are both Ice takers, the fund is divided between them and certain favored employees—the box office men, the house manager, the producer's general manager, and perhaps others. There is no set rule. If the theatre owner and producer are men who obey the law, the employees' group get that much more. The whole business is a cash business; probably no one knows all the ramifications. The recipients frequently put the cash in secret safe deposit boxes. One man noted for his Ice grabs kept the location *so* secret that when he died not even his widow knew where they were. She found herself almost penniless, although there was surely a vast amount of cash stashed away somewhere.

Although Ice is obviously part of the gross box office receipts, certain people never, to my knowledge, share in it: dramatists, composers, lyricists, directors, stars, and any others whose compensation is based on a percentage of such gross receipts; also the investors in the play. (Stars who have been given house seat privileges sometimes sell their rights to speculators.) In short, the people who create the entertainment and the people who supply the capital for production are all excluded. *That is the tragic part.* If they could participate in

Ice—let alone speculative profit—the theatre would quickly become a healthier place financially.

But the self-righteous attitude of the public in regard to theatre ticket speculation is one that cannot be explained nor argued away. It is a popular delusion and an extraordinary madness of the crowd. The complete absurdity of the situation becomes apparent when just two facts are considered.

First, speculation in World Series baseball tickets, big football game tickets, and some film tickets is known to exist just as much as theatre ticket speculation; *no* outcry ever arises. Second, it is not illegal to *pay* more than the legal top price, which is saying that a man who pays over money in an illegal transaction is innocent of any wrong, only the taker is a wrongdoer. I once suggested that paying more than the legal top *should* be made a misdemeanor. I made the suggestion only to prove that the politicians were not really interested in preventing speculation, and the complete disregard of the suggestion did prove it. (People who can afford to pay $25 a ticket are also able to give campaign contributions; no politician wants to inconvenience *them*.)

How this all came to pass is a fascinating but lengthy story, not germane to the present discussion. Suffice it to say that the statutes were enacted because of a clamor by well-meaning, naive do-gooders; they are as unenforceable as the prohibition laws were. They remain on the books because politicians feel that if they voted for repeal, an ignorant electorate with no understanding of the matter might vote against the legislators some future day. Moreover, the group of Ice takers inside the industry quietly support the politicos who keep the laws in force.

Almost every industry has its own "rotten apple," but the effect is often minor. The disastrous effects of Ice, however, are hard to overestimate. In typical rotten-apple fashion it began to breed more and more rottenness elsewhere. Kickbacks became much more common, particularly with the staffs of unsuccessful producers who had no hit throwing off Ice. As the cost of musicals mounted, kickbacks became almost an accepted thing. When Samrock undertook his first big outside musical show, he was startled by the way suppliers *routinely* asked him how big a cut he demanded. One scenery builder, now out of business, presented his bid in two parts, one for scenery, one for the kickback.

Another snide trick of producers was to pocket advertising rebates; if a producer had several shows on during a year, the newspapers would add up all the lineage and if the total reached a certain figure would send a check for a rebate. Producers frequently did not bother to allocate the rebate among the backers of the various plays; they pocketed the whole amount!

All of this reacted against both producers and theatre owners when it came to negotiations with the theatrical unions. These had grown in number and power during the war. Almost everybody who worked as an employee was a member of some union; moreover, unheard of elsewhere, the *owners* of scenery-building shops were allowed to keep their union membership. They could, therefore, keep their prices high; if business fell off, they went to work temporarily as stagehands. And stagehands were tough; during the wartime wage freeze they calmly announced that their members needed an extra amount per week as "expense money." It was a clear violation of wage controls, but if it wasn't paid, the show was forced to close.

The union negotiators in 1948 were well aware of Ice, kickbacks, rebates, and the like. It was pretty hard to convince them that their members should accept low wages in order to keep production and running costs down. Indeed, it was *impossible*. The current Lords of the Broadway Manor were beginning to reap the whirlwind which their long-time arrogance had sown.

Our Company was known to be a top-flight producing company that had both stature and dignity. Our members did not take Ice; we did not cheat our investors by pocketing advertising rebates. As to the unions—Samrock quickly became an important figure in the union world; we got no unwarranted favors, but neither were we subjected to unfair demands.

What might be called "the extracurricular record" of the playwright members and of the Company itself also worked in our favor. These men were not merely playwrights. Sidney Howard, the short-lived founder-member, first came into prominence through an investigation of the drug traffic. Rice's record with the American Civil Liberties Union was well known. Maxwell Anderson was one of the few dramatists who went to the front during World War II to work on the problems of morale. Sherwood not only organized the Stop Hitler Now campaign; he headed the Office of War Information for a time and was chosen by President Roosevelt for some extremely important special investigations. (Bob told me that in 1944 he was sent to see General MacArthur on a very important issue. The general was then losing favor with many people, who thought him, outside of his war duties, arrogant and stupid. Bob himself was dubious; hence he was amazed to hear from MacArthur his plans to make Japan a capitalistic democracy if he were given charge of the occupation—plans which eventually were largely carried out.)

The Company was known to have been generous in providing

Maxwell Anderson in the barracks at Fort Bragg. "He is a kind, quiet, unassuming fellow who seems to prefer the companionship of enlisted men to officers"—Sgt. Lloyd Shearer. Later, Max donned a uniform and went to the Pacific.
(*United States Army*)

benefits for various charities. Sherwood wrote, free of charge, the introduction to an anti-Nazi film, *Pastor Hall*, at the request of Mrs. Roosevelt. We strongly supported the growing antiracist movement in America, unhesitatingly cancelling road performances when we discovered a city or theatre was imposing ugly restrictions. Rice was one of the first to foresee, and warn against, the vices that would spring from the Martin Dies Committee, later called the House Un-American Activities Committee.

We gave money and time to long-range theatrical projects, paying the costs for a young producer to tour certain road theatres to see whether their stages would make possible an economy plan he had devised. (He found that they wouldn't.)

One long-range plan dragged on in a way that produced a most curious result. Sherwood wrote a film script for the Council of the Living Theatre designed to increase general interest in the theatre. The Council could not raise the money to produce it; the project languished. Then new members came on the Council Board and some of them strove to revive this project, although they had no real knowledge of the past effort. They hired new writers; these proved unsatisfactory. One bright day the new head of the Council asked Bob if he would revise a new film script. As he read it he began to have a strange *déjà vu* feeling. It was a loose and very bad revision of his own first script!

Some greatly desired experiments were dropped because we did not have the necessary funds available. Elmer Rice urged again and again that we rent a theatre and put on a series of revivals of the members' previous successes, but he would not believe either Samrock or me when we told him how much money would have to be raised for such a project; hence, it never got off the ground.

We explored the idea of having our own film company. Fiorello La Guardia was then mayor; he was eager to make New York a film-producing center. When one of his aides heard of our discussions he arranged for me to meet the mayor and discuss the matter. I was a great admirer of "the Little Flower," but this meeting was a disappointment. I explained how much, and what kind of, capital a film-producing company would need. His countenance began, and continued, to fall as I talked. Unlike Rice, he believed me; what troubled him was that he had never given that phase of the matter any real thought.

We retained a popular lecturer, Clayton Hamilton, to address the suburban clubs on our plans; I have always felt that we never gave this idea a fair trial. We worked out plans for preopening sales of tickets very similar to a plan which Harold Prince put into operation in the late sixties.

Our riskiest experiment was undertaken early in our history. In 1939, after *Abe Lincoln in Illinois* had run over 400 performances, Rice persuaded the rest of us to move it to a larger theatre and adopt a ticket price scale of $1.10, 85¢, and 50¢ (tax included). The purpose of this was expressed, rather grandiloquently, by Rice in a press release which he wrote for the Company: "to bring back the theatre to those who are hungry for it, and to introduce it to those who have never tasted its delights."

I opposed this experiment because it was clear to me that if the demand for tickets to *Abe* continued to be as great as it had been, we would simply be increasing the profits of the speculators. However, the demand wasn't that great; far from it, we never had a capacity week and we closed the production after eight weeks with a loss of $15,000.

The public knew little of all this. But Broadway did, and they respected the Company for it.

Sherwood in the Pacific. Max, in a memorial poem, spoke of Bob as "Tall. Lean. Gangling. Watchful."
(*Theatre Collection, New York Public Library*)

Touching Bottom and an Unexpected Rescue

Despite our ten-year record, we were in trouble; deep trouble, deeper than we realized. I should have realized it, but I was in the middle of a real *Sturm und Drang* period of my personal life. Carly and I had faced the fact that our marriage was irretrievably "worn out"; not a little shattered, I undertook a rugged Freudian analysis; eventually, I went to Reno; we were divorced; and in 1949 I married Mary Mason. She was a successful stage and radio actress, the star of a bearable radio serial, "Maudie's Diary." After our marriage, she gave up acting, dropped her stage name, and, as Betty Wharton, became a professional theatre librarian on the staff of the Lincoln Center Performing Arts Library. More important, we have literally "lived happily ever after."

There was some basis for minimizing the Company's troubles and looking at things through the famous mythical rose-tinted glasses.

Sherwood had arranged for two current musical comedy giants, Irving Berlin and Moss Hart, to join him as co-producers of a show for which he would write the book. The Company would have only a small stake, but it would derive weekly payments of "office charges." Elmer was working on three plays, including a revision of his play *Not for Children*. Best of all, Max and Kurt had acquired the stage rights to Alan Paton's distinguished book *Cry the Beloved Country* and were making it into a musical. They had written a wonderful song, "Lost in the Stars," and decided to use it as a title song.

It was not long before the rose-tinted glasses began to fade into a less attractive color. The Sherwood-Berlin-Hart musical soon ran into rough seas. It was titled *Miss Liberty*. The story involves two newspaper tycoons of the late 1880s fighting for circulation; one of them, as a publicity stunt, sends a young man to Paris to find the girl who was the model for the Statue of Liberty. A beautiful girl is palmed off on him. He falls in love with her and brings her to the States; she is accompanied by her mother who professes to despise Americans. Complications ensue; at the end, there is one effective scene before the famous statue.

Bob was trying to bring something fresh and original to the musical theatre; he wanted to get away from "Boy Meets Girl" stories; but freshness and originality do not alone make a good libretto, and Bob was inexperienced in this field. The notion that the young man, let alone his astute world-famous employer, could be fooled by the young girl was preposterous; it was well known that Bartholdi had worked on the statue for years. There were other inconsistencies and unbelievable aspects. But such was Bob's standing that Berlin and Hart accepted his script, praised it, and went to work with it. A mutual admiration society grew up; Bob would tell us how wonderful Berlin's songs were and what good casting ideas Hart had. *We* thought the casting was all wrong and were worried about the book from the start; as Kurt put it, "Bob thinks it's too easy."

The play opened in Philadelphia. I was accompanied by Burt Shevelove, destined to become famous as a triple-threat man in both theatre and TV—director, author, lyricist. This time there was no chill *slowly* settling down on us; disaster began *leaping* at one almost as soon as the curtain went up and, with rare breaks, it continued to do so. Actors hired for their acting ability were made to dance; dancers were given songs; the only person who seemed to surmount everything was Ethel Griffis, a seventy-odd-year-old actress playing the mother. She received great applause for a song, "Only for Americans," an excellent Berlin composition but rather confusing to the audience, since it heaped scorn on America when the mother was eager to have the young man take her and her daughter to that very place.

Shevelove and I walked sadly out of the theatre. He said, thoughtfully, "Well, I guess when three of the biggest men in the theatre make a mistake it's got to be one of the biggest mistakes ever seen."

Newspapers usually do not pay much attention to tryout openings. But the three names involved here were so big that the tryout was

An all-star cast of creative artistic and producing talent: Joe Hyman, Oliver Smith (in a rare moment of exhaustion), Jerome Robbins, Irving Berlin, Victor Samrock, Moss Hart, and Jay Blackton in the foreground. (*Graphic House*)

deemed national news, and the wires carried such headlines as "Play by three famous theatre men lays big egg." The word-of-mouth was equally bad.

But the trio was a trio of famous professionals and, undaunted— well, somewhat daunted—they went to work to fix it. They put Hart in charge and loyally supported his decisions for changes. Somehow or other, it was whipped into a shape that enabled it to run for nearly forty weeks—not all of them profitable—but quite an achievement for a play blasted to pieces out of town.

I took my elder daughter to the New York opening. She was always a demanding theatregoer; she thought not only the book but also the score was below par—it *wasn't* one of Berlin's best. "I think," she said, acidly, "that Mister Berlin has unconsciously plagiarized every composer he knows, including Irving Berlin." This was unfair, but none of the songs ever attained the standing of a big Berlin hit such as "White Christmas" or "Easter Parade."

The Company, Sherwood, and Moss Hart recouped their investments in the show by reason of a surprising action on the part of Berlin. He purchased the film rights for $187,000. I was told that this action was inspired by his desire to say no Berlin show ever failed financially. Another story was to the effect that his obsessive hatred of agency commissions prompted the action. Someone had tentatively offered $200,000, subject to a commission of $15,000; he thereupon offered $187,000, with no commission payable, which was readily accepted. Personally, I find either story hard to believe, but, then, I can't see why he should have bought the film rights at all. People *do* do funny things.

Although we didn't say so—at least, not very loudly—we were all shaken by the declining quality of Sherwood's work. The Greek play had passed away for good, and another script, with the unhappy title *Girls with Dogs*, was quickly consigned to that limbo from which it never should have come. We made excuses for *Miss Liberty*, saying, as Kurt did, that Bob thought a musical script was too easy, and that in Philadelphia he was suffering from his great curse, *tic douloureux*. But *Girls with Dogs* defied any excuses. Then Philip Barry died, leaving an unfinished script; his widow asked Bob to finish it.

Naturally, he hesitated, remembering Polly Howard and *Madam, Will You Walk*. But Ellen Barry, Phil's widow, turned out to be the exception that proves the rule. She accepted the fact that Barry had not fully decided just how he wanted to develop the story, and gave Bob *carte blanche* to go ahead. But his first revision really scared us; it seemed to all of us to be as indecisive as Barry's draft; the characters did inconsistent things from inconsistent motives.

Bob left for England after finishing this first revision. It was his favorite vacation spot and Mrs. Sherwood had made their house there a showplace, yet homelike. Bob also did a great deal of writing there.

I had not had a chance to discuss the first version with Bob in person. I knew he planned to do some work on it in England. With no little trepidation I decided to try an experiment. I wrote a long letter in whch I made no general criticism, but simply asked about each unmotivated or inconsistent action—why did he, or she, or they, do that? Bob never answered the letter, nor commented on it; presumably, he didn't like it, but, being Bob, he read it exactly as he would read a critical newspaper review. And back came a second revision in which the change for the better was magical. I cabled him, using that word; he did tell other people about the cable, so apparently my letter had had an effect.

We were all hopeful that Sherwood was himself again, but the play proved to be unsuccessful. However, this seemed more the fault of Barry's conception—or lack of conception. A startling event had obviously played a part in Barry's thinking; James V. Forrestal, serving with great acclaim as Secretary of the Navy, had suddenly resigned and withdrawn from the world of action. (He ended by committing suicide.) The protagonist of *Second Threshold* was just such a man, although *he* pulled out of his depression. But neither Barry nor Sherwood was able to make the man really interesting to the audience, and certainly he exhibited no trace of the brilliance attributed to him by the other characters.

The Company later co-produced a play, *The Emperor's Clothes*, in

Sherwood and James V. Forrestal. Forrestal's suicide was undoubtedly a factor in Philip Barry's conception of *Second Threshold*. (*Collection of Mrs. Robert E. Sherwood*)

which the leading character was described as a giant among scholars, but he never said or did anything that would have raised him above the stature of a midget. Anyone desiring to write a play about a great and brilliant man should study Shaw's *Major Barbara;* the protagonist, Andrew Undershaft, is first merely *described* as dominating, but he then appears and *does* overpower everyone within his first ten speeches.

In the meantime, *Lost in the Stars* began its career with a favorable omen: Rouben Mamoulian agreed to direct it. Mamoulian had achieved top-of-the-basket prominence both as a stage and a film director. His stage successes included *Porgy and Bess* and *Oklahoma!* But he also had had some ghastly failures. We were told by those who knew his work best that the time to get him was after a bad flop; he was a phoenixlike director who rose from ashes sturdier than before. We were lucky to get him when we did; he had just had a failure with *The Leaf and the Bough;* he gave us a first-rate job.

Alan Paton, Kurt Weill, and Maxwell Anderson.
(*Hugelmeyer*)

Parenthetically, one of the most striking facets of his personality was his charm for women. This was all the more remarkable in that Rouben was clearly not a man who would ever be cast for the role of a "handsome hero," and some people found his foreign accent hard to take. But there were rumors of a list of romantic attachments that included such beauties as Greta Garbo and Marlene Dietrich. No full-blooded male could look at a man with such a reputation without a feeling of deep awe.

Lost in the Stars was the first major musical to deal bluntly with the problems of racism. It was a plea to mankind to believe that blacks and whites *could* become friends and to recognize that a black man could have as much dignity as a white man. Unfortunately, there was

Rouben Mamoulian.
(*Hugelmeyer*)

not available at the time any black actor who could both sing Weill's music and project the strength of character required. We finally settled on Todd Duncan, who had infinite charm but never could be mistaken for a tower of strength.

At the first run-through Bob and Elmer were obviously unhappy with Duncan's personality; although not so obviously, so were Max and Kurt. Mamoulian tried to cheer up everyone. "We must make him sing as soon as possible," he declared, "then he'll be a big hit." Max rewrote Duncan's opening scene and cut it down so that he could quickly sing the song "Thousands and Thousands of Miles." He received tremendous applause—it is a tremendous song—and it looked as if Mamoulian's prophecy would come true. But it didn't— quite. Audiences did accept Duncan, but he did not turn into the kind of star who packed the house. And the failure to pack the house brought about the strangest and eventually most tragic contretemps I have ever witnessed among theatre professionals.

The critical notices were excellent. However, Max was going through a smug period and acted as if such a result had been certain from the start. Kurt began to take the same attitude. Hence, it was a rude shock when, after not too many weeks, the play began having empty seats. Thereupon they began summoning Samrock and Fields to meetings where they demanded to know why Vic and Bill were permitting this to happen. I couldn't believe my ears when Vic and Bill described these meetings to me:—two veteran theatre men ordering a press agent and business manager to see that the house sold out! It was *Street Scene* all over again, only worse. Max became more and more irascible and Kurt more and more excitable. Bill said to me, "I'm scared that Kurt is going to have a heart attack." He died from just such an attack on April 3, 1950.

This was the worst blow yet. Sidney Howard's death and Sam Behrman's resignation left gaping holes, but one could hope to fill those holes—indeed, Robert Anderson did fill one of them. But there were no two Kurt Weills.

Very few people in America appreciated the extent of his genius; he could compose for grand opera, comic opera, symphonic orchestra, musical comedy, concert recital, what you will. It was through Kurt that I became *convinced* that American music publishers were *not* the geniuses they held themselves out to be. I had done considerable work with Kurt's American publisher; when he heard a new score, he readily pontificated as to which songs would become popular and which would not. He was wrong just as often as right.

I never realized until Kurt's death just how wrong this man could be. Representing Kurt's widow, the lovely Lotte Lenya, I asked him

Lost in the Stars. Kurt had no objection to the injection into a play a little of what was then called razzmatazz. He could compose for this as easily as he could for pathos.
(*PIX*)

to appraise Kurt's works—*catalogue* is the peculiar word used to encompass the entire body of work. He declared that of course "September Song" was valuable, any child could know that—and that *Down in the Valley* was also extremely good. (I do not believe I have met ten persons who ever heard this score.) The rest of the catalogue, he opined, was *of little or no value.* Happily, Kurt's widow paid no attention to the publisher, and there are now available recordings of many of his songs. Moreover, while *Down in the Valley* never became famous, a revival of *The Threepenny Opera* was a six-year sensation and the song "Mack the Knife" was heard as widely as "September Song."

The Big Slide

Kurt's death initiated a slide to the very bottom in the Company's affairs. There was an accompanying tiny gleam of sunshine; Sidney Kingsley had a new play which he asked us to co-produce.

The play was a dramatization of Arthur Koestler's successful book *Darkness at Noon*, an all-out attack of Communism in Russia. Kingsley did a masterful job of adaptation; the casting was skillful, even to the unknowns; it chalked up 186 performances in New York and had a road tour of 31 weeks. It gave Sidney another New York Drama Critics' Circle Award. But, like *Anne of the Thousand Days*, it did not fill our coffers, and, strangely enough, it had no great appeal to the Company's members. No playwright member attended the out-of-town opening.

Perhaps the play was too intellectual. Certainly it did not teem with emotion. Koestler had rather dragged in a love story, and Sidney did his best to give this phase of the book dramatic impact. But even this didn't work; it would not have enticed Goldwyn as a good answer to his standard question, "Who loves who?" But I think the lack of enthusiasm of the Company members stemmed from their increasingly morbid concern with their own affairs.

The first of Elmer's three plays (only two were ever finished) was titled *Love among the Ruins*; it created all kinds of trouble before Elmer withdrew it. Bill Fields, from conscious or subconscious motivation, came to call it *Lost in the Ruins*. I believe its inspiration was the reverse of Kanin's *The Smile of the World*; Betty Field was much younger than Elmer; this play showed that such a marriage could be, and remain under stress, an overpowering love match. It was a simple, direct story, simply told; the characters were clearly defined; alas, it was a perfect illustration of one of those plays that Howard Lindsay described as ones that "just aren't any damn good."

This script quickly *forced* us to face our deepest trouble; Company plays were no longer easily financed. We should have learned this from *Lost in the Stars*; the playwright members had to invest their own money to complete its financing. But we attributed this to the fact that black casts were considered bad financial risks, and only people of the most liberal tendencies were willing to back such shows. Race relations were still pretty bad in 1949. People told jokes such as the story of the farmer talking about a pest of insects known as chiggers who was asked by a do-gooder to say Chigro. Elmer's play presented no such problems; we couldn't raise money for *it* because potential backers insisted on reading it and then said a clear and decisive no.

No one wanted to say bluntly that something was lacking in our members' current scripts, but we all had subconscious qualms. Morale was becoming nonexistent; despair was becoming the order of the day. Excerpts from a few letters make this clear.

August 25, 1950

Dear Bob:

Knowing that you are working, I am very reluctant to add to your burdens, but the present state of the Playwrights' Company is so unsatisfactory that I think you will want time to ponder the situation, in order to be ready with some constructive suggestions upon your return.

The immediate problem that brings the whole complex into focus is the difficulty we are having in financing *Love among the Ruins*. The response from our regular investors has been so negative as to make it almost a certainty that we shall have to look to some other source. But what that source is to be is far from clear.

The organization, geared to handle the work of five authors has become top-heavy. Its maintenance, on the present setup, is not only a burdensome financial strain, but a tiring psychic one. As the fellow said, none of us is getting any younger. Barring atomic bombs and hot-rod drivers, we all should still have a good many creative years ahead of us. But our creativeness is not going to be helped by the ever-present consciousness of financial problems and the uncertainty of getting our plays produced. If the company cannot relieve us of all that, then what is the excuse for its existence?

It seems to me that if we are to continue as a full-time organization we must get some other authors in. Hardly a new thought! We've discussed it endlessly and got nowhere; but I think the time has come when we must really do something about it, especially in view of Sam's firm decision not to rejoin the company. Of course, the question is, as always, who. I'm not ready to come up with the answer.

I'm hoping you'll have some good ideas. I know we've got to do something!

Excuse the length of this! I'll omit gossip and chitchat and just say we're all hoping for a new play from you.

Best.

Elmer

ANDERSON TO WHARTON

August 30, 1950

Dear John—

Thanks for your two letters. Victor called me today and we agreed on Thurs. eve next week for a dinner meeting. I've been having a rough time trying to write a play and at the moment am not sure that there'll be anything of mine to put on in an arena or any other kind of stage with or without financing. Still we ought to discuss the financing problem in general, and I ought to find out a few things to tell our stockholders. My present thought is that maybe we should all leave the theatre together and try to make a living at something else. But we can discuss that too.

Yours,

Max

RICE TO WHARTON

August 31, 1950

I'm sorry to be such a headache to everybody. Maybe if you could just [get] me a job as a law-clerk, it would settle everything.

Yours,

Elmer

(Rice was a member of the New York Bar.)

SHERWOOD TO RICE

August 30, 1950

Dear Elmer,

Your letter certainly paints a depressing picture, and I am not the one to say it is in any way exaggerated. The work that I did with the Committee of Theatrical Producers, and sub-committees thereof, last winter shocked me profoundly as I learned a lot more than I had known before of the appalling economic conditions of the theatre. The record of our own company for success and failure in the past four years has been considerably above average for reputable producers and yet, as you say, an investor in all six productions would have barely broken even. You can add to that such collateral productions as *Love Story* and *Miss Liberty* and the narrow margin is wiped out, although both looked like attractive propositions for investors. The terrible fact is that unless you can turn out a *Life with Father, Oklahoma!, Harvey*, or *South Pacific*, you may as well be dead. Why anyone should now invest in the theatre—except to promote a cutie or add to the losses on the income tax or both—is beyond me.

I do not believe there are measures to be taken within our own organization that will answer the problem except by folding up and going off, individually, bag on stick, to seek our fortunes in other fields. I for one feel a bit too aged for that. Furthermore, if there were no Playwrights Co., I can't believe that I'd have any interest left in working in the theatre.

Madeline and I send our very best to you and Betty.

Yours,

R.E.S.

Claude Rains and Kim Hunter in *Darkness at Noon.* The traps for a dramatist are endless. Rains was a proven star, but, even with the lovely Miss Hunter by his side, he proved to be utterly unromantic.
(*Alfredo Valente*)

Elmer was naturally frustrated and angry about *Love among the Ruins*. He suggested ways of raising money which would have violated the rules of the Securities and Exchange Commission, which, unknown to Elmer, had obtained some control of theatrical financing. While Victor and Bill and I were figuratively scratching our heads over this he suddenly came up with a revised script of his old play *Not for Children* and announced that his wife Betty Field, and a male star, Elliott Nugent, had agreed to play in it. This precipitated a monumental crisis.

During the 1947 dry spell, in desperation, I had one day revived an earlier suggestion—the possibility of revising and producing this play. I now bitterly regretted my suggestion. It was all too clearly enough of an avant-garde play to scare off the usual backer, in spite of the names of Elliott Nugent and Betty Field. However, Sidney Kingsley was arranging to produce another play through the Company, *Darkness at Noon;* we did raise our share of the financing for that, and I had hopes that these backers would put something in *Not for Chil-*

Walter J. Palance in *Darkness at Noon*, before he became known as Jack. (*Alfredo Valente*)

*dren.*They didn't. It looked as if we might have to cancel the production; it would have spelled FINIS for the Company. A sudden inspiration came to me.

The Rescue

A Midwesterner had recently come to New York and financed and produced a Shakespearian revival. He had also volunteered to try to help the struggling American National Theater and Academy, and had given it some help. Obviously, he wanted to become involved in the New York theatre. I had met him and given some slight advice on an ANTA matter. I had found him charming and very smart. I put on my hat, went to his office, and laid some not altogether attractive cards on the table.

We *desperately* needed money to complete the financing of *Not for Children.* Admittedly, it was an unusually risky venture. But if he would supply the end money, I would make sure that he met and worked with the playwright members and I believed that he would like them and that they would like him enough to result in his becoming a member of the Company. Today I can't understand why I felt so sure this would happen, but I did feel sure and apparently somehow conveyed a sense of surety, for he accepted my proposal and in a short time Roger L. Stevens became a member of the Company.

Roger was not asked to become a member only for money reasons; we never invited anyone to membership unless we admired him and found him congenial. The following letter which I wrote to Max makes this clear.

January 4, 1951

Dear Max,

I am sorry that there was a mixup about the meeting yesterday. We did not transact any actual business. We congratulated Bob, listened to his report on *Darkness at Noon* and discussed Elmer's production.

It is in connection with the latter that I called the meeting. In raising the money for this I asked Roger Stevens to invest $20,000 which he has done. I told him that I wanted him to meet you and Bob and Elmer, to attend rehearsals and to generally be "one of the family" in connection with this production. I feel that Stevens is the type of man who should be encouraged in the theatre and I believe that if all of us come to like him and he likes us he could become a member and be of enormous help to The Playwrights' Company in many ways.

I thought I should tell you this so that you will not be surprised if he appears at readings, rehearsals and run throughs and if I invite him to join the group for discussions afterward.

Sincerely,

John

The addition of Roger to the membership immediately gave the Company an aura of financial stability. He was known to be a fabulously successful real estate operator; the press printed stories of how he bought the Empire State Building; millions upon millions were involved. To the vast majority of unsung and underpaid theatre workers, anyone with as much as $10,000 in the bank was considered rich. In their minds, a man who could buy the Empire State Building must have money enough to pay off the national debt.

In 1951 he radiated aggressive creativity and a simplistic personal charm. Everyone in the theatre took an instant liking to him. The Wharton and the Stevens families quickly became close friends. We all went to Europe in 1952. We went by boat, leaving from the Jersey side. It was a gray, cloudy day; suddenly the sun broke through and a shaft of light seemed to fall directly on the Empire State Building. Roger summoned us to the deck with the excitement of a child to point out how impressive his new toy was; you could almost hear him saying to himself, "And I own it." It *was* impressive, and his pleasure in it was irresistibly contagious.

In London Alfred de Liagre was co-producing a play with Hugh Beaumont, who was at the time the most important person in the British theatre. De Liagre invited us to an opening night party at Beaumont's house. Beaumont had started his career as an office boy for the music publishing firm of Chappell, Ltd., but his small house and its furnishings looked like a *pied-à-terre* of a fastidious scion of the aristocracy. The guests included theatrical folk of top rank from England and America; I recall particularly Alfred Lunt and Lynn Fontanne talking with a group which included the Littlers, extremely important figures in the London theatre. My wife later told me that Mrs. Littler had recalled to Miss Fontanne that they had met before; it turned out to have been in the bomb shelter of the Savoy Hotel. London still had vivid recollections of the war.

> Roger L. Stevens. After joining the Company he quickly became one of the best known and most popular men in the theatre. At one time the Shuberts suggested that he buy their entire holdings (valued at considerable millions) and become their "successor" in running the American theatre.
> (*The New York* Times)

Beaumont had heard of the Company, and he made a tentative date with Roger and me to hear more about it. There was a mix-up which annoyed Roger and he was inclined to let the matter drop. I decided that a connection with Beaumont was worth the loss of a little dignity and put the meeting together again. By the end of one talk we had all become friends; Roger and Beaumont eventually co-produced many plays. I never went to London thereafter without seeing Binkie, as everyone called him, until his untimely death in 1973.

Roger was not one of the inherited rich. He had made his money by hard work and creative ingenuity, although he seldom talked about the latter. But he was quite ready to apply both of those qualities to the problems of the theatre in general and to the Company in particular.

He was always eager to experiment. He arranged for the Company to try out *Mr. Pickwick* at a university, having the sets and costumes made in the college workshops. This was an immense saving. Unfortunately, Fields, and, to my surprise, Samrock, too, opposed this idea and insisted on having the production built all over again. Bill always opposed anything new and different; Victor had some sound reasons; but the experiment, in any event, was too many years ahead of its time.

Roger's favorite field for creativity was finance, particularly schemes enabling one to "do the mostest with the leastest" amount of cash. The real estate business was famous for schemes of this sort. I once asked him if $100,000 was enough of a sum to make one noticed in New York real estate; he brushed it off. "I mean $100,000 *cash*," I added. "Oh," said Roger, "*that's* quite something else again."

He thought the so-called "Wharton Agreement" which was used for financing most productions was old-fashioned and inadequate. He came to call it "John Wharton's old-auntie method." But his own little-cash methods also showed their faults—more and more as time went on.

His first financial activity for us was devising a most complicated setup for the Company. It involved affiliation with two other corporations—Whitehead-Stevens, Inc., and Producers Theatre, Inc., in which Robert Whitehead, an eminent producer, and Robert Dowling, a real estate mogul, had interests. None of the playwright members understood the setup. They took Roger's word, and mine, that it seemed the best way to assure financing for their plays. This was the fact; but it was assurance gained at a high price; the Company's participation in profits was reduced to an extent which not only our members but also our other stockholders never found explicable. Later, he devised still more complicated plans.

Early in our acquaintance I detected an underlying neurotic quality in Roger—perhaps because it was similar to my own brand of neuroticism. My partner, Louis Weiss, used to say that it took a neurot to spot a neurot. Roger's subconscious problems were to burst out in a strange, unexpected way; but that was later, much later.

CHAPTER

XV

Riptide

An odd fantasy once crossed my mind. In it everyone connected with the Company was sitting in a modern version of Belshazzar's palace. An invisible hand wrote on the wall:—

"January, 1950. Neither Anderson, nor Behrman, nor Rice, nor Sherwood will ever write an original, successful 'important' play again."

If such a fantasy had been real, would—*could*—even one of us have believed that prediction? These men had reached the mature age of fifty to sixty; it should have been the period of their greatest creativity. Shaw wrote *Saint Joan* when he was over sixty-five; Goethe was pushing eighty when he wrote Part II of *Faust*. Conceding that the four were not equivalent geniuses to Shaw and Goethe, still, one might have expected that one of them would produce something of high import. Instead, they regressed. What happened? *What* happened? *What happened?*

Of course, creativity *can* just burn out at any age. But I think there was another, deeper cause.

A profound change was subtly taking place in our country. It is hard to describe. As good a place as any to start from may be Act III, Scene 1 of *Abe Lincoln in Illinois*, which Sherwood wrote from one of the famous Lincoln-Douglas debates. Douglas, then a judge, closes his speech with these words:

> We can go on as we have done, increasing in wealth, in population, in *power*, until we shall be the admiration and the terror of the world!

In his answering speech, Lincoln begins his peroration as follows:

> The Judge said that we may be "the terror of the world." I don't think we want to be that. I think we would prefer to be the encouragement of the world, the proof that man is at last worthy to be free.

These two opposing points of view have always had their adherents. Throughout recorded history the Douglas point of view has almost always been the dominant one. The ruling classes have shown a predilection for killing; animals in peacetime, human beings in wartime. They have never had much trouble in finding subordinate class adherents to assist in the killing, and in the rape, torture, and massacres which were (and still are) accepted accompaniments to

Raymond Massey and Albert Phillips in *Abe Lincoln in Illinois*. The beginning of the Lincoln-Douglas debate.
(*Vandamm*)

war. To be a "world power" means a military power to these people.
But in the 1890s, the period in which our members were born, the
adherents to the Lincolnesque thesis began a movement for world
peace and world brotherhood that eventually eclipsed the Douglas
point of view, and for fifty years made our country unique in its
international policies.

The movement was smug, naive, somewhat self-deluded—reread
the Beveridge quotation in Chapter I—but it *was* the ideal of the
dominant majority. We believed in democracy, the Bill of Rights, the
Four Freedoms; we believed that war was evil; it had to be fought if
your country was attacked—but *only* then. Many Americans deplored the use of the atomic bomb (which, ironically enough, *did*, for
a short time, make us the terror of the world), and we talked glibly
and nonsensically about the peacetime uses of atomic energy:—auto
motors little bigger than thimbles, steamships powered by cigar-box-
sized generators; also, somehow it would increase the food supply of
the whole world. Yes, we did talk that way; we forget the foolish
things we say—in 1946 we considered ourselves to be *the* supreme
technicians; many Americans said that the Russians *couldn't* build an
automobile!

But we had reason to be proud of ourselves, too. At the end of
World War I we had sought neither territory nor indemnity; President Wilson asked only for a League of Nations, which a powerful
minority political clique prevented us from joining. At the end of
World War II we repeated this program, and we did join the United
Nations. We set up democracies in West Germany and Japan. The
Marshall Plan in 1948 was the greatest act of international charity in
the history of mankind. Most Americans, including our liberal playwrights, felt that now was the time to redouble our efforts to realize
our ideal of world peace and brotherhood and to prove that man was
at last worthy to be free. We were realistic enough to realize that
there was plenty to be done before the proof was achieved; poverty,
racism, and corruption were still widespread; we all saw *that*. To try
to eliminate all this was our top priority.

What we did *not* see was the fact that a profound change was on
the way. The adherents of the Lincolnesque ideals were slowly
becoming a minority; the adherents to the age-old Douglas point of
view were becoming the majority. President Truman's administration
was quietly taking the steps that led into a "Cold War"—and a hot
one in Korea. The enemy, they told us, was Communism, particularly
Russian Communism, which, so we began to hear, was about to
conquer the whole world and impose Communism by force—and also
by the use of fifth columns—in all the democracies. When, in 1949,

the Russians produced, to the astonishment of many Americans, a nuclear explosion, the adherents to the Douglas philosophy began to grow clearly and unmistakably into the dominant majority.

I do not wish even to raise the question of whether the instigators of the Cold War were right or wrong. What I am concerned with here is showing what the public outburst against Communism did to the American entertainment world. When the House Un-American Activities Committee (HUAC) stepped up its anti-Communist campaign, and when Senator Joseph McCarthy in 1950 spearheaded a drive by his Senate subcommittee, the whole entertainment industry was shaken to its roots.

The situation had some confusing aspects. Clearly, there *were* a few American citizens—a tiny group at that time—who were devout Communists and followed the "Moscow line"—perhaps they dreamed of overthrowing the American Government, by force if necessary— as unlikely a dream as anyone can imagine. There was a slightly larger group who, in a muddled way, believed that Communist economic methods were superior to capitalism. A still larger group had explored Communist theories and organization during the 1930s depression and had long since become disenchanted.

McCarthy and HUAC launched a campaign calculated to make all of these people outcasts and pariahs by public denunciation. The campaign was soon extended to include any radical, or indeed anyone who expressed a view that did not damn Communists the world over. State Department officials who expressed the view (honest and *correct*) that Mao Tse-tung would defeat Chiang Kai-shek found their careers ruined when McCarthy and HUAC turned their guns on them and proclaimed them Communists.

Of course, the campaigners wanted publicity, and a sure way to get publicity was to attack people in the theatre, films, radio, and TV. And these people were accused on the flimsiest evidence. A book entitled *Red Channels* was published, which listed (often inaccurately) every activity or affiliation of countless workers in TV and radio which conceivably could be construed as pro-Communist. The New York Court of Appeals, in a decision which could only have resulted from bigotry, held that this was not libelous even when it clearly ruined a man's livelihood. For the mere listing in *Red Channels* inevitably meant that the person named could get no employment in films, radio, or TV. *Denials were given short shrift.*

To the credit of Broadway, most producers and theatre owners, including the Shuberts, refused to be intimidated. But the dramatists were bewildered—as were all of us who were against McCarthyism. We found ourselves helpless against the tide of prejudice which grew

Red Channels

The Report of
COMMUNIST INFLUENCE IN RADIO AND TELEVISION

Published By
COUNTERATTACK
THE NEWSLETTER OF FACTS TO COMBAT COMMUNISM
55 West 42 Street, New York 18, N. Y.
$1.00 per copy

The publication which viciously but effectively set countless Americans against their fellow citizens on the basis of flimsy evidence.

stronger and stronger. Most of the liberals simply did not know what to write about. Certainly there was no incentive for Sherwood to write a play designed to inspire an audience to enter public service when State Department career men were being ruined by false accusations. Nor for Max to try to analyze honor when HUAC suddenly adopted one of the most un-American and dishonorable rules ever promulgated: *the test of a citizen's loyalty was his willingness to squeal on the friends of his youth.*

The only dramatist of note who used the theatre as a place of protest was Arthur Miller. He wrote a new version of Ibsen's story of prejudice on the rampage, *An Enemy of the People.* He followed this with *The Crucible* in which he epitomized the situation in one line: *Is only the accuser holy now? The Crucible* dealt with the witch hunts of Salem. It is now considered by some critics to be Miller's best play to date, but such was the climate when it was produced that the reviewers tended to denigrate it as mere counter-propaganda. Miller was hounded by HUAC for years; my partner, Lloyd Garrison, and I undertook his defense, cleared his name, and kept him out of jail.

No other dramatist, including the Company members, came out with a protest play; indeed, there was hardly a play of *any* importance during this period. I do not believe it was fear. Sherwood wrote a preface for a book attacking *Red Channels*, and Rice, who had predicted just such a wave of bigotry years before, labored hard and long with the American Civil Liberties Union. To this day, I feel it was bewilderment—liberals were asking, "What has happened to our country; how dare we call ourselves the Land of the Free; what will be the end of it all?"

The internal impact on the Company was sad and disturbing. The entire climate was one that promoted dissension, and a serious brouhaha developed between Elmer and Max. The Dramatists Guild took under consideration a proposal that it should defend any member who was listed in *Red Channels*. Elmer was strongly in favor of the proposal; Max took a most surprising stand. Although he had just written *Barefoot in Athens*, a play extolling Socrates, he refused to see any great wrong in HUAC's actions or the publication of *Red Channels*. It was a bad time in Max's life. He was personally unhappy. He was beset by tax problems. He was boiling with hatred of the critics who had given bad notices to *Barefoot*, and the hatred spilled over and took in not only Communism but also everything and everyone in any way connected with it. He really believed that all the left-wingers were planning to overthrow the government by force and establish totalitarianism in America. He was, consciously and unconsciously, seeking objects on which to vent his wrath.

Max made some valid points. There *were* real Communists listed in *Red Channels;* he would not want to see himself committed to defend *them*. These people were traitors in his mind; he reserved the right to judge them accordingly. He was terribly upset by the situation; he wrote Elmer to assure him that he, Max, was troubled no end by their disagreement, but also to reiterate his views. Elmer replied as follows:

February 4, 1952

Dear Max:

I was very glad to get your letter, because I, too, have been greatly troubled by the fact that two such wholehearted believers in democracy should be so diametrically opposed upon a fundamental issue. I welcome the opportunity to clarify my position, though it is a tough subject to handle in a letter of reasonable length. However, I'll take a stab at it.

In the first place, you evidently believe that membership in the Communist Party is a crime and that Communists are criminals. You have every right to that opinion, but it is not the law of the land. No statute and no court opinion says so. The House Un-American Activities Committee was vested with broad powers of investigation and has been conducting hearings for a dozen years or so. The only reason for the creation of such committees is the gathering of information to form a basis for remedial legislation. Yet the Committee has never come up with a bill outlawing the Communist Party, or if it has, it has never reached the floor of the House. The United States Supreme Court has had numerous opportunities (in deportation and other cases) to declare the Party illegal. It has never done so. On the contrary, it has repeatedly side-stepped the issue. The latest and best opportunity was in its review of the conviction of the Communist leaders under the Smith Act. What did the Court do? It decided, six to two, that the Act was constitutional and that, therefore the conviction must be affirmed. Two of the judges, Douglas and Black, emphatically expressed the opinion that the Act violates the Bill of Rights. Two members of the majority, Jackson and Frankfurter, went out of their way to say that while they believed the Act to be constitutional, they deplored its passage and regarded it as a dangerous threat to free speech.

What about the act itself? Its passage was opposed by the American Civil Liberties Union and by innumerable other liberal groups and individuals. Even Tom Dewey made an issue of it and debated it with Stassen in the 1948 Oregon primary election, with the result that Stassen was practically eliminated as a candidate for the Republican nomination. I am not a Dewey man (believe it or not!) but I certainly applauded him when he said that there are more than enough laws on the books to convict anybody who is guilty of espionage, sabotage, sedition and treason. You seem to think that the conviction of the Communist leaders makes communism a crime. That is not the fact, these men were not charged with any overt act. They were not even charged with the advocacy of overt acts. They were charged with *conspiring* to advocate, a crime new to the annals of American jurisprudence and one that dangerously imperils the basic American principle of freedom of discussion.

I have no greater love for the Communists than you have. But—largely, I suppose, because of my legal training and my long years of activity in the civil liberties' field—I have a deep devotion to the principles of the Bill of Rights and to the Anglo-American system of law. To me that means that a man is innocent until proved guilty; that the burden of proof is upon his accusers; that an accused person shall have the right to be confronted with the evidence against him and to cross-examine his accusers. In constitutional terms, it means the right to unlimited expression of opinion, even of opinion that is repugnant to the majority and that threatens established institutions. (I seem to remember a recent play, in which a fellow named Socrates held out for the right to question anything, even though his questioning might weaken the authority or integrity of the state.) I am talking, of course, of opinion, dogma, doctrine, propaganda, not acts of violence. This is not a theoretical difference, but a fundamental one. Free speech means free speech. If the American people want to vote themselves a Communist regime, they have the right to do so. Further—and this is the crux of it—if American institutions cannot withstand Communist propaganda, they cannot be very vital or very deeply rooted. I happen to believe in the validity of American institutions and in their ability to resist even organized attempts to destroy them.

Let's move on to *Red Channels*. You say that it includes innocents, border-line cases and thorough-going Communists. Undoubtedly, that is true. But what really frightens me is that an honest, objective, fair-minded man is willing to say who belongs in which category on no more evidence than is afforded by an arbitrary, malicious and unverified array of charges and insinuations. Surely you wouldn't want yourself judged in this *a priori* fashion. I have been and I know the dangers that inhere in this kind of thing.

I think I've gone into this situation a little more deeply than you have. I happen to know that most of the *Red Channels* "citations" are taken direct from the report of the California Tenney Committee (a juvenile delinquent brother of the House Committee). I am cited thirteen times—pretty good for a guy who has openly been attacking Soviet imperialism and the principles of the American Communist Party, for years and years. (Also cited is a certain Maxwell Anderson; Hollywood Writers' Mobilization, 1945; Sponsor, National Council for Soviet-American Friendship, 1948; Signer of letter protesting against methods of Thomas Committee, 1948).

My citations include: Membership of the Board of Directors of the ACLU; membership of the National Institute of Arts and Letters; sponsorship of the American tour of the Artof Theatre; signer of a congratulatory telegram to the Moscow Art Theatre on its 50th anniversary; sponsorship of the Film and Photo League, which Sidney Howard asked me to join in 1935 and which I've never heard of since; and others of a similar nature.

Ever since my withdrawal from the Celanese Theatre, I have been sniped at by Counterattack (i.e. *Red Channels*) and linked with organizations, some of which I resigned from years ago and others that I have never even heard of. The point of all this is that if you didn't happen to know me and judged my political opinions on the basis of the Tenney report and Counterattack, you would undoubtedly put me down, at the very least, as an ardent Soviet sympathizer. . . . Fortunately, it wouldn't affect my livelihood—and wouldn't even if the theatre afforded a livelihood. But the theatre still affords a free forum. I'm afraid it won't much longer though, if the principle of political proscription continues to make headway.

How closely have you followed what is going on in this country? Do you know that academic freedom is in grave danger? Teachers no longer think it safe to express any unorthodox opinion. Students shy away from joining any liberal campus organization. Text-books are being fine-combed for "subversive" doctrine. Our public services are deteriorating because men of quality are unwilling to assume positions that subject them to the indignities of investigations, loyalty tests, McCarthyite snooping, name-calling and slander. Under the McCarren Act, foreign scientists and educators are being denied admission to the United States (and the opinion spreads in intellectual circles abroad that we have renounced freedom of thought). Fear and suspicion are everywhere. Hush-hush and don't stick your neck out are the orders of the day. I see and hear it, everywhere I go; and the agenda of the ACLU bristle with new evidences of censorship and the repression of opinions and ideas.

You say that the Authors' League is always defending the left-wingers. The same charge is constantly made against the American Civil Liberties Union (though it has defended such strange fish as Gerald Smith and Jehovah's Witnesses and offered to defend Kirkpatrick, if anyone tried to suppress *Red Channels*). But all that proves is that the left-wingers are under fire. No one is attacking Cardinal Spellman, Herbert Hoover, Mary Pickford or Mrs. Harrison Williams. You think the reds on the League Council are using me. I don't agree. . . .

I feel that somehow I have said both too much and too little. This is a thorny subject. Also, it involves deep emotions and that doesn't always make for the clearest thinking. But I think what it all boils down to is this: We both are deeply concerned about the preservation of freedom and the defeat of totalitarianism. You believe that the American Communists gravely threaten these

objectives. I believe that a far greater danger lies in yielding to
fear and thereby irreparably impairing the very freedom that we
want to preserve. I doubt if we'll ever reach an agreement, but
we may reach an understanding of each other's point of view;
and I guess that's better than nothing.

Yours,

Elmer

Looking back, it now seems clear that McCarthyism was only the
most striking sign of the changes going on in America. Political
power was passing to men who were fascinated by the old-fashioned
game of international power politics. The power of the military
increased everywhere; as usual, attempts to repress criticism of the
government went along with this. A repetition of the past six thousand years was growing up, except that twentieth-century politicians
kept justifying their actions by telling the electorate that everything
they did was in the cause of peace—world peace was, it seems, to be
achieved by perpetual wars to prevent other wars. The dominant
majority in America was changing beyond recognition from the
dominant majority of the period 1890 to 1948.

On top of all the foregoing, American dramatists had to face the
fact that the artistic revolution which began with painting, then
passed to sculpture, music, the dance, and the novel, was now bearing
down on the drama. The "well-made" play was on its way out in the
minds and pens of a number of voluble drama reviewers—their
fulsome praise was reserved for an entirely different type of play.

And yet, I still find it surprising that neither Anderson, nor Behrman, nor Rice, nor Sherwood was able to adapt to these conditions.
But neither were most of the other important playwrights of their
generation. Clifford Odets wrote *The Country Girl*, a fine play, but
nothing of importance compared to *Awake and Sing* or *Waiting for
Lefty*. Sidney Kingsley's *Night Life* failed completely. Lillian Hell-
man's plays lacked any theme of great importance. Thornton Wilder
was silent. Eugene O'Neill was dying; *he* proclaimed the belief that
the insects would inherit the earth.

Perhaps the only answer is that Man cannot adapt to too *sudden* a
change. He burns out.

CHAPTER
XVI

The Second Blooming

In July of 1951 the tint of our glasses was even rosier than in 1948. Our balance sheet might show the Company to be at its financial nadir; but were we downhearted?—no! We concluded the legal formalities of making Stevens a member, confidently put Samrock and Fields back on regular salary, and figuratively raised a banner proclaiming three productions for the coming season. To Broadway we looked as powerful and as desirable a producing company as in 1938.

And, indeed, for playwrights who wanted the most control possible over their plays, the Company *was* the most powerful and most desirable. Much of this was due to Sherwood, whose talents—*totally against his will*—were undergoing a strange metamorphosis.

If Sherwood had decided, in 1951, to become an independent producer, he could have made a fortune for himself and his backers. During the next five years he exhibited an almost eerie ability to spot scripts that had the making of hits, and, more important, to detect the weak spots and show how to correct them. Unfortunately, this ability did not become apparent until the three-company deal had been made; our Company did not get the full financial benefit of his work.

However, the Company, during this period, *was* a playwrights' company and the top producer for dramatists who wanted to have the final say on their productions. Stevens assured financing. Samrock

The members in 1951. Sherwood was still the dominant figure.
(*PIX*)

was admittedly unsurpassed on the business end. Fields was second to none as a press agent. My law firm had a theatre-wide reputation for efficiency. And if a dramatist wanted help and advice on the artistic side, it was available from men—particularly Sherwood—whose judgment he was bound to respect.

Many of the popular playwrights of the day recognized these factors and brought at least one of their plays to the Company. In the years 1951–55 inclusive, we produced or co-produced eleven plays by nonmembers. The script of one play struck everyone as so important that, before it opened, on Sherwood's urging, we elected the author, Robert Anderson, a member. The play, *Tea and Sympathy*, turned out to be the Company's longest running play. Of the eleven plays, one won both the Pulitzer Prize and the New York Drama Critics' Circle Award. Two won awards for the best foreign play. Another received the Critics' Award; still another the Antoinette Perry Award. Two of the failures were near misses. Much of this success was due to Sherwood.

I still have a vivid recollection of Bob's first big contribution to an outside play, *The Fourposter*. This is a two-character play about a marriage, written by a curious fellow named Jan de Hartog. (He lived on a boat and denied citizenship in any nation, presumably to try to escape taxes.) It is not a very profound play, but it is an honest portrayal of certain common marriage problems and audiences can recognize themselves in one or another part of it.

Hume Cronyn and his wife, the lovely Jessica Tandy, had co-starred successfully in a summer-stock tour. Cronyn suggested to Samrock that the Company produce it in New York, with the talented but erratic José Ferrer directing. It was clearly a good bet, but our finances were low. Thereupon Roger volunteered to take a look-see.

The events of the day of the look-see, as recounted by Samrock, sound like the scenario of an old-time silent-film comedy. The play was in Falmouth, Massachusetts; Roger said he would drive Victor and Mrs. Stevens up in time for dinner and the show. Victor duly appeared at the agreed-upon starting place and found Mrs. Stevens sitting in the back of the car with a large poodle by her side. Roger, it appeared, had explained that he had to finish a real estate transaction and would be "a little late."

Both Samrock and Mrs. Stevens knew what "a little late" could mean in Roger's life. (He is the only man I ever knew who actually missed a boat for Europe.) As the time passed, both of them began to exhibit signs of nervousness; only the dog remained seemingly unperturbed. Roger finally appeared and they drove off, exceeding the speed limit wherever there was a sufficient stretch of road to warrant it.

Despite the speed, it was evident that they were going to be late for the show, even without dinner. Roger pulled up by a roadside stand and ordered four hamburgers. The attendant who brought them out asked which of the three people was having the extra one. "Nonsense," said Roger, and pointed to the dog.

Eventually, exhausted and still a bit hungry, they arrived in time for the final act. This was, as can be imagined, a bit confusing to people who had never seen the show. But Roger was now the unperturbed one. Backstage he congratulated the Cronyns and announced

Hume Cronyn and Jessica Tandy, another highly skilled, delightful married couple, in *The Fourposter*. Cronyn eventually gave the only portrayal of Polonius that made me believe the character was a wise royal adviser. Miss Tandy in *The Voice* held spellbound an audience that could see only her mouth.
(*Friedman-Abeles*)

that he would see to it that the Company raised the money for production.

We were all delighted and went to the opening night of the tryout in Wilmington with high hopes. To our disappointment, there was a big problem.

It is hard to describe what was wrong; in the terms of Hollywood, "the play had the cutes"; the honesty of the writing seemed to have gone. After the performance we gathered for the usual postopening discussion. Various ideas were put forward; Bob kept silent. Cronyn and Ferrer arrived, Ferrer looking very cocky; he was soon betraying contemptuous annoyance at suggestions that all was not well. Bob continued to keep silent for some time. Then he suddenly unleashed a shower of criticism and suggestions that blew Ferrer and Cronyn off their feet.

Ferrer was outraged and tried to leave, but Cronyn made him stay. They listened and, *mirabile dictu*, they acted on the advice. *The Fourposter* became another of the Company's long running plays.

Another incident of this production which stays in my memory is the beginning of a highly successful road tour in Chicago, after a

José Ferrer and the Cronyns, before Sherwood struck.
(*Friedman-Abeles*)

year's run in New York. The audience was enchanted; they obviously found the play fresh and gay. I went backstage and congratulated Hume and Jessie, dwelling particularly on the spontaneity of their performances. Hume smiled. "You wouldn't believe how many days of hard, dull, repetitive rehearsal it took to achieve that spontaneity."

Bob enthusiastically approved the Company's decision to produce Sam Taylor's play *Sabrina Fair*. But he felt a lot of hard work was still needed, and he pitched in and helped to do it. Even so, all was not well. Although Margaret Sullavan, a star of both films and stage, was playing the lead, and the magnetic Joseph Cotten was her male opposite, it was clear, on the night of the tryout opening in New Haven, that the play did not "grab the audience." No one, not even Bob, could see why, for it was a witty, charming story; yet audiences simply did not dig it. In the customary meeting in the Taft Hotel we pondered the problem; no one had an answer.

The playwright John van Druten and Walter Starkie, van Druten's current producer, came to see the play and made what seemed a curious suggestion. Bob said, "Let's try it." This was the suggestion: there should be a prologue in which the character played by Miss Sullavan should make a speech about the play, explaining that it was something of a Cinderella story. Mr. Taylor wrote the following charming speech; Miss Sullavan delivered it expertly; it *worked*. Audiences loved the play and Miss Sullavan, and it ran for 317 performances and has been played in stock literally countless times.

Prologue Speech of *SABRINA FAIR*

The music, which is lightly gay and nostalgic and eighteenth century, fades down until it is almost gone. The stage is in darkness. A pool of light appears slowly, and in it there stands a girl in a simple dress, looking very much as though she were about to go off to a party of sixteen-year-olds.

THE GIRL (MISS SULLAVAN) SPEAKS.

> Once upon a time,
> In a part of America called the North Shore of Long Island,
> Not far from New York,
> Lived a very small girl on a very large estate.
> The house on the grounds had many rooms, and many servants,
> And in the garage were many cars,
> And out on the water were many boats.
> There were gardeners in the gardens,
> And a chauffeur to drive the cars,
> And a boatman who hauled out the boats in the fall

Margaret Sullavan and Bill Fields during rehearsals of *Sabrina Fair*.
Maggie astounded everyone who met her by her simple, direct friendliness,
unlike any other film star I ever knew. Yet, as she once told me, she was
subject to devastating "black rages."
(*Friedman-Abeles*)

> And scraped their bottoms in winter
> And put them back in the spring.
> From the windows of her room
> The girl could look out on an indoor tennis court
> And an outdoor tennis court; an indoor swimming pool
> And an outdoor swimming pool
> And a pool in the garden for goldfish.
> Life was pleasant here,
> For this was about as close to heaven as one could get
> On Long Island.
> But then one day the girl grew up
> And went beyond the walls of the grounds
> And found the world.

(The light fades out, the girl disappears, the music is gone.)

It seems strange that so simple a change could so completely trans-
form the fate of a play, but it can. The most famous example is
Disraeli, in which the English actor George Arliss starred with
enormous success. The story of the play pits Disraeli against a man
named Probert. In the climactic scene, Probert admits his defeat and
declares it is outrageous that a man like Disraeli should have such
power. He then walks out; Disraeli, literally and metaphorically,

becomes the center of the stage. In its tryout, the curtain came down on this scene as Probert was making his exit. There was mild applause; enough customers came to assure a run, but there was no sign of a smash hit. The author thereupon decided to add two lines.

He put Disraeli's ward, a charming young girl, into the final scene. When Probert walks off, she bursts out, "Oh, Mr. Disraeli, thank God you *do* have such power." Disraeli replies, "I haven't, dear child, but *he* doesn't know that." Curtain. Those two lines made all the difference. Word of mouth very quickly built the play into a sensational success.

The Company's production of *Ondine* would never have reached New York if it had not been for Bob. It is a strange fantastic play,

Margaret Sullavan and Joseph Cotton during rehearsals of *Sabrina Fair*. Maggie presented a unique problem when it came to costumes; she improved the clothes, rather than vice versa. A producer's wife who shopped with Maggie for her clothes in a working-girl role almost gave up; they would select a cheap, ready-made dress, but when Maggie put it on, it looked like *haute couture*.
(*Friedman-Abeles*)

Margaret Sullavan, Luella Gear, Scott McKay, and Cathleen Nesbitt in *Sabrina Fair*.
(*Vandamm*)

based on legends of knights in armor, on white horses, meeting fairy sprites. Producing it at all was a very risky venture. But Audrey Hepburn, by then a movie star of no mean proportions, agreed to star in it with her husband-to-be, Mel Ferrer, also a movie star, and Alfred

Audrey Hepburn in *Ondine*. Already a movie star, she was only twenty-five when she played Ondine for the Company. When we were wracking our brains to find some way to persuade her to continue the run, her mother said, "Simply tell her she *must* stay; she is an obedient child." Mama was wrong in this case; the obedient child was in love, and she followed her fiance, Mel Ferrer, to Italy.
(*Theatre Collection, New York Public Library*)

AUDREY HEPBURN

Lunt agreed to direct. Again, Bob pitched in to help with some tricky problems.

There was a run-through before the play left for a Boston tryout. We all thought that Lunt had done a superb job, and we saw the makings of a smash hit. Max, who had been so upset by the critical reaction to his play *Barefoot in Athens* that he wanted to renounce the theatre found this run-through enough of an inspiration to reverse his decision. He wrote Bob to this effect:

February 7, 1954

Dear Bob—

. . . I'm beginning to get a glow out of something else that has come about casually. When I saw Alfred at work and remembered what magic he and Lynn have I began automatically to think of plots they might play. And, thanks be, a story has occurred to me I think they'd like. I haven't begun work on it, or even planned it, and I know that others will probably play it if it's written, but it's a good idea with some nobility and some fun in it. Maybe I'll have it when I come east.

I've been happier about *Ondine* than about anything else in the theatre for years.

Max

But Hepburn and Ferrer were not satisfied.

When the play opened in Boston there was such a blowup between Lunt and Ferrer that the former packed up and went home to Wisconsin. It took not only Sherwood but everyone else concerned to persuade him to come back. Then Miss Hepburn flared up. At eleven o'clock one morning, as Bob was dawdling over morning

Alfred Lunt, Mel Ferrer, and Audrey Hepburn at a very early rehearsal of *Ondine;* no hint of the gathering storm. (*Friedman-Abeles*)

coffee in his New York apartment, Miss Hepburn suddenly appeared, having flown down on an early plane. It was touch and go whether she would continue. Bob never gave us the details of the interview, but he clearly was able to reassure her. She made an enormous personal success in the play, so great that it was impossible to find anyone to replace her when she left at the end of the season to follow Ferrer to Italy and marry him there.

We had an opening night party after the Broadway premiere; everyone was optimistic, radiating friendliness to all. This led one lady to ask Lunt an extraordinarily naive question—"Did you learn anything from working with a movie star like Mel Ferrer?" "Yes, madam," replied Alfred, briskly, "I learned that you cannot make a knight-errant out of a horse's ass."

Despite Lunt's dour comment, the play was a sellout. Bob must have derived some satisfaction from such an accomplishment, but he really had no desire to produce other people's plays. On February 8, 1954, he wrote me the following letter; the only unpleasant letter of his that I recall:

Dear John:

. . . I must confess that I feel pretty bitter about the extent to which I have been forced to take the rap in connection with the production of *Ondine*. After all of the troubles I had with *Sabrina Fair* I announced that I was not going to go through with this kind of work again, as I have had so many problems of my own during recent months. I am now in real trouble with *Pontius Pilate* [a TV script] as I have had no time to do the final revisions that I contemplated, and God knows when I shall get the time, as I have to return to Boston this afternoon. Not one other member of the Playwrights' Company has been near *Ondine* since it opened in Boston despite the fact that, as you know, the troubles there have been of an extraordinarily harassing kind. (I have just heard that Roger is going to Boston this afternoon.) It seems to me that I have been imposed upon to an outrageous extent and left to do all the dirty work on two successive productions. I hate this kind of work and am not qualified for it by nature or temperament. I have no ambition to become famous as the poor man's Terry Helburn [co-director of The Theatre Guild]. I have a life of my own to live—and also a living of my own to earn. I simply cannot afford to remain in the Company on these terms.

Yours,

Bob

Audrey Hepburn in *Ondine*. She was appealing standing, sitting, or even crawling.
(*Milton H. Greene*)

Roger suggested that Bob receive special compensation for what he had done, but Bob declined. He wanted to get back to being a writer and earn money from his work as such. Of course he continued to take an interest in Company productions, but thereafter he never gave them quite so much attention.

Sherwood also insisted on rigorous compliance with the policy of giving the playwright final say on all problems relating to his play. This policy had its severest test with *Cat on a Hot Tin Roof* by Tennessee Williams. We received word that the New York City License Commissioner was threatening to close the play on moral grounds. This, of course, squarely raised the question of censorship; every member of the Company, including Sherwood, opposed censorship. Elmer Rice was fanatic; he demanded that the Company take a stand against the commissioner. Williams was indignant, too, but he told me privately that he did not wish to take a stand that might close the play.

This *was* a peculiarly infuriating case. The City License Commissioner was charged with the duty of seeing that physical theatres were safe and sound; no one expected him to exercise artistic censorship. But if he chose to interpret the law as giving him that power, he could revoke the theatre's license. By the time you fought it out through an ordinary court trial, the play would be dead.

At first I judged that a court might issue an injunction restraining the commissioner from acting on such an interpretation, but on looking further into the facts I found a troublesome aspect. There were children in the play and the charge of moral unfitness had emanated from the Children's Aid Society, a top-drawer New York charity. Judges, rightly, support anyone defending children. I felt bound to tell Tennessee that I feared a court test; he decided that he

Ben Gazzara and Barbara Bel
Geddes as the tormented hus-
band and wife in *Cat on a Hot
Tin Roof*.
(*Theatre Collection,
New York Public Library*)

wanted to settle the matter if settlement were possible. Bob insisted
that the author's decision must prevail.

The commissioner announced that he was coming to see the play
himself on a Monday evening. Victor Samrock betook himself to the
theatre to make sure that the children's dressing room was in apple-
pie order and that there were no demoralizing influences around. He

Paul Newman and Elizabeth
Taylor in the same roles on
the screen.
(*Theatre Collection,
New York Public Library*)

found one, and ordered its removal; it was a calendar, owned by a stagehand, showing Marilyn Monroe in twelve various stages of undress. Today, I imagine, the ten-year-olds might have bought such a calendar for themselves.

In any event, the commissioner found that the children's physical surroundings were satisfactory, but he refused to give up his claim that he could censor the script. Bill, Victor, and I finally got him to agree that all he needed were two or three innocuous changes; apparently he felt that he had to tell the Children's Aid Society that he had accomplished *something*. Williams agreed to the changes and the play went on to profit and glory. Elmer never admitted that he was satisfied, although he didn't insist on the Company rejecting the profits.

But what Sherwood could do for outside playwrights he could not

Tennessee Williams receiving the New York Drama Critics' Circle Award from Walter Kerr.
(*Friedman-Abeles*)

The children in *Cat* who provoked a censorship problem.
(*Zinn Arthur*)

do for his fellow-members—nor, worst of all, himself. During the
1951–55 period, Elmer had two failures; he then remained sterile for
four years. Max Anderson wrote only one success; it was neither
original nor important, simply the dramatization of the book *The Bad
Seed*. His original play *Barefoot in Athens* was a failure; he started
and dropped two other plays. In February of 1954 his depression was
such that he wrote me the following letter.

February 27, 1954

Dear John—

I am hopeful that there'll be a play. If there isn't it will be
because it takes more courage to write each succeeding play than
the one preceding needed, and maybe there isn't sufficient heart
for it.

But I'll try. Best to you—and those you see about.

Yours

Max

I think Sherwood agonized more than either of the other two over
his inability to write. His fame as a playwright had put him above the
others; the fall was further and harder. He once remarked sort of
wistfully and sorrowfully, "I still seem to be touted as the great

Nancy Kelly and Patty McCormack in *The Bad Seed*. This was Max's one fling with real "mellerdrama," and very succesful it was, too. (*Fred Fehl*)

American playwright. I guess the only way I could change things would be to have a play produced." He was right. The Company presented a posthumous production of his play *Small War on Murray Hill*. It failed. A prominent critic thereupon wrote a review in which he declared that Sherwood never had any ability worth mentioning.

Bob did not stop trying to write. But we all began to tremble when he sent us a new script. There are certain scenes which are called "obligatory scenes"; the author has set the stage for some kind of confrontation for which the audience waits eagerly; the scene between Hamlet and his mother is world famous. Bob simply could not write these scenes any more. In his unproduced play *The Better Angels* I waited for the scene where the non-Mormon heroine would face things out with an aggressive young fanatic. When the scene came, the young Mormon simply lost his fanaticism and aggression.

Nor could he seem to pick out one theme and develop it. *The Better Angels* also posed a fascinating problem of loyalties. The hero is a Virginia army officer; when the Civil War breaks out, he is astounded and bewildered by having to choose between the Virginia he knows and the Union of states and people he has never seen. It is, of course, a major problem of war and peace today; can one develop a loyalty to something larger than the nation? Bob, having posed this fascinating question, let the story wander off to nowhere.

He also tried his hand at television drama, with no more success. He wrote one piece of magazine fiction of which the less said the better. After *The Best Years of Our Lives*, he had no great success with films. He was asked to write a movie script of *War and Peace* and undertook an overtaxing trip to Yugoslavia where the filming was to take place. But the whole venture fell through.

This was a particularly maddening disaster. The film company was not one of the major companies; no one knew its financial condition. Bob's agent therefore demanded an advance payment of $20,000 before Bob went to Yugoslavia. The company assured the agent that the check was on the way, and Bob boarded his plane. I was out of town and shortly received a phone call from my partner, Norman Zelenko, who was handling the matter in my absence. In horrified tones he informed me that the check turned out to be for only $10,000. "But that's not the worst of it," he fairly moaned, "The Agency refused to accept the check and sent it back to the film company. When they phoned me about the $10,000, I told them *never* to refuse money of any amount from a film company of that

Two enchanting young people: Daniel Massey and Patricia Bosworth in *Small War on Murray Hill*. Danny became a star like his father, Raymond; Miss Bosworth, alas, forsook the stage and became a successful writer.
(*Friedman-Abeles*)

sort. But it was too late. Bob may never get anything now."

He didn't.

In some odd fashion, our personal relations reached their height during this period. Bob and I became closer and closer friends. One day I told him that I was troubled by some financial gimmick that Roger was talking about; I felt it cut too deeply into Company policy. "Indeed," I said, "I'm afraid it might impair the relationship between you and me."

Without hesitation, and without any break in speech, Bob replied, "*That* would be impossible."

I have never forgotten his saying those four words.

On November 11, 1955, he wrote in his diary, "When I try to write I feel I am going to die." Three days later he died from a heart attack.

One of his last achievements had been to secure the election of Max to the American Academy of Arts and Letters. After Bob's death Max wrote a tribute to Bob and read it at the Academy's annual meeting:

> Back in the early twenties
> Met a young giant.
> As I remember it
> He was lounging against a wall
> Chatting with cronies
> Somewhere in the theatre district.
> Tall. Six foot seven I heard later.
> Lean. Gangling. Watchful.
> A lot of structural steel
> In that suave leaning tower.
> He put out a hand that had a grip in it.
> Spoke slowly. Said few words.
> Syllables carefully articulated.
> Made rounded sentences when he made any.
> Mordant.
> Kindly.
> A long head. A long face, looking down.
> Astute.
>
> Next meeting.
> He'd written a play and I went to see it.
> I said to myself
> Some of these lines are better than Shaw.
> Just as witty and more blood in them.
> High tension. High voltage. High comedy.

We talked a bit.
He smiled slowly from up there where he lived
Six foot seven.
He was somewhat dazed.
The play was a hit.
He could quit writing for a boss.
Could write as he pleased.

When *Petrified Forest* opened I was in San Francisco.
Read about it.
Sent him a wire.
That does it. That's the kind of play I'd like to write.
Later *Idiot's Delight* was on
With the Lunts—
The whole town infected with its laughter.
It took all the prizes
And deserved them.
Never heard such a glissando of wit.

Bob was president of the Dramatists' Guild
in 1937.
After a tough session
Bob and I sat down with Elmer Rice
To have a drink (not that we drank much).
One of us said
Why don't we produce our own plays?
Well, we were pleased with the idea.
Talked with Sidney Howard and Sam Behrman.
They came in with us.
We made up the Playwrights' Company.
Abe Lincoln in Illinois was Bob's first contribution.

From that time on
We met regularly.
It seemed sometimes
That was what our office was for.
We put on plays
But what mattered most
Was talking things over with tough-minded men
Working at the same trade.
Alchemy was our business.
Trying to transmute Broadway into gold.
That result was (and is) mostly frustration.
Or fool's gold.
Sometimes there was a glint of the real metal.

We tried not to worry ourselves.
Bob made a sort of center,
A rallying standard.
If he wasn't there nothing was transacted
Except Transactions.

  When he was there
  The sparks flew.
  Mostly in fun.
  Sam and Elmer were fast with their rapiers,
  But Bob was quick also,
  And his reach was—
  Well, figure it out,
  Six foot seven.
  One of the Playwrights said
  About a play of his:
  "I can't put it off.
  I'll be sitting on tenterhooks
  Till it's produced."
  "What," I asked,
  "Are tenterhooks?"
  Bob turned to me gravely.
  "The upholstery of the anxious seat," he said.

The earth is now altered.
The city is emptier and colder.
Some of its meaning has gone
Out of Broadway,
Out of Fifth Avenue.
Out of the familiar windows along the Street.
Somewhere at a frequented table,
Someone is ordering a Dubonnet cocktail.
No doubt
Someone is speaking slowly
With laconic wit.
But it's not Bob, and the earth is diminished and not the same.
Sherwood is dead.
Those who were younger than he
Are still younger.
Those who were older,
I among them,
Are much older now.

Sherwood.
(Collection of Mrs. Robert E. Sherwood)

CHAPTER XVII

The Sixth Playwright

After Sherwood's death the Company disintegrated at an astonishingly rapid pace. It was a remarkable example of what can happen to a group of people when the leadership changes. The Company continued, in name, for another five years, but it might as well have been called the Tom, Dick, and Harry Producing Company; the resemblance to The Playwrights Producing Company, Inc., was minimal. The top leadership passed to Roger Stevens, who, despite his abilities, was, of course, not a playwright.

The Company is listed on the records as producer or co-producer of over twenty plays in the next five years, but only three were new plays written by members. The other plays were mostly selected by Stevens without much consultation with the playwright members, who often did not bother to read the scripts or to go to the plays when they were produced. Often we had no personal acquaintance with the co-producer. Roger was trying to accomplish an almost impossible task: to keep alive a Company that would produce the plays of three playwrights who were only occasionally writing plays that were producible, let alone money making. That he was able to do it at all is greatly to his credit.

Sherwood was primarily a playwright; as we have seen, he had no desire to be a producer. Stevens was a producer. Sherwood dominated the Company until the day of his death, even though he failed to write a successful play. In the mysterious way that leadership works, its wonders to perform, the Company under Sherwood was a playwrights' company; under Stevens, just another Broadway producer.

If Robert Anderson had been ten years older at the time of Sherwood's death, the story might have been different. He quite clearly had leadership qualities; they stuck out all over in his connection with the thriving New Dramatists Committee; later, he headed the Dramatists Guild. But the outrageous fortune that lurked just around the corner throughout the whole life of the Company here once again came into view. Anderson's seven years as a member were marked by a series of unusual events which prevented the Company from getting the full benefit of his talents.

He had studied theatrical writing in his college days, and thereafter at the New School for Social Research. He had taught playwriting. He had adapted plays for radio and television, as well as working on originals. He could, therefore, analyze a script as skillfully as any playwright member except Sherwood. This ability gave an ironic touch to the very beginning of his membership.

"I was steeped in the work of Max Anderson, Rice, and Sherwood," he told me, "and admired their plays no end. On my election as a member, all three sent me scripts of new plays. And I didn't like *a single one of the three.* In fact, I thought they were quite bad, no, very bad. I was embarrassed beyond belief. Could I start my career with the Company by telling this unpleasant fact to these distinguished men? I asked Phyllis [his wife] and Audrey [Audrey Wood, his agent]. They were pretty puzzled, too, but finally advised me that I *should* say what I thought; if the members hadn't wanted my honest opinion they wouldn't have asked me to join. Fortunately for me, nobody except the author in question liked any of the scripts, so I was not a minority of one. But it was an unhappy affair."

It was an unhappy affair that was to be repeated. Max, Elmer, and Bob Sherwood continued to write scripts that he did not like and had good reason for disliking. And he came to think that some of the scripts which Roger Stevens found were just "trash." Obviously, it was not easy for him to decide just what to say.

While puzzling over this he became involved in another contretemps—of minor importance but unusual enough to mention. Such a situation had never come up before, nor did it thereafter. It emanated from two of our stockholders, Mr. and Mrs. Howard Cullman.

Howard Cullman was a curious character, charming and considerate on most occasions, utterly insensitive on others. He and his brother, Joseph, who was ten years his senior, had inherited a flourishing tobacco concern. Howard quickly realized that in this field he was dwarfed by Joe, who was the ablest all-around businessman I

have ever known. He thereupon decided to make a career in other fields, and he was extremely successful in all of them, notably the chairmanship of the Port Authority of New York. This surprised many of his peers who thought him superficial. They overlooked talents that were rare in the business world. He had a peculiar genius for publicity; this enabled him to get things done which other men who might have a far better intellectual understanding of the particular problem were unable to accomplish.

In 1938 he decided to try theatrical financing. He backed a play, *Dance Night*, which failed completely and returned to him not one penny of his investment. My first wife, Carly Wharton, at that time was undertaking to raise the money for a play which evoked little interest in script form; she persuaded Howard to invest $5,000. The play was *Life with Father;* he never had again a percentage profit to equal it. He thereupon decided to make small investments and spread them widely; this permitted him to publicize himself as a monumental backer of plays. The total Cullman investment in the Company was $5,000.

Mrs. Cullman was a shrewd judge of theatrical properties. She suggested to her husband that they acquire the rights to a book, *Don't Go Near the Water*, and get someone to dramatize it. This would, of course, entitle them to a larger share of any profits. They asked Bob Anderson if he would take on the assignment.

Bob naturally took the position that this was a Company matter, whereupon both Mr. and Mrs. Cullman launched into a diatribe against the Company, which left our new member bewildered, astounded, and unhappy. Victor Samrock immediately rushed to the rescue and tried to dissipate each of the Cullman complaints by specific answers; later, Roger took the laboring oar and did a brilliant job in restoring peace, sweetness, and light. The author of the book then got a release from the Cullmans and sold the book to the movies.

It is strange what trifles can stick in one's mind concerning a person with whom one has had really important connections. Howard Cullman was for a long time a client of my partner, Arthur Cohen, and we were involved in many important nontheatrical legal problems. Yet, what occurs to me when his name is mentioned is the fact that he always pronounced the word "bonanza" as "bonzana." Incidentally I also remember that Roger Stevens used to pronounce "idea" as "idee." Maybe all of us have our favorite mispronunciations; I recall a time when I pronounced words beginning with *wh* as though they

Robert Anderson.
(Alexander Bender)

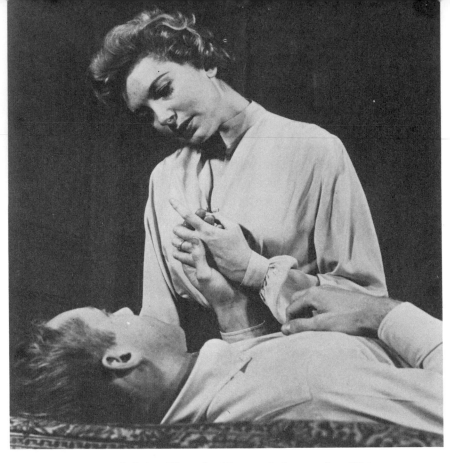

Deborah Kerr and John Kerr in *Tea and Sympathy*. This scene was criticized for being unduly "suggestive"; today it would probably be played in the nude. Still, as Ann Corio, a famous strip-tease artist, points out, suggestibility, if properly done is infinitely more effective than the act itself: "A woman who knows how to do it can take off her gloves in a way that will make a man ask her to marry him."
(*Theatre Collection, New York Public Library*)

began with *w*. When people pointed out that I was mispronouncing my own name, I overcompensated—sometimes asking for a glass of "whater." I wonder what mine are today.

Such things were minor. The major events which kept Bob Anderson from creative writing were three in number. The first was a peculiarly contemptible sort of plagiarism suit. Bob's wife, Phyllis, was a play agent, but she did not represent Bob. The plaintiffs alleged that they had submitted a script to Phyllis and that she, in "breach of trust," had given it to her husband and *Tea and Sympathy* had been copied from it. Actually, *Tea and Sympathy* had been written before Phyllis ever saw the other script, and the plaintiffs eventually withdrew the suit. But, although he paid no damages, it cost Bob a pretty penny for legal services. The Company could do little to help defend the suit; it did pay one-quarter of the law bill.

If you ever have the good fortune to write a successful play and the bad fortune to be sued for plagiarism, you will be surprised by the amount of shock it produces. For willful plagiarism is a form of stealing—theft of another person's creative work—and to be *charged* with theft does something to the nervous system that is hard to describe. There have been people who were never able to write again after going through a plagiarism suit.

In Bob Anderson's case it was peculiarly shattering because his wife was drawn into it. And if ever there was a completely honorable woman—one who could really qualify in every way as Caesar's wife—it was Phyllis. No wonder he was temporarily stopped short in the field of creative writing.

Fortunately for Bob, the success of *Tea and Sympathy* produced results which kept him busy. Unfortunately for the Company, these results were the second factor in denying the Company the full benefit of his talents. They kept him from writing a new play for five years. In 1953 the ending of *Tea and Sympathy*, a proposal of adultery, caused serious censorship problems in Hollywood and London. Hard to believe? Yes. But true. Bob had to go to California and London to work out the film version and the English production. He also went to Paris, where Ingrid Bergman played the star role; happily, the Parisians did *not* raise censorship problems.

But the third factor dwarfed the other two put together. Phyllis contracted cancer—a terminal case—and the doctors ordered Bob not to tell her.

Phyllis was a remarkable person in many ways. She was a play agent who delighted in working with young, unestablished playwrights. In that special field she was superior to anyone else; somehow this work resulted in her being the only agent in history to have a theatre named after her. She was not only a skillful agent; she radiated humanity. Her clients adored her.

So did Bob. When the fact that her illness was terminal was made clear, the strain on him was, as can be imagined, almost unbearable. That he could do any work at all is extraordinary. She died just about three years after the opening of *Tea and Sympathy*.

I shall never forget the brief memorial service held for her. For one thing, you could almost literally say that the air was heavy with grief. *Everyone* there was stricken. But what I remember most clearly were the remarks made by Elia Kazan: "But there is no comfort. The fact is still there; she's gone. It's a tragedy and it's stunning and final."

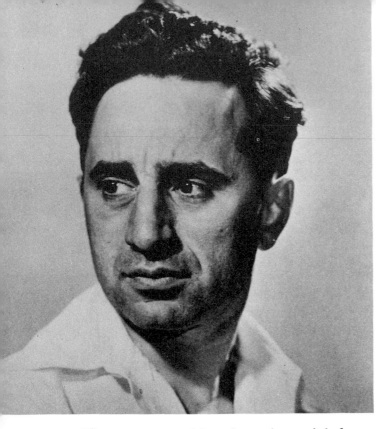

Elia Kazan. One of the greatest directors of a great theatrical era. (*G. Maillard Kesslere*)

There was something about the straightforward presentation of this stark truth that was unbelievably impressive.

After her death, three years went by before Bob had a new play on Broadway. In the interval he did some film work, including the film-script of *The Nun's Story* for Audrey Hepburn. But it was an unhappy period. He described it in a letter to me written in 1957:

July 10, 1957

Dear John:

The last seven months have been strange ones for me. I suppose this was inevitable not only after Phyllis' death, but after the five years of anxiety and sadness that led up to it.

As you know, I took off for Paris on December 9th. My doctors advised this as a good idea. The Paris production of *Tea and Sympathy* would give me a reason for going and a focus. It almost seemed providential that it should be there when I needed it.

When I came back after the Christmas season, I tried to settle down to work on a play, but found I couldn't concentrate, and found I couldn't get any objectivity on subject matter. Also I found I didn't care about anything at all. This is what troubled me most, since a person not only can't write, but can't live very well without caring about something. My doctors said I was still

Phyllis Anderson.
(Theatre Collection, New York Public Library)

in a state of shock and exhaustion and that I shouldn't rush it
. . . but that I should work. The only thing left for me to do
was a movie, which would keep me busy but on something
objective.

New York was still very sad for me, and as a matter of fact
still is. So after three weeks there reading books for movie
adaptations, I decided on *The Nun's Story*, and left for California. I spent six weeks out here conferring with Fred Zinnemann on the picture. This trip proved wonderful for me. I
gained back my fifteen pounds, and I had a very positive feeling.

I then returned to New York and immediately became depressed again, so took off for London for the opening there of
Tea, and then Paris for a week, and then joined Fred Zinnemann
on our background tour for *The Nun's Story*.

Jean Louis Phillipe and Ingrid Bergman in the Paris production (1953) of *Tea and Sympathy*. Miss Bergman played the role of the American professor's wife in French. With a Swedish accent? (*Collection of Robert Anderson*)

June 12th I returned to New York, and went up to Connecticut to our cottage there to set to and write the screenplay. But I found that place was too full of memories, since that was the place I had taken care of Phyllis most of last summer . . . Gadge and Molly [Kazan] asked me to live with them for the summer, but I decided again that the best thing is to get away from all associations, and so I came out here. I have been writing very well here, at about the rate of ten pages of script a day. Except for occasional moments, I find I can keep from being depressed . . . and I feel that this spell of work should give me a good groundwork to get back into my own work. It may be that I might decide to stay here until I have managed to write a play . . . or I may not. The important thing for me will be to keep the wheels turning now that I am in motion again.

As I told you, I have turned down a number of very attractive movie offers, and several offers to sign writer-director contracts with studios. I still see myself as a playwright, but this movie writing in the past three years has been a crutch for me to keep busy and occupied.

Audrey Hepburn in *The Nun's Story*, for which Robert Anderson wrote the filmscript.
(*Theatre Collection, New York Public Library*)

I cannot promise a play . . . but rest assured that as soon as the script of the movie is finished, I shall concentrate on nothing else. It is the one thing I need to get back on my feet, to feel that I am functioning again.

My best to Betty . . . and Keep in touch.

Best,
Bob

In 1958 he wrote more cheerfully. He had finished the playscript of *Silent Night, Lonely Night.*

Dear John:

As for the play . . . More people wanting to do it, but My God, how to get them all together at the same time with the same director. As you know Barbara and Dick Widmark would do it with Gadge . . . but Gadge won't do it, so that knocks out that very good team . . . Josh won't do it with either of them . . . and in asking them who else they might do it with, they came up with nobody . . . Now Hank Fonda has fallen in love with the play . . . and says he must do it. But he has some kind of commitment with Mankiewitz for a play, but this may be ironed out soon . . . But he's selling the play hard around town . . . every person I meet who knows him says, "Christ, what kind of play have you written . . . Hank has flipped." So that's good. He's the first one who's really said here I am . . . hold the play for me . . . Maria Schell is still here and eager . . . Margaret Sullavan liked the play, but was depressed by the ending . . . All the time Josh has been no help at all. He told me to go out and get a cast, and if he liked it, he'd do it. I told him this wasn't much of a help, and he said he didn't have the time or energy to do anything more . . . I don't call this really going with a play, the way, apparently Fonda is willing to go with it . . . Wish to Hell Gadge would change his mind, but I know he won't. Very strange since he admires it so.

Anyway, that's the story at the moment. I'll probably be out here at least another month . . . If I can stay sane. Lots of friends, but I guess grinding away at something I'm not too keen about takes its toll.

Best to you all . . . and keep in touch.

Bob

Henry Fonda became more and more enthusiastic over the play and Barbara Bel Geddes, the star of *Cat on a Hot Tin Roof*, also enthused. Fonda assured Bob that he wanted to buy the movie rights for himself, so that he could be sure of starring in the picture as well as the play. As a result, a fabulous preproduction offer for the rights was turned down.

But in the theatre you can't count on anything or anybody.

From the beginning of rehearsals Fonda's enthusiasm began to decline. The play, finally titled *Silent Night, Lonely Night*, opened in New York to lukewarm notices. Fonda was not well; he could not give his best performance. The slow pace of Peter Glenville's direction did not help. Brooks Atkinson called it "slow and ruminative"; to me, there were simply constant meaningless pauses. I wanted to get

Henry Fonda and Barbara Bel Geddes in *Silent Night, Lonely Night*. Barbara inherited from her father, the inspired designer Norman Bel Geddes, a wistful, almost childlike quality which, added to her beauty, made her exceptionally appealing. During the 1930s depression, Norman devised a horse-racing game which he set up in his studio and required his guests to play. We had to buy chips marked $5, $50, and $100. "You see," he explained shyly but delightedly, "it's more fun that way. When we settle up, we'll divide everything by 1,000."
(*Friedman-Abeles*)

up on the stage and, metaphorically, push the action along. Despite this, the audience reaction was not bad; business showed signs of life. *Then Fonda went completely sour on the play, infected Miss Bel Geddes; they refused to take any cut in salary; the play closed; the fabulous movie offer was lost.*

At that time Bob Anderson was almost exactly the same age as was Bob Sherwood when he launched the Company. I have not the slightest doubt that Anderson could have relaunched it if there had been available four playwrights of his age, talent, and point of view. He had not only the talent but also the intellectual attainment necessary to consolidate the leadership of such a venture. He had the necessary charm. There was no pomposity in him; he could laugh at himself and enjoy the laugh.

He once recounted to my wife and me, with great glee, the story of an "embarrassing moment" in Rome. He had arranged a dinner party at a swank restaurant in Rome, the Hostaria dell'Orso; Audrey Hepburn, at the height of her fame, was the guest of honor. The dinner went off fine; he felt he had impressed her as a sophisticated host. Then the bill was presented to him; he confidently took out a Diners Club Card and placed it on the tray.

"Credit cards were fairly new," he said, "I thought the possession of one showed a smart up-to-dateness. But no—the waiter stared at the card mistrustfully until he began to attract the attention of all the guests. I began to feel embarrassed; to my relief, the waiter suddenly took the bill and card and disappeared. But he returned shortly with the restaurant manager who was exuding such gloom that all conversation stopped and my embarrassment doubled.

"Finally, the manager spoke. Fixing me with a stare of unalloyed suspicion he nonetheless said they *could* honor the card, but they wouldn't pay the 7 percent discount; I would have to pay that in addition to the amount on the bill. By this time I felt that all the guests were secretly laughing at me; I was so uncomfortable that I would have paid 70 percent; all I wanted was to get it over and done with."

Happily, Miss Hepburn was not disturbed. She and her husband became good friends of Bob. Her friendship continued after her divorce and remarriage. I hope he will lure her back to the stage in an original play.

Just after the opening of *Silent Night, Lonely Night* Bob married the charming, vivacious film, stage, and TV star Teresa Wright. They share a curious predilection—the purchase of houses. They live in a lovely old house in the little town of Bridgewater, Connecticut. *In a neighboring town,* Bob owns another house where he does his

Bob and Teresa Anderson.
(*Friedman-Abeles*)

writing. Teresa owns a smaller house in Bridgewater, for what
purpose I have never made out. On a motor trip through Maine they
spied an old farmhouse which they couldn't resist buying and on a

Mr. and Mrs. Cullman. Both of them were shrewd judges of a play's profit
possibilities, but everyone makes mistakes in this field; they rejected *My
Fair Lady*.
(Collection of Mrs. Howard Cullman)

Robert Anderson, the sole surviving playwright member, at the author's
75th birthday party, where he scored a personal comedy success equal to
Arthur Miller's (see page 174).
(Friedman-Abeles)

trip to Portugal they were prevented from buying a house there only by pressure of business in America that sent them home before they could make an offer.

The marriage seems to have stimulated Bob's ever-present willingness to experiment along new lines. For a long time the wiseacres pontificated that one-act plays could not succeed on Broadway. He challenged this by presenting a bill of four one-act plays under the cumbersome title *You Know I Can't Hear You When the Water's Running*. It was an enormous success. It was, incidentally, the first use of suggested male nudity, done so skillfully that no one found it salacious. In 1972 he decided to try his hand at the novel; the manuscript was literally gobbled up by the first publisher to see it.

The novel, *After*, opens with a story of the years during which a wife suffered and finally died from cancer; it stresses the impact on both wife and husband. It is obviously suggested by Phyllis's last years, but a reader need not have known Phyllis to be overwhelmed by it. I have never read anything more affecting and effective.

I look forward with confidence to more fresh, original, and dramatic work from Robert Anderson.

XVIII

A Broadway Gőtterdammerung

There is a now neglected essay by Bernard Shaw titled "The Perfect Wagnerite." It gives a Shavian explanation of "The Ring of the Niebelungen" which would, I feel sure, have surprised Richard Wagner. Basically, according to Shaw, in most of the libretti Wagner was preaching the glories of something very like Fabian Socialism. I doubt this, but there is no denying one point which Shaw makes at the end: after Siegfried has died and the mightiest of funeral dirges has been played, the libretto of *Götterdammerung* relates a mess of uninteresting bickering and senseless tragedy that has only occasional relevance to the great mythological story. One is rather glad when the gods' castle finally bursts into flames and comes to its final end.

If an opera were ever made of The Playwrights Producing Company, Inc. a funeral march should be played as of November 14, 1955, the day of Sherwood's death. The castle didn't burn up until June 30, 1960, but the earlier date was the real date of the Company's demise. What happened between those two dates was largely irrelevant to the real story.

But a few loose ends should be tied off.

The outstanding internal change was that the neuroticism in Roger which I had suspected became a reality in a strange and surprising way. From being close to the most popular man in the theatre he suddenly became known as one of the most difficult to deal with. Many people found him incredibly rude. I knew from unhappy personal experience that neuroses can take most undesirable forms; I have been very, very difficult myself for long stretches of time. I sympathized with Roger, but I didn't know what to do about it. I could only hope that it would eventually burn itself out.

This hope was fulfilled. In the 1960s he threw the bulk of his energy into getting the Johnson administration to set up the National Endowment for the Arts. He succeeded, was appointed the first Administrator, and did a magnificent job. Later, he raised the money for, and became the first head of, the Kennedy Center for the Performing Arts. Obviously, he regained his old-time charm and turned it on the politicos.

But that was all later. In the late 1950s he wasn't any fun to work with.

His no-cash policies began to come to roost on Victor Samrock's head. The latter was accustomed to paying suppliers on the dot;

Time Remembered. What I myself remember most vividly is that at a time when a drama could be done for $50,000, the sets alone for this one cost $60,000. They *were* beautiful.
(*Vandamm*)

suddenly, promised funds did not materialize and Victor had to stall. Eventually, Roger always saw to it that all bills were paid, but sometimes "eventually" was a long time coming.

Max and Elmer became irritated with Roger's policies to the extent of threatening to resign unless certain changes were made. This dispute was quickly patched up, but it was only a patch job.

The gods continued to be unfair. Roger brought to the Company many top-flight directors, actors, dramatists, and co-producers. The aura of success hung on. But this precipitated another curious contretemps.

Trouble developed with outside stockholders other than the Cullmans. While Sherwood was alive, his friends treated their investment as nonbusiness and paid little attention to it. After his death they began to look at the situation with different eyes—jaundiced ones. They wanted to know why the Company made so little money out of so many solid hits. The answer, of course, was that Roger's setup was designed to assure production of members' plays and payment of Company overhead, but did not give a large share of the profits of any play to the Company. As early as January 1954 I had made up and presented to the Board a schedule showing the Company's profit participation in three successes:

Tea and Sympathy	10½%
Sabrina Fair	20%
Ondine	35%

(The arrangements for *Cat on a Hot Tin Roof* and *Tiger at the Gates* were not much more favorable.)

When I finished the presentation I was not exactly convulsed with joy; neither was anyone else. I should have stopped and asked myself this question—"What have Roger and I wrought?" But the Company had become such an integral part of my life that I went blindly ahead. However, it soon became clear that we had better buy out our investors. By sacrificing a large Company investment we were able to raise enough to pay them *in cash* the par value of their preferred stock and $15 per share for the Class A Stock which had gone to them for $1 per share. So each of them made *some* profit and was glad to call it quits.

It was a tiny profit, after twenty years. On the other hand, it was downright miraculous that there was any profit at all when one considered the string of calamities the Company had suffered.

Howard's death, Sherwood's absorption by the war effort and the Hopkins biography, Arthur Byron's collapse, Halliday's illness, Lem Ward's death, Behrman's resignation, the sudden jump in costs, Kurt

Dame Judith Anderson and Mildred Dunnock in the avant-garde play *In the Summer House*. It missed success by a hairsbreadth.
(*Graphic House*)

Weill's death, and finally Sherwood's death; quite a list! In only one year—the first—was the Company able to proceed on the assumption underlying its formation—that five active playwrights could give the Company at least three plays a year to produce, and that these would generate more profit than loss. *Abe Lincoln* and *No Time for Comedy* yielded large profits; *Knickerbocker Holiday* was no disaster; only *American Landscape* flopped. The profit *far* exceeded the loss.

Compared to those happy days, the Company, as far as members were concerned, was indeed a dismal scene in the late 1950s.

Elmer began to dislike Roger more and more; he privately called him "the tycoon." Matters came to a climax when Roger refused to finance Elmer's play *Cue for Passion*, unless he could find a co-producer; he finally brought in a lady with no experience and gave her co-production credit. The play, on opening, appeared to be a hit, but audiences dwindled. It was a crusher for Elmer and also a crusher to any further relationship with Roger.

Max calmly accepted an assignment from Guthrie McClintic to dramatize a book, *The Day the Money Stopped*. This had been highly touted by the book reviewers as a sure-fire hit play because it was almost all dialogue—very good dialogue. Book reviewers seldom understand that it takes more than dialogue to make a play. To our

John Kerr and Diana Wynyard in *Cue for Passion*, Elmer's reworking of the Hamlet theme. Its failure was the last straw for Elmer; he never had another play produced.
(*Friedman-Abeles*)

horror, Max accepted the reviewers' view. He merely copied the dialogue; the result was disaster. It was a totally different Maxwell Anderson from the one who had written *The Eve of St. Mark* and *Joan of Lorraine*.

He died in 1959—happy in his private life with his new wife, Gilda—unhappy and frustrated as a dramatist, but still struggling to recover his old-time greatness. At his funeral Bob Anderson, in a moving address, presented a brilliant picture of the true Maxwell Anderson.

"I have been spending a lot of time with Max the last two days . . . I suppose most of us have . . . thinking about what he had meant to me and the Theatre . . . reading parts of his plays and essays . . . just remembering and coming again to the realization that he was that kind of man by which other men are measured.

"Max first touched my life importantly long before I knew him as a man . . . back in the mid-thirties, when he was one of

Julie Harris in *The Country Wife*, a play that has attracted many a star to its many revivals. The dynamic Miss Harris held her own with any of them.

the leaders of that stunning generation of playwrights who were making our drama the most exciting in the world.

"It was a great time for a young man to become aware of the American theatre and American playwrights. Like hundreds of other college boys, I wrote my first play in blank verse and on an Elizabethan subject in frank imitation of Max. I wrote my Senior Honor's Thesis on Maxwell Anderson, and I remember using on the title page that ringing passage from the preface to *Winterset:*

> "I believe with Goethe that dramatic poetry is man's greatest achievement on his earth so far, and I believe with the early Bernard Shaw that the theatre is essentially a cathedral of the spirit, devoted to the exaltation of men and boasting an apostolic succession of inspired high priests which extends further into the past than the Christian line founded by St. Peter."

"On my graduation from the University, I don't remember what the speaker said. Something Max had written was far more important.

> "To the young people of this country, I wish to say: if you practice an art, be proud of it, and make it proud of you. If you now hesitate on the threshold of your maturity, wondering what rewards you should seek, wondering perhaps whether there are any rewards beyond the opportunity to feed and sleep and

The first birthday celebration of *The Pleasure of His Company*, co-produced by Frederick Brisson and the Company. Mr. and Mrs. Brisson (Rosalind Russell) with co-stars Cyril Ritchard and Cornelia Otis Skinner prepare to drink a toast to the continued prosperity of the comedy; *L to R*, Mr. Brisson, Miss Skinner, Miss Russell, Mr. Ritchard.

(*Vandamm*)

breed, turn to the art which has moved you most readily. It may break your heart, it may drive you half mad, it may betray you into unrealizable ambitions or blind you to mercantile opportunities with its wandering fires. But it will fill your heart before it breaks it; it will make you a person in your own right; it will open the temple doors to you and enable you to walk with those who have come nearest among men to what men may sometime be."

"I next remember Max after the war, around 1949, when he climbed the five flights of stairs to a room over the Hudson Theatre to talk to the first group of New Dramatists . . . young unproduced playwrights who gathered together once a week to learn more about playwriting.

"It was my first glimpse of Max, and I was not disappointed. As always he was shy, quiet, brief in his responses . . . and with that smile, that sad, wise, kind smile which seemed to say that he accepted life as he had found it, happy, tragic, rewarding and bitter.

"Sometime during the evening, Howard Lindsay, who was conducting the session, started to name some of Max's plays . . . *What Price Glory?*, *Mary of Scotland*, *Both Your Houses*, *Elizabeth the Queen*, *Valley Forge* . . . and we looked at Max, who looked somewhat surprised . . . *High Tor*, *The Wingless Victory*, *The Masque of Kings*, *Saturday's Children*, *Winterset* . . . and we looked at each other and shook our heads . . . *Knickerbocker Holiday*, *Star Wagon*, *Key Largo*, *Anne of the Thousand Days*, *Joan of Lorraine* . . . and as the list went on, we smiled, smiles of wonder and admiration . . . smiles that were close to tears. . . .

"Last Spring at the Theatre Guild Party, I sat at a table with Max and Gilda. And towards the end of a festive, lighthearted evening during which there had been songs and moments from Theatre Guild plays . . . suddenly, there on the stage were Helen Hayes and Helen Mencken in the last scene from *Mary of Scotland*.

"It was a great moment. It was as though we had all forgotten the excitement and splendor and sweep of words and poetry . . . and we were being reminded as only the theatre can remind you, so that you can say nothing, but can only stand and applaud until your hands hurt . . . When the ovation eventually was over, I looked across at Max and by a senseless bobbing of the head tried to convey how I felt . . . And he said, with that lovely air of surprise . . . 'It sounded all right, didn't it?' . . .

Richard Burton and Susan Strasberg in *Time Remembered*. Burton's first appearance on the American stage; a very successful first.
(*Theatre Collection, New York Public Library*)

Author Morton Wishengrad and director Peter Hall with co-stars Siobhan McKenna, Joan Blondell, and Art Carney during a rehearsal of *The Rope Dancers*.
(*Friedman-Abeles*)

"The last memory I have of Max is a few weeks ago at a meeting of The Playwrights' Company, that company where in the great days he had been so happy with his friends and peers, Bob Sherwood, Elmer Rice, S. N. Behrman, Sidney Howard, Kurt Weill and John Wharton . . . John Wharton was presiding at the meeting, and towards the end he asked us each what we were working on, and Max smiled and admitted that he was working on a new musical, that he had a new play already finished, and was mapping out another.

"After the meeting broke up, Max asked me to come to Stamford one day and have lunch and see his house by the water . . . I said I would. Maybe we should wait for the weather to get better, and we could sit on his seawall and discuss playwriting and the state of the world . . . He said that would be fine. Maybe in the Spring . . . And we waved good-bye to each other and left."

After Max's death Elmer became still more disenchanted with the Company. He resigned from the Board of Directors and demanded that the Company be dissolved.

No one objected to Elmer's demand, although Bob Anderson asked that it be postponed until the presentation of *Silent Night, Lonely Night*. During the postponement Roger arranged for the Company to produce what was to be the final play; it was written by Gore Vidal and entitled *The Best Man*.

Oddly enough, this last play, like our first play, dealt with presidential candidates. But the difference in approach was startling! *Abe Lincoln in Illinois* dealt with candidates who, wisely or unwisely, were driven by moral fervor. *The Best Man* showed candidates who flung around unproved accusations of mental instability and homosexuality. It was a clear example of how the cynicism which grew up in the 1950s was replacing the idealism of the first half of the twentieth century.

No one born after 1930—which means almost a majority of Americans today (1974)—really understands that fifty-year period. Part of the period is getting nostalgic attention, but there is little or no study of it by those searching for a social philosophy. When such study becomes prevalent, the playwrights of the twenties, thirties, and forties will regain their old importance. People will understand what Max Anderson meant when he talked of trying to help men clear up the confusion in their lives, what warning was implicit in Rice's *Adding Machine* and *American Landscape*, what Sherwood meant by dedication to public service. (And could any title for the Indochina

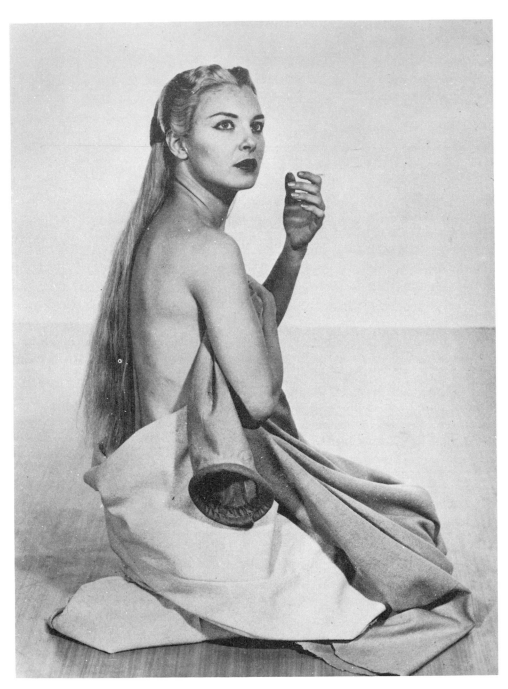

Joanne Woodward in *The Lovers*.
(*Friedman-Abeles*)

Helen Hayes and Helen Menken in *Mary of Scotland.* "It sounded all right."
(*Vandamm*)

wars have been more apt than *Idiot's Delight?*) These men were liberals in the true sense of the word. They believed that people were capable of improvement and that perhaps the greatest feature of that improvement would be a reduction in Man's inhumanity to Man. And they expressed their beliefs in a dramatic form that anyone could understand.

This point of view and this style of writing are almost unknown in the American theatre today (1974). Clarity of theme is no longer regarded by critics as a necessity—not even a desideratum. Praise may be heaped on an abstruse play which the author defiantly refuses to explain.

Man's inhumanity to Man is pretty much taken for granted. There is an insatiable interest in the "losers" of society. A good example is the current increase in the popularity of certain plays by the great Eugene O'Neill. No one has ever approached O'Neill's skill in por-

The Best Man, which did not exactly increase your admiration for presidential candidates. (*Friedman-Abeles*)

Our audiences remained distinguished. (*David Workman*)

traying losers: alcoholics, bums, outcasts, frustrated failures. *The Iceman Cometh* and *A Moon for the Misbegotten* are masterpieces of such portrayals; however, neither play holds out hope of any betterment; O'Neill, as Brooks Atkinson has pointed out, came to believe that life was tragic and could *not* be changed. In the glow of the 1940s both of these plays were largely dismissed as "tired" or "thin" pieces of work. Revived posthumously in the 1970s they received praise which would have amazed O'Neill himself. Obviously, the critical and audience climate had undergone a 180 degree change. When the change comes full circle, as it will, the "winners" portrayed in the pre-1950 dramas will again attract attention.

The Best Man was a solid hit, but its enthusiastic reception did not stop the filing of a Certificate of Dissolution on June 30, 1960, exactly twenty-two years after the filing of the original Certificate of Incorporation. So we were unique to the end. I know of no other producing organization that brought its legal existence to an end just after producing a play destined to run for over five hundred performances.

EPILOGUE

What of the Future?

In 1952 I received a letter from Sherwood in which he declared that "I often stop to wonder what the hell it is that has kept the Playwrights Company together this long through so many vicissitudes and so much inactivity (particularly on my part)." Today the answer seems pretty clear to me.

Men and women are "herd animals"; they instinctively form into groups, herds, flocks, packs. (Human complexity is such that the same people can behave like a wolf pack at one time and a flock of sheep at other times.)

Children instinctively form into cliques or gangs. When they grow up they seek to become part of some organization, the greater the better, and immediately give it their loyalty. This "desire to belong" explains why a corporation can have thousands of loyal employees, why Vermont farmers and Texas oil men can be loyal to the United States of America. The most successful herds have a leader who inspires trust and emulation.

Max, Elmer, Bob, and, later, Kurt and Bob Anderson stuck to the Company through its many unhappy, as well as the happy, periods because of what they got from "belonging." The cooperation, stimulation, plain pleasure of friendships, outweighed what must have been deep frustrations. Samrock, Fields, and I, each in his own way, had the same loyalty. Today I am clear that Roger Stevens and I made a great mistake when we promoted the Playwrights Company–Producers Theatre–Whitehead–Stevens combination idea. Somehow it split up and destroyed the instinctive loyalty.

I have been asked whether I think there could be a new and more successful Playwrights Producing Company. My answer is an emphatic yes, *if* it can attract the loyalty of its members to the degree that our Company did. I do not believe that *just any* five or more dramatists could so organize. They would have to admire each other's work, have the same general social philosophy, and—I think—all desire to write what I have called "important plays."

Many a dramatist has said that playwriting is a lonely profession. Our Company proved that it does not *have to be* lonely. Moreover, such group membership can be immensely stimulating—both the Company and the New Dramatists Committee, which we helped to spawn, prove that. I hope that any reader of this book who determines to try his hand at playwriting can find a "group"—particularly if he wants to write serious and "important" plays.

The question of what will be deemed "important" over the next twenty years is a question for which there is today no ready answer. All over the world, but particularly in America, men, women, and children are having to learn to adapt themselves to changes coming at a breathless speed. What seems important today can be forgotten a year—even a month—later. Never before have playwrights had to write for an audience in an equivalent state of turmoil. Change there has always been, but never before at this speed.

Of course, a few basic human conflicts are eternal—Man's penchant for creation versus his penchant for destruction. No one has ever described the penchant for destruction more graphically or pessimistically than Leonardo da Vinci in his "Prophecies."

On earth creatures shall be seen who are constantly killing one another. Their wickedness shall be limitless; their violence shall destroy the world's vast forests; and even after they have been sated, they shall in no wise suspend their desire to spread carnage, tribulations, and banishment among all living beings. Their overreaching pride shall impel them to lift themselves toward heaven. Nothing shall remain on the earth, or under the earth, or in the waters, that shall not be hunted down and slain, and what is in one country, dragged away into another; and their bodies shall become the tomb and the thoroughfare for all the living things they have ruined. O Earth, what restrains you from opening up and from engulfing them as one, into the deep fissures of your chasms; so that the face of heaven no longer beholds so cruel and abominable a monster!

SELZ

The Playwrights Producing Company, Inc., a producing company to put on its own plays: Maxwell Anderson, S. N. Behrman, Robert Sherwood, Sidney Howard, and Elmer Rice. Caricature by Irma Selz, 1938. (*James Graham and Sons, Inc.*)

No playwright is likely to arise who can explain *how* to stop modern barbarism on such a scale. But the point of view, the approach, can give importance to the dramatist. G.K. Chesterton's book on Bernard Shaw closes with a tribute which was applicable to the days of our Company and remains applicable today. Chesterton felt, in 1909, quite correctly, that there was a death and destruction tide rising in Europe, although it was hard for him really to believe it. But he ended his book by saying:

> . . . . this shall be written of our time; that when the spirit who denies besieged the last citadel, blaspheming life itself, there were some, there was one especially, whose voice was heard and whose spear was never broken.

APPENDIX A

Basic Agreement for the Incorporation of

the Playwrights' Company

AGREEMENT made and entered into this 12th day of April, 1938 between MAXWELL ANDERSON, S.N. BEHRMAN, SIDNEY HOWARD, ELMER RICE and ROBERT E. SHERWOOD (herein collectively called "the playwrights"), and JOHN F. WHARTON (herein called "Wharton").

Each of the playwrights has for a number of years been engaged in writing plays which have been produced in New York City and elsewhere. The playwrights desire to organize a corporation by which plays hereafter written by the playwrights may be produced and exploited in the manner herein set forth; such corporation also to have the power to produce plays written by other dramatists. The parties desire that Wharton be associated with the enterprise in the manner herein set forth.

1. The playwrights desire to start with a capital of Fifty thousand ($50,000) dollars, but to make provision for the raising of additional capital from outside parties. They desire that those who subscribe the capital, whether themselves alone or with outside parties included, shall receive a preference for the repayment of the capital and be entitled to fifty (50%) per cent of the profits of the enterprise, and to that end it is proposed to create a class of stock which will receive fifty (50%) per cent of the profits regardless of the number of shares issued. It is further intended that Wharton shall receive a ten (10%) per cent interest in the profits of the enterprise for the services to be rendered by him hereunder and the remaining profits shall be divided equally among the playwrights for their management services. To carry out this intent:

The parties agree to cause to be incorporated under the laws of the State of Delaware as soon as practicable after July 1, 1938 a corporation (herein referred to as "the corporation"), whose certificate of incorporation shall provide for:

(a) Full powers to engage in all kinds of theatrical and entertainment enterprises:

(b) An authorized capital stock consisting of:

(1) Fifteen hundred (1500) shares of four (4%) per cent Non-Cumulative Non-Participating Preferred Stock of the par value of One Hundred ($100.) dollars per share, preferred to the extent of One Hundred ($100.) dollars per share upon dissolution;

(2) Fifteen hundred (1500) shares of Class A Stock of the par value of One ($1.) dollar per share, entitled as a class to one half of the profits after preferred dividends, and fifteen hundred (1500) shares of Class B stock of the par value of One ($1.) dollar per share, likewise entitled to one half of such profits. No dividend shall be declared on the Class B Stock unless at the same time a dividend is declared on the Class A Stock as a class in an amount equal to the amount so declared on the Class B Stock as a class, plus the aggregate of such amounts, if any, that shall have been paid as compensation, for services rendered merely as executive officers, to the holders of Class B Stock since the last dividend declared on the Class A Stock. The Class B Stock shall have exclusive voting power for the election of directors, but otherwise the voting power shall be exercised both by the Class A Stock and by the Class B Stock, each share of each such class to have one vote.

(c) A Board of Directors to be not less than six (6) nor more than nine (9) in number;

(d) Such further provisions as Wharton and Rice shall consider advisable.

2. Each of the playwrights agree to subscribe for one hundred (100) shares of the Preferred Stock at One hundred ($100.) dollars per share, one hundred (100) shares of the Class A Stock at One ($1.) dollar per share, and two hundred and forty (240) shares of the Class B Stock at One ($1.) dollar per share. Wharton agrees to subscribe for three hundred (300) shares of the Class B Stock at One ($1.) dollar per share. Payment for said shares shall be made in cash upon request from time to time against delivery of certificates for the stock so subscribed for at any time after the incorporation of the corporation.

Upon consummation of the foregoing, the outstanding securities will be held as follows:

Preferred Stock	No. of Shares
Anderson	100
Behrman	100
Howard	100
Rice	100
Sherwood	100

Class A Stock entitled as a class to fifty (50%) per cent of the profits	No. of Shares
Anderson	100
Behrman	100
Howard	100
Rice	100
Sherwood	100

Class B Stock entitled as a class to fifty (50%) per cent of the profits	No. of Shares
Anderson	240
Behrman	240
Howard	240
Rice	240
Sherwood	240
Wharton	300

In the event that the corporation desires to obtain additional capital from other persons, no Class B Stock shall be sold to such persons, but Preferred Stock and Class A Stock shall be sold at such prices as the Board of Directors shall from time to time determine.

3. The first Board of Directors of the corporation shall be six (6) in number and shall consist of the parties hereto. The directors shall be elected by cumulative voting to assure that each of the parties can continue as a director.

4. The corporation shall be obligated to accept for production any play written hereafter and during the term of this agreement by any of the playwrights which, in the opinion of the Board of Directors, conforms to the following:

(a) The budget of estimated production cost as approved by the Board of Directors (including the amount of Actors' Equity or Stagehands' Union deposits or guarantees, but not including any estimated out-of-town loss) shall not exceed Twenty-five thousand ($25,000) dollars;

(b) The budget of estimated weekly operating cost as approved by the Board of Directors shall indicate that the corporation's share of maximum possible box office receipts for five (5) consecutive weeks would exceed the operating costs for said five (5) weeks by an amount equal to the estimated production cost, exclusive of such deposits or guarantees.

5. Each of the playwrights agrees to offer to the corporation the production rights for each play that shall hereafter be completed by

him at any time from the date hereof until the expiration of the term of this agreement (or until his earlier withdrawal pursuant to paragraph "14" of this agreement). In the event that any such play so submitted is not one which the corporation is obligated to accept for production pursuant to paragraph "4" hereof, the Board of Directors by vote (exclusive of the playwright submitting the play) of a majority of a quorum, may, nevertheless, within thirty (30) days after submission, accept such play for production. Upon the acceptance of any play for production, the corporation and the author of the play shall enter into a standard production contract of The Dramatists' Guild providing for:

(a) Payment to the author of royalties of ten (10%) per cent of the gross weekly box office receipts;

(b) Payment of advance royalties in the minimum amount provided in the Minimum Basic Agreement;

(c) The expiration of the producing rights in the corporation in the event that the play is not placed in rehearsal by the January 1st following the execution of said Dramatists' Guild contract;

(d) The interest of the corporation in subsidiary rights shall be forty (40%) per cent with respect to motion picture, radio and television, and foreign presentation (other than Great Britain) rights, and shall be fifty (50%) per cent with respect to other subsidiary rights.

Playwrights agree to adopt a policy of writing plays which, so far as possible, do not require unavailable stars or outside management. (It is understood and agreed, however, that Maxwell Anderson is now at work on a play which he has agreed to submit to Alfred Lunt and Lynn Fontanne, and if Mr. Lunt and Miss Fontanne object to production by this corporation he is to be free to have it produced elsewhere.) In the event that any playwright shall feel that special circumstances (such as the fact that a star actor or a director whom he requires for his play is under exclusive contract to an outside manager or in other ways committed to such outside manager) render it impossible, in his opinion, for his play to be properly presented by the corporation, he shall be free to make outside arrangements, but only with the management which can supply such star or other necessary personnel, and in such event he shall endeavor to obtain for the corporation an interest in such production.

The corporation shall have the right to produce and exploit plays written by dramatists other than the playwrights entitled to the benefit of this contract.

6. In the event that the corporation shall accept for production any play of any of the playwrights hereunder but shall fail to produce the play within the period therefor provided, or in the event that the corporation shall not accept for production, because of budget limitations, any play submitted to it hereunder, the author of said play shall (upon the expiration of said production period or upon the decision not

to accept for production, as the case may be) have full right to make whatever arrangements he may desire with any other persons whatsoever with respect to the production of said play, and neither the corporation nor the other parties hereto shall have any interest whatsoever in said play.

7. In the production of any play the author thereof shall, subject to the financial restrictions set forth in paragraphs "8" and "9" hereof, have complete control of all matters dealing with the artistic side of the production, such as determination of choice of cast, director, designer, selection of properties, sets, size of theatre, and other like matters. The Board of Directors by vote (excluding the author of the play in question) of a majority of a quorum, shall be empowered to decide all other questions, including decisions as to road tours and organization of companies other than the original New York company, determination of time of closing the play, determination of terms of English production, price of tickets, decisions as to prior out-of-town runs, theatre terms, amounts to be spent for, and the nature of, publicity and advertising. In the event that a play is placed in rehearsal and a question arises as to whether further rewriting is necessary, the Board by a majority vote (including the author in question) of a quorum, may pass upon the question of withdrawal and reopening. The Board of Directors shall also determine all matters relating to the leasing and equipment of an office, the employment of an office staff, the employment of a press agent, business manager, auditor, and all other matters relating to the business operations of the corporation. The Board of Directors, acting by a majority vote of the entire Board, shall have authority, except as restricted by law, to delegate any of its powers to an Executive Committee or other committee or to a business manager and/or any other officer or employee of the corporation, by resolution defining the extent to which such authority is delegated, and any action properly taken by such committee or person pursuant to such resolution shall be binding upon the corporation and its stockholders.

Nothing in this agreement is intended or shall be construed to diminish or vary in any manner the rights of each of the playwrights as an Author under the Minimum Basic Agreement with respect to each of his plays that shall be produced hereunder.

8. No expenditures shall be made or incurred nor shall any commitments or contracts be made by or on behalf of the corporation (unless approved by the Board of Directors or a duly appointed committee) with respect to any play unless and until the author shall have delivered to each of the other playwrights a script which the author deems complete and until the Board of Directors or a duly appointed committee shall have determined that the budget of estimated production cost and budget of estimated operating cost are satisfactory.

9. No expenditures shall be made or incurred, nor shall any commitments or contracts be entered into by or on behalf of the corporation, with respect to any play which shall cause to be exceeded any of

the items set forth on the budgets with respect to said play, unless specific approval thereto shall have been given by the Board of Directors or by a business manager or other person in whom the Board of Directors shall, by resolution, have vested such authority.

10. Each of the playwrights shall have the right to direct the production of any or all of his plays to be produced hereunder. In the event that any playwright shall so direct any play, he shall receive compensation in the amount of Two thousand ($2,000.) dollars for such services.

11. Each of the playwrights agrees to be available to New York City from August 1st to February 15th in each year during the term of this agreement and to render services to the best of his ability and to devote such time as shall be necessary therefor to the corporation in connection with matters relating to casting, changes in script, and any other matters relating to the production of plays and general operations of the corporation that shall arise in connection with any of the plays hereunder. It is understood that if at any time any of the playwrights shall be of the opinion that the writing, rehearsal or production of one or more of his own plays requires his full time and attention for any period of time, such playwright may devote his exclusive time thereto during said period of time and shall not be required to render his services to the corporation during said period in connection with other plays.

12. Wharton agrees to act as counsel for the corporation during the term of this agreement and as such counsel to render all necessary legal services other than those involving litigation or services of an extraordinary nature, such as merger with any producing organization, reorganization of the Company, etc., and in addition, to supervise the financial affairs of the corporation and to accept as full compensation for such service the rights conferred upon him by reason of the issuance to him of three hundred (300) shares of the Class B Stock of the corporation as set forth above.

13. In the event that (a) any of the playwrights shall fail to submit to the corporation at least one (1) completed manuscript of a new play during the twenty-four (24) month period beginning with February 1st, 1938, and during each twenty-four (24) month period beginning on any February 1st after 1938, or (b) Wharton shall cease to practice law or shall fail or refuse to render his services hereunder, or (c) any playwright or Wharton shall die during the term of this agreement, then and in any of such events the corporation and/or the playwrights entitled to the benefits of this contract shall have the right, but not the obligation, to purchase from such playwright or from Wharton, as the case may be, all stock in the corporation held by such person and to pay for the same in cash the value of such stock determined as stated below, said right to be exercisable within thirty (30) days after such determination of value.

14. Any playwright shall have the right to withdraw from this agreement and terminate his obligation to submit new plays and render services hereunder as of February 1, 1940 or as of any February 1st

thereafter. Said right shall be exercisable by notice in writing delivered to the corporation not less than thirty (30) days prior to the effective date thereof. Upon receipt of such notice by the corporation, then the corporation and/or the playwrights entitled to the benefits of this contract shall acquire the right, but not the obligation, to purchase from said playwright all stock in the corporation held by him and to pay for the same in cash the value of such stock determined as stated below, such right to be exercisable within thirty (30) days after the determination of such value.

15. The parties shall have the right from time to time to admit one or more additional playwrights to the benefits of this contract, provided that (a) the admission of each such additional playwright shall have been approved in writing by all the playwrights then entitled to the benefits of this contract, (b) each such additional playwright shall agree to purchase from the playwrights Class B Stock in such amounts as they shall respectively desire to sell to him and to pay for such stock the value thereof as determined by the Board of Directors, and (c) each such additional playwright shall agree to be bound by all the provisions of this agreement provided with respect to the playwrights to the same extent as if a party hereto at the time of execution hereof. Each such new playwright shall have the right to subscribe for Preferred Stock, if any be unissued, of the corporation at par in an amount not exceeding the amount then held by any of the other playwrights and shall also have the right to purchase one (1) share of Class A Stock with respect to each share of Preferred Stock so purchased and to pay for such Class A Stock the value thereof as determined by the Board of Directors.

16. The corporation shall adopt by-laws consistent with the provisions of this agreement and in such form as Wharton and Rice shall consider advisable.

17. The name of the corporation shall be selected by all the parties to this agreement, and all plays produced by the corporation shall be presented under that name.

18. No compensation shall be paid to any holder of Class B Stock for his services as an executive officer except in the last month of any fiscal year and in no case shall the aggregate of such compensation so paid exceed fifty per cent (50%) of the estimated net profits for said fiscal year.

19. The parties agree that on or before the issuance of stock in the corporation to them they will enter into an agreement, in such form and with such provisions as Wharton and Rice shall deem advisable, restraining the transferability of such stock and providing for a reasonable opportunity to the corporation and/or the playwrights entitled to the benefits of this contract to acquire, at the value determined as set forth below, any stock which any of the parties hereto shall desire to transfer. Such agreement may prescribe the method of exercising the rights set out in Paragraphs "13" and "14" hereof. Said agreement shall also provide that all certificates for stock issued to the parties shall bear a legend referring to the restrictions upon the transferability of said certificate.

20. Whenever under any of the provisions of this agreement it shall become necessary to determine the value of any of the stock of the corporation (except where, by the provisions hereof such determination is to be made by the Board of Directors of the corporation), then, if the seller and the purchaser or purchasers shall be unable within a reasonable time to agree upon a value, said value shall be determined and settled by arbitration in New York City by abritrators appointed by the American Abritration Association and in accordance with the rules of said Association as then in effect.

21. The terms of this agreement shall be from the date hereof until such date as (a) four (4) or more of the playwrights shall have died or withdrawn pursuant to paragraph "14" above, or (b) such earlier date as all the playwrights then entitled to the benefits of this contract shall in writing fix as the date of termination.

22. The phrase "the playwrights entitled to the benefits of this contract" wherever used herein shall be construed to apply to all playwrights who (a) are original parties to this agreement or shall have subsequently admitted pursuant to paragraph "15" hereof, and (b) who at the time in question are alive, have not become subject to the provisions of clause "(a)" of paragraph "13" and have not withdrawn pursuant to the provisions of paragraph "14."

23. The corporation shall promptly after its organization assume all the obligations to be performed by the corporation hereunder, by executing the instrument hereto annexed. Upon the execution of such instrument, the corporation shall be deemed a party to this agreement and entitled to all the rights and privileges and subject to all the obligations and liabilities of this agreement with the same full force and effect as if the corporation were originally a party hereto at the date of execution hereof.

WITNESS due execution of this agreement the day and year first above written.

MAXWELL ANDERSON [Signed]

S.N. BEHRMAN [Signed]

SIDNEY HOWARD [Signed]

ELMER RICE [Signed]

ROBERT E. SHERWOOD [Signed]

JOHN F. WHARTON [Signed]

APPENDIX B

A Chronological Record of the Productions

and the Co-Productions of the

Playwrights Producing Company, Inc., 1938–1960

ABE LINCOLN IN ILLINOIS

By Robert E. Sherwood
Direction: Elmer Rice
Scenery: Jo Mielziner
Costumes: Rose Bogdanoff

Tryout: Washington and Baltimore
New York: Plymouth Theatre
October 15, 1938
472 performances
Tour: 32 weeks

CAST

Mentor Graham	Frank Andrews
Abe Lincoln	Raymond Massey
Ann Rutledge	Adele Longmire
Judith	Iris Whitney
Ben Mattling	George Christie
Judge Bowling Green	Arthur Griffin
Ninian Edwards	Lewis Martin
Joshua Speed	Calvin Thomas
Trum Cogdal	Harry Levian
Jack Armstrong	Howard daSilva
Bab	Everett Charlton
Feargus	David Clarke
Jasp	Kevin McCarthy
Seth Gale	Herbert Rudley
Nancy Green	Lillian Foster
William Herndon	Wendell K. Phillips
Elizabeth Edwards	May Collins
Mary Todd	Muriel Kirkland
The Edwards' Maid	Dorothy Allan
Jimmy Gale	Howard Sherman
Aggie Gale	Marion Rooney
Gobey	Hubert Brown
Stephen A. Douglas	Albert Phillips
Willie Lincoln	Lex Parrish
Tad Lincoln	Lloyd Barry
Robert Lincoln	John Payne
The Lincolns' Maid	Iris Whitney
Crimmin	Frank Tweddell
Barrick	John Gerard
Sturveson	Thomas F. Tracey

Jed .... Harry Levian
Phil .... Kevin McCarthy
Kavanagh .... Glenn Coulter
Ogleby .... John Triggs
Donner .... David Clarke
Cavalry Captain .... Everett Charlton
Soldiers, Railroad Men, Townspeople: Stuart McClure, Allen Shaw,
    Phillip Caplan, David Hewes, Dearon Darnay, Harrison
    Woodhull, Robert Fitzsimmons, Joseph Wiseman, Walter
    Kapp, George Malcolm, Bert Schorr, Augusta Dabney, Bette
    Benfield, Ann Stevenson.

KNICKERBOCKER HOLIDAY

Book and lyrics by Maxwell
   Anderson
Music by Kurt Weill
Direction: Joshua Logan
Scenery: Jo Mielziner
Dances: Carl Randall and
   Edwin Denby
Costumes: Frank Bevan

Tryout: Hartford, Boston, and
   Washington
New York: Barrymore Theatre
   October 19, 1938
   168 performances
Tour: 9 weeks

CAST

Washington Irving .... Ray Middleton
Anthony Corlear .... Harry Meehan
Tienhoven .... Mark Smith
Vanderbilt .... George Watts
Roosevelt .... Francis Pierlot
DePeyster .... Charles Arnt
DeVries .... John E. Young
Van Rensselaer .... James Phillips
Van Cortlandt, Jr. .... Richard Cowdery
Tina Tienhoven .... Jeanne Madden
Brom Broeck .... Richard Kollmar
Tenpin .... Clarence Nordstrom
Schermerhorn .... Howard Freeman
Pieter Stuyvesant .... Walter Huston
General Poffenburgh .... Donald Black
Mistress Schermerhorn .... Edith Angold
Citizens of New Amsterdam—Helen Carroll, Jane Brotherton,
    Carol Deis, Robert Arnold, Bruce Hamilton, Ruth Mamel,
    William Marel, Margaret MacLaren, Robert Rounseville,
    Rufus Smith, Margaret Stewart, Erika Zaranova, William
    Wahlert.
Soldiers—Albert Allen, Matthias Ammann, Dow Fonda, Warde
    Peters.

AMERICAN LANDSCAPE

By Elmer Rice
Direction: Elmer Rice
Scenery: Aline Bernstein
Costumes: Aline Bernstein

Tryout: Boston
New York: Cort Theatre
December 3, 1938
43 performances

CAST

Captain Anthony Dale .... George Macready
Betty Kutno .... Patricia Palmer
Frances Dale Spinner .... Rachel Hartzell
Gerald Spinner .... Donald Cook
Carlotta Dale .... Phoebe Foster
William Fiske .... Howard Miller
Captain Frank Dale .... Charles Waldron
Constance Dale .... Sylvia Weld
Joe Kutno .... Theodore Newton
Captain Samuel Dale .... Charles Dingle
Klaus Stillgebauer .... Alfred A. Hesse
Moll Flanders .... Isobel Elsom
Captain Heinrich Kleinschmidt .... Con MacSunday
Harriet Beecher Stowe .... Lillian Foster
Paul Kutno .... Jules Bennett
Abby Kutno .... Ethel Intropidi
Nils Karenson .... Aage Steenshorne
Henri Dupont .... Pierre d'Ennery
Patrick O'Brien .... J. Hammond Dailey
Reverend Jasper Washington .... Emory Richardson

NO TIME FOR COMEDY

By S. N. Behrman
Co-production with
   Katharine Cornell
Direction: Guthrie McClintic
Scenery: Jo Mielziner
Costumes: Valentina

Tryout: Indianapolis, Louisville,
   Cincinnati, Columbus, and
   Baltimore
New York: Barrymore Theatre
April 17, 1939
185 performances
Tour: 32 weeks

CAST

Clementine .... Gee Gee James
Linda Esterbrook .... Katharine Cornell
Philo Smith .... John Williams
Gaylord Esterbrook .... Laurence Olivier
Amanda Smith .... Margalo Gillmore
Robert .... Peter Robinson
Makepeace Lovell .... Robert Flemyng

MADAM, WILL YOU WALK

By Sidney Howard
Direction: Margaret Webster
Scenery: Robert Edmond Jones
Costumes: Mildred Manning

Tryout: Baltimore (November 13, 1939) and Washington (Closed out of town)

CAST

Officer Mallon .... Tom Tully
Mrs. Broderick .... Lucia Seger
Broderick .... John L. Kearney
Father Christy .... Lloyd Gough
Mrs. Fanaghy .... Sara Allgood
Judge Moskowitz .... Florenz Ames
Miss Auchincloss .... Ellen Hall
Delia .... Ruth Yorke
Mr. Dockweiler .... Keenan Wynn
Mary Coyle .... Peggy Conklin
Dr. Brightlee .... George M. Cohan
Scupper .... Arthur Kennedy
Two Boys { .... Edmund Howland
          .... Eugene Schiel
Alderman Coyle .... Lawrence C. O'Brien
Sailor .... Frank Downing
Sailor's Girl .... Evelyn Mars
The Magistrate .... Edward McNamara
The Clerk .... Maurice Manson
Policemen { .... John Pote
           .... Charles Christensen
Spectators, Reporters, Photographers: Tom Squire, Larry Gates, Kenneth Ferril, Mildred Dunnock, Alice Teague, Ann Davidson, George Whyte.

KEY LARGO

By Maxwell Anderson
Direction: Guthrie McClintic
Scenery: Jo Mielziner
Costumes: Helene Pons

Tryout: Indianapolis, Columbus, Cleveland, Buffalo, and Boston
New York: Barrymore Theatre November 27, 1939
105 performances
Tour: 13 weeks

CAST

Victor d'Alcala .... Jose Ferrer
Nimmo .... Charles Ellis
Jerry .... James Gregory
Monte .... Alfred Etcheverry
King McCloud .... Paul Muni
Sheriff Gash .... Ralph Theodore
D'Alcala .... Howard Johnsrud

Alegre d'Alcala .... Uta Hagen
Gage .... Crahan Denton
Corky .... Richard Cowdery
Murillo .... Frederic Tozere
Hunk .... Karl Malden
Priscilla .... Eve Abbott
Killarney .... Ruth March
Mrs. Aaronson .... Goldie Hannelin
Mr. Aaronson .... Richard Bishop
Mrs. Wheeler .... Ethel Jackson
Mr. Wheeler .... Richard Barbee
Osceola Horn .... William Challee
First Man Tourist .... John Fearnley
First Woman Tourist .... Norma Millay
Second Woman Tourist .... Helen Carroll
John Horn .... Averell Harris
Sam .... Hudson Shotwell

TWO ON AN ISLAND

By Elmer Rice   *Tryout:* New Haven and Boston
Direction: Elmer Rice   *New York:* Broadhurst Theatre
Scenery: Jo Mielziner   January 20, 1940
Costumes: Helene Pons   96 performances

CAST

William Flynn .... Robert Williams
Samuel Brodsky .... Martin Ritt
A Red-Cap .... Earl Sydnor
Mary Ward .... Betty Field
John Thompson .... John Craven
A Policeman .... Edward Downes
Clifton Ross .... Earl McDonald
The Sightseeing Guide .... Howard da Silva
The Driver .... Robert O'Brien
Mrs. Dora Levy .... Dora Weissman
Dixie Bushby .... Arthur L. Sachs
Middle-Western Man .... Roderick Maybee
Middle-Western Woman .... Roberta Bellinger
Frederic Winthrop .... Whitner Bissell
Lawrence Ormont .... Luther Adler
Martha Johnson .... Terry Harris
An Actor .... Charles Polacheck
Heinz Kaltbart .... Rudolf Weiss
Dorothy Clark .... Martha Hodge
Katherine Winthrop Holmes .... Joan Wetmore
Martin Blake .... Herschel Bentley
A Cashier .... Norma Green
Gracie Mullen .... Ann Thomas
A Married Couple .... {Sara Peyton
                                           {John Philliber
Helen Ormont .... Harriet MacGibbon
Sonia Taranova .... Eva Langbord
Mrs. Ballinger .... Frederica Going
A Museum Attendant .... Charles La Torre
Another Married Couple .... {John Triggs
                                         {Dorothy Darling
Ruth Ormont .... Helen Renee
A Hindu .... Larri Lauria

A Waiter .... Aage Steenshorne
Another Married Couple .... { Sellwyn Myers
{ Lucille Sears
Fred .... Don Shelton
Dolly .... Adele Longmire
Mrs. Williams .... Mary Michael
New Yorkers and Out-of-Towners: Roberta Bellinger, Alvin Chil-
    dress, Dorothy Darling, Evelyn Davis, Virginia Girvin, Fred-
    erica Going, Terry Harris, Eva Langbord, Charles La Torre,
    Larri Lauria, Adele Longmire, Assotta Marshall, Roderick
    Maybee, Sellwyn Myers, Mary Michael, Robert O'Brien, Sara
    Peyton, John Philliber, Hilary Phillips, Arthur L. Sachs,
    Lucille Sears, Don Shelton, Aage Steenshorne, Earl Sydnor,
    Joan Wetmore, Robert Williams.

THERE SHALL BE NO NIGHT

By Robert E. Sherwood   *Tryout:* Providence, Boston,
Co-production with   Baltimore, and Washington
   The Theatre Guild   *New York:* Alvin Theatre
Direction: Alfred Lunt   April 29, 1940
Scenery: Richard Whorf   181 performances
Costumes: Valentina   *Tour:* 38 weeks

CAST

Dr. Kaarlo Valkonen .... Alfred Lunt
Miranda Valkonen .... Lynn Fontanne
Dave Corween .... Richard Whorf
Uncle Waldemar .... Sydney Greenstreet
Gus Shuman .... Brooks West
Erik Valkonen .... Montgomery Clift
Kaatri Alquist .... Elisabeth Fraser
Dr. Ziemssen .... Maurice Colbourne
Major Rutkowski .... Edward Raquello
Joe Burnett .... Charles Ansley
Ben Gichner .... Thomas Gomez
Frank Olmstead .... William Le Massena
Sergeant Gosden .... Claude Horton
Lempi .... Phyllis Thaxter
Ilma .... Charva Chester
Photographer .... Ralph Nelson
Photographer .... Robert Downing

JOURNEY TO JERUSALEM

By Maxwell Anderson
Direction: Elmer Rice
Scenery: Jo Mielziner
Costumes: Millia Davenport

New York: National Theatre
October 10, 1940
17 performances

CAST

Marius	Arthur L. Sachs
The Greek Woman	Fay Baker
Herod	Frederic Tozere
The Soothsayer	Joseph V. De Santis
Mira	Alice Reinheart
Joseph	Horace Braham
Jacob	Ronny Liss
Miriam	Arlene Francis
Jeshua	Sidney Lumet
The Beggar	Joseph Wiseman
Shadrach	Charles De Sheim
Cassia	Terry Harris
Reba	Jeannette Chinley
Jesse	Edwin Vail
Zebulon	Alan Manson
The Centurion	Karl Malden
Ishmael	Arnold Moss
The Robber	Paul Genge
The Scribe	Henry Lascoe
The Porter	Walter Kapp
Gennesareth	David Leonard
Malachi	Joseph Kramm
Abbas	Charles Ellis
Chorazim	George Fairchild
Hanan	Byron McGrath
The Dove Woman	Juliet Talbot
The 1st Money Changer	Arnon Ben-Ami
The 2nd Money Changer	Joseph Wiseman
The Pharisee	Henry Walden
The Fruit Seller	Joseph Blanton
The Matzoth Seller	Katherine Cody
Flaccus	Paul Genge
Festus	James Gregory

FLIGHT TO THE WEST

By Elmer Rice
Direction: Elmer Rice
Scenery: Jo Mielziner
Costumes: Helene Pons

Tryout: Princeton, Washington,
and Boston
New York: Guild Theatre
December 30, 1940
136 performances

CAST

Richard Banning	Kevin McCarthy
1st Portuguese Mechanic	John Triggs
2nd Portuguese Mechanic	Harald Dyrenforth

August Himmelreich .... Rudolph Weiss
Thomas Hickey .... Paul Mann
Edmund Dickensen .... Don Nevins
Marie Dickensen .... Lydia St. Clair
Lisette Dickensen .... Helen Renee
Louise Frayne .... Constance McKay
Colonel Archibald Gage .... James Seeley
Count Paul Vasilich Vronoff .... Boris Marshalov
Frau Clara Rosenthal .... Eleanora Mendelssohn
Dr. Hermann Walther .... Paul Hernried
Howard Ingraham .... Arnold Moss
Hope Talcott Nathan .... Betty Field
Charles Nathan .... Hugh Marlowe
Captain George McNab .... Karl Malden
Captain Arthur Hawkes .... Grandon Rhodes
1st Corporal .... John Triggs
2nd Corporal .... Harald Dyrenforth

THE TALLEY METHOD

By S. N. Behrman
Direction: Elmer Rice
Scenery: Jo Mielziner
Costumes: Valentina

Tryout: Boston, Cleveland,
Baltimore, New Haven,
and Philadelphia
New York: Henry Miller Theatre
February 24, 1941
56 performances

CAST

Avis Talley .... Claire Niesen
Philip Talley .... Dean Harens
Cy Blodgett .... Hiram Sherman
Enid Fuller .... Ina Claire
Mary .... Lida Kane
Manfred Geist .... Ernst Deutsch
Dr. Axton Talley .... Philip Merivale

CANDLE IN THE WIND

By Maxwell Anderson
Co-production with
  The Theatre Guild
Direction: Alfred Lunt
Scenery: Jo Mielziner
Costumes: Valentina

Tryout: Boston, Baltimore, and
Washington
New York: Shubert Theatre
October 22, 1941
95 performances
Tour: 20 weeks

CAST

Fargeau .... Philip White
Henri .... Benedict MacQuarrie
Deseze .... Robert Harrison

Charlotte	Leona Roberts
Mercy	Nell Harrison
Madeline Guest	Helen Hayes
Maisie Tompkins	Evelyn Varden
Raoul St. Cloud	Louis Borell
German Captain	Harro Meller
German Lieutenant	Knud Kreuger
Col. Erfurt	John Wengraf
Lieut. Schoen	Tornio Selwart
Corporal Behrens	Mario Gang
Madame Fleury	Michelette Burani
M. Fleury	Stanley Jessup
First Guard	Brian Connaught
Second Guard	Ferdi Hoffman
Cissie	Lotte Lenya
Corporal Mueller	Joseph Wiseman
Third Guard	George Andre
Fourth Guard	Guy Moneypenny
Corporal Schultz	William Malten
Captain	Bruce Fernald

THE EVE OF ST. MARK

By Maxwell Anderson
Direction: Lem Ward
Scenery: Howard Bay

Tryout: Boston
New York: Cort Theatre
October 7, 1942
306 performances
Tour: 28 weeks

CAST

Deckman West	Matt Crowley
Cy	Grover Burgess
Nell West	Aline MacMahon
Neil West	Carl Gose
Zip West	Clifford Carpenter
Ralph West	Edwin Cooper
Pete Feller	Stanley G. Wood
Janet Feller	Mary Rolfe
Private Quizz West	William Prince
Private Thomas Mulveroy	Eddie O'Shea
Private Shevlin	David Pressman
Corporal Tate	Charles Mendick
Private Francis Marion	James Monks
Private Glinka	Martin Ritt
Sergeant Ruby	George Mathews
Sergeant Kriven	Robert Williams
Lill Bird	Joann Dolan
Sal Bird	Toni Favor
Waiter	Charles Ellis
Flash	Dorothea Freed
Dimples	Beatrice Manley
A Guard	Kent Adams
Pepita	Joven E. Rola

THE PIRATE

By S.N. Behrman
Co-production with
  The Theatre Guild
Direction: John C. Wilson
Scenery: Lemuel Ayres
Costumes: Miles White

Tryout: Madison, Milwaukee,
  Cleveland, Indianapolis,
  Cincinnati, Pittsburgh,
  Washington, Boston, and
  Philadelphia
New York: Martin Beck Theatre
  November 25, 1942
  176 performances

CAST

Pedro Vargas .... Alan Reed
Manuela .... Lynn Fontanne
Isabella .... Lea Penman
Mango Seller .... Juanita Hall
Ines ....Estelle Winwood
Capucho .... James O'Neill
Fisherboy .... Albert Popwell
Trillo .... Maurice Ellis
Don Bolo .... Walter Mosby
Estaban .... Robert Emhardt
Serafin .... Alfred Lunt
The Hermit .... William Le Massena
Lizarda .... Muriel Rahn
Viceroy .... Clarence Derwent
Maid to Isabella .... Inez Matthews
Viceroy's Guards .... Guy Moneypenny, Peter Garey
Maids to Manuela .... Ruby Greene, Anna Jackson, Lavinia White
Members of Serafin's Troupe, Soldiers and Townspeople: David
    Bethea, Bruce Howard, Martha Jones, Jules Johnson, Clare
    Keith, Fredye Marshall, Charles Swain, Elois Uggams, Joseph
    Washington, Carol Wilson, Jeffrey Etheridge.
Musicians: Emilio Denti, Emmet Matthews, John Dixon, Adolphus
    Cheatham, Wilbur De Paris, Eddie Gibbs, John Brown, Max
    Rich, Herbert Cowens.

THE PATRIOTS

By Sidney Kingsley
Co-production with
  Rowland Stebbins
Direction: Shepard Traube
Scenery: Howard Bay
Costumes: Rose Bogdanoff and
    Toni Ward

New York: National Theatre
  January 29, 1943
  172 performances
Tour: 24 weeks

CAST

Captain .... Byron Russell
Thomas Jefferson .... Raymond Edward Johnson

Patsy	Madge Evans
Martha	Frances Reid
Doctor	Ross Matthew
James Madison	John Souther
Alexander Hamilton	House Jameson
George Washington	Cecil Humphreys
Sergeant	Victor Southwick
Colonel Humphrey	Francis Compton
Jacob	Thomas Dillon
Ned	George Mitchell
Mat	Philip White
James Monroe	Judson Laire
Mrs. Hamilton	Peg La Centra
Henry Knox	Henry Mowbray
Butler	Robert Lance
Mr. Fenno	Roland Alexander
Jupiter	Doe Doe Green
Mrs. Conrad	Leslie Bingham
Frontiersman	John Stephen
Thomas Jefferson Randolph	Billy Nevard
Anne Randolph	Hope Lange
George Washington Lafayette	Jack Lloyd

A NEW LIFE

By Elmer Rice
Direction: Elmer Rice
Scenery: Howard Bay
Costumes: Rose Bogdanoff

Tryout: Baltimore and Washington
New York: Royale Theatre
September 15, 1943
69 performances

CAST

Theodore Emery	Sanford McCauley
Miss Hanson	Alice Thomson
Miss Devore	Coleen Ward
Miss Murphy	Ann Driscoll
Miss Weatherby	Sara Peyton
George Sheridan	Kenneth Tobey
Lillian Sheridan	Timmie Hyler
Esther Zuckerman	Dorothy Darling
Mollie Kleinberger	Dora Weissman
Edith Charles Cleghorne	Betty Field
Olive Rapallo	Ann Thomas
Gustave Jensen	John Ireland
Dr. Lyman Acton	Blaine Cordner
Miss Kingsley	Frederica Going
Samuel Cleghorne	Walter N. Greaza
Isabelle Cleghorne	Merle Maddern
Millicent Prince	Joan Wetmore
Grover C. Charles	Arthur Griffin
Miss Swift	Terry Harris
An Anesthetist	Elizabeth Dewing
Captain Cleghorne	George Lambert
Ruth Emery	Helen Kingstead
Miss Woolley	Shirley Gale

STORM OPERATION

By Maxwell Anderson
Direction: Michael Gordon
Scenery: Howard Bay

Tryout: Baltimore, Pittsburgh, and
Cleveland
New York: Belasco Theatre
January 11, 1944
23 performances

CAST

1st Sgt. Peter Moldau .... Myron McCormick
Abe .... Joseph Dorn
Winkle .... Alan Schneider
Simeon, a Technical Sgt. .... Cy Howard
Mart, a Technical Sgt. .... Millard Mitchell
Dougie .... Michael Ames
Bread Seller .... Maurice Doner
The Muezzin .... Nehem Simone
Stefano .... Carlo Respighi
Lt. Thomasina Grey .... Gertrude Musgrove
Lt. Kathryn Byrne .... Dorothea Freed
Lt. Dammartin .... Walter Kohler
Corp. Ticker .... Bertram Tanswell
Capt. Sutton .... Bramwell Fletcher
Mabroukha .... Sara Anderson
Arab Guide .... Maurice Doner
Chuck, Technical Sgt. .... Charles Ellis
Corp. Hermann Geist .... Louis Fabien
Squillini .... Nick Dennis
Arab Boy .... Neil Towner
Arab Women: Marianne Bier, Julie O'Brien, Elizabeth Inglise, Lela Vanti.

THE RUGGED PATH

By Robert E. Sherwood
Direction: Garson Kanin
Scenery: Jo Mielziner
Costumes: Valentina

Tryout: Providence, Washington,
and Boston
New York: Plymouth Theatre
November 10, 1945
81 performances

CAST

Jamieson .... Emory Richardson
Hazel .... Kay Loring
Major General MacGlorn .... Ernest Woodward
Morey Vinion .... Spencer Tracy
Harriet Vinion .... Martha Sleeper
George Bowsmith .... Clinton Sundberg
Leggatt Burt .... Lawrence Fletcher
Charlie .... Henry Lascoe
Pete Kenneally .... Ralph Cullinan
Fred .... Nick Dennis
Gil Hartnick .... Rex Williams

Edith Bowsmith	Jan Sterling
Firth	Theodore Leavitt
Albok	Paul Alberts
Dix	Sandy Campbell
Stapler	Lynn Shubert
Kavanagh	Sam Sweet
Ship's Doctor	Howard Ferguson
Costanzo	William Sands
Guffey	David Stone
Hal Fleury	Gordon Nelson
Colonel Rainsford	Clay Clement
Gregorio Felizardo	Vito Christi
Doctor Querin	Edward Raquello

DREAM GIRL

By Elmer Rice
Direction: Elmer Rice
Scenery: Jo Mielziner
Costumes: Billy Livingston

Tryout: New Haven and Boston
New York: Coronet Theatre
December 14, 1945
348 performances
Tour: 19 weeks

CAST

Georgina Allerton	Betty Field
Lucy Allerton	Evelyn Varden
Radio Announcer	Keene Crockett
Dr. J. Gilmore Percival	William A. Lee
George Allerton	William A. Lee
Miriam Allerton Lucas	Sonya Stokowski
The Obstetrician	William A. Lee
The Nurse	Evelyn Varden
Jim Lucas	Kevin O'Shea
Claire Blakeley	Helen Marcy
A Stout Woman	Philippa Bevans
The Doctor	Don Stevens
Clark Redfield	Wendell Corey
A Policeman	James Gregory
The Judge	William A. Lee
The District Attorney	Keene Crockett
George Hand	Edmon Ryan
Bert	Don Stevens
A Mexican	Wendell Corey
Two Other Mexicans	{ David Pressman / James Gregory
A Waiter	Stuart Nedd
Arabella	Sonya Stokowski
Luigi, a Waiter	David Pressman
An Usher	Gaynelle Nixon
Miss Delehanty	Helen Bennett
Antonio	Don Stevens
Salarino	Robert Fletcher
A Theatre Manager	William A. Lee
A Head-waiter	Keene Crockett
A Waiter	Robert Fletcher
Justice of the Peace Billings	William A. Lee
A Chauffeur	Stuart Nedd

TRUCKLINE CAFE

By Maxwell Anderson
Co-production with Harold
   Clurman and Elia Kazan
Direction: Harold Clurman
Scenery: Boris Aronson
Costumes: Millia Davenport

Tryout: Baltimore, Md.
New York: Belasco Theatre
   February 27, 1946
   13 performances

CAST

Toby	Frank Overton
Kip	Ralph Theadore
Stew	John Sweet
Maurice	Kevin McCarthy
Min	June Walker
Wing Commander Hern	David Manners
Anne	Virginia Gilmore
Stag	Karl Malden
Angie	Irene Dailey
Celeste	Joanne Tree
Patrolman Gray	Robert Simon
Evvie Garrett	Joann Dolan
Hutch	Kenneth Tobey
Matt	Louis A. Florence
June	Jutta Wolf
Sissie	Leila Ernst
Tory McRae	Ann Shepherd
Sage McRae	Marlon Brando
Man With a Pail	Lou Gilbert
The Breadman	Peter Hobbs
Janet	Peggy Meredith
Mildred	June March
Bimi	Richard Paul
Tuffy Garrett	Eugene Steiner
First Man	Solen Hayes
First Woman	Lorraine Kirby
Mort	Richard Waring
Second Man	Joseph Adams
Second Woman	Rose Steiner
First Girl	Ann Morgan
Second Girl	Gloria Stroock

JOAN OF LORRAINE

By Maxwell Anderson
Direction: Margo Jones and
       Sam Wanamaker
Scenery: Lee Simonson
Costumes: Lee Simonson

Tryout: Washington
New York: Alvin Theatre
   November 18, 1946
   199 performances

CAST

Jimmy Masters, the Director (The Inquisitor)	Sam Wanamaker

Al, the Stage Manager .... Gilmore Bush
Mary Grey .... Ingrid Bergman
    (Joan)
Abbey .... Lewis Martin
    (Jacques D'Arc) (Cauchon, Bishop of Beauvais)
Jo Cordwell .... Bruce Hall
    (Jean D'Arc)
Dollner .... Kenneth Tobey
    (Pierre D'Arc)
Charles Elling .... Charles Ellis
    (Durand Laxart)
Farwell .... Arthur L. Sachs
    (Jean de Metz) (The Executioner)
Garder .... Peter Hobbs
    (Bertrand de Poulengy)
Sheppard .... Berry Kroeger
    (Alain Chartier)
Les Ward .... Romney Brent
    (The Dauphin)
Tessie .... Timothy Lynn Kearse
    Ass't. Stage Manager (Aurore)
Jeffson .... Roger De Koven
Kipner .... Harry Irvine
    (Regnault de Chartres, Archbishop of Rheims)
Long .... Kevin McCarthy
    (Dunois, Bastard of Orleans)
Noble .... Martin Rudy
    (La Hire)
Quirke .... Brooks West
    (St. Michael) (D'Estivet)
Miss Reeves .... Ann Coray
    (St. Catherine)
Miss Sadler .... Joanna Roos
    (St. Margaret)
Champlain .... Joseph Wiseman
    (Father Massieu)
Smith .... Stephen Roberts
    (Thomas de Courcelles)
Marie, the Costumer .... Lotte Stavisky
Electrician .... Himself

STREET SCENE

Book by Elmer Rice
Music by Kurt Weill
Lyrics by Langston Hughes
Co-production with Dwight Deere
  Wiman
Direction: Charles Friedman
Scenery: Jo Mielziner
Costumes: Lucinda Ballard
Choreography: Hanya Hohm

Tryout: Philadelphia
New York: Adelphi Theatre
January 9, 1947
148 performances

CAST

Abraham Kaplan .... Irving Kaufman
Greta Fiorentino .... Helen Arden
Carl Olsen .... Wilson Smith
Emma Jones .... Hope Emerson
Olga Olsen .... Ellen Repp

Shirley Kaplan	Norma Chambers
Henry Davis	Creighton Thompson
Willie Maurrant	Peter Griffith
Anna Maurrant	Polyna Stoska
Sam Kaplan	Brian Sullivan
Daniel Buchanan	Remo Lota
Frank Maurrant	Norman Cordon
George Jones	David E. Thomas
Steve Sankey	Lauren Gilbert
Lippo Fiorentino	Sydney Rayner
Jennie Hildebrand	Beverly Janis
Second Graduate	Zosia Gruchala
Third Graduate	Marion Covey
Mary Hildebrand	Juliana Gallagher
Charlie Hildebrand	Bennett Burrill
Laura Hildebrand	Elen Lane
Grace Davis	Helen Ferguson
First Policeman	Ernest Taylor
Rose Maurrant	Anne Jeffreys
Harry Easter	Don Saxon
Mae Jones	Sheila Bond
Dick McGann	Danny Daniels
Vincent Jones	Robert Pierson
Dr. John Wilson	Edwin G. O'Connor
Officer Harry Murphy	Norman Thomson
A Milkman	Russell George
A Music Pupil	Joyce Carrol
City Marshall James Henry	Randolph Symonette
Fred Cullen	Paul Lilly
An Old Clothes Man	Edward Reichert
An Interne	Roy Munsell
An Ambulance Driver	John Sweet
First Nursemaid	Peggy Turnley
Second Nursemaid	Ellen Carleen
A Married Couple	{ Bette Van / Joseph E. Scandur

Passersby, Neighbors, Children, etc.: Aza Bard, Diana Donne, Juanita Hall, Marie Leidal, Biruta Ramoska, Marcella Uhl, Larry Baker, Tom Barragan, Mel Bartell, Victor Clarke, Bobby Horn, Wilson Woodbeck.

ANNE OF THE THOUSAND DAYS

By Maxwell Anderson
Co-production with Leland Hayward
Direction: H.C. Potter
Scenery: Jo Mielziner
Costumes: Motley

Tryout: Philadelphia and Baltimore
New York: Shubert Theatre
December 8, 1948
288 performances
Tour: 10 weeks

CAST

Anne Boleyn	Joyce Redman
Henry	Rex Harrison
Cardinal Wolsey	Percy Waram
Thomas Boleyn	Charles Francis
Servant	Ludlow Maury
Henry Norris	Allan Stevenson
Mark Smeaton	John Merivale

Duke of Norfolk .... John Williams
Percy, Earl of Northumberland .... Robert Duke
Elizabeth Boleyn .... Viola Keats
Serving Woman .... Kathleen Bolton
Servant .... Cecil Clovelly
Mary Boleyn .... Louise Platt
Madge Shelton .... Margaret Garland
Jane Seymour .... Monica Lang
Sir Thomas More .... Russell Gaige
Thomas Cromwell .... Wendell K. Phillips
Bishop Fisher .... Harry Irvine
Prior Houghton .... George Collier
A Messenger .... Harry Selby
Bailiff .... Fred Ayres Cotton
Bailiff .... Harold McGee
Clerk .... Terence Anderson
Singers: Richard Leone, Frank Myers, Donald Conrad.
Musicians: Harold McGee, Malcolm Wells, Charles Ellis.

THE SMILE OF THE WORLD

By Garson Kanin
Direction: Garson Kanin
Scenery: Donald Oenslager
Costumes: Mainbocher and
    Forrest Thayer

Tryout: New Haven and
    Philadelphia
New York: Hudson Theatre
    January 12, 1949
    5 performances

CAST

Josef Boros .... Boris Marshalov
Mrs. Boros .... Elizabeth Dewing
Petey .... Sam Jackson
Evelyn .... Ruby Dee
Sara Boulting .... Ruth Gordon
Sam Fenn .... Warren Stevens
Justice Reuben Boulting .... Otto Kruger
Stewart .... Ossie Davis
Alice Widmayer .... Laura Pierpont

LOST IN THE STARS

Book and lyrics by
    Maxwell Anderson
Music by Kurt Weill
Direction: Rouben Mamoulian
Scenery: George Jenkins
Costumes: Anna Hill Johnstone

New York: Music Box Theatre
    October 30, 1949
    281 performances
Tour: 14 weeks

CAST

Leader .... Frank Roane
Answerer .... Joseph James

Nita .... Elayne Richards
Grace Kumalo .... Gertrude Jeannette
Stephen Kumalo .... Todd Duncan
The Young Man .... Lavern French
The Young Woman .... Mabel Hart
James Jarvis .... Leslie Banks
Edward Jarvis .... Judson Rees
Arthur Jarvis .... John Morley
John Kumalo .... Warren Coleman
Paulus .... Charles McRae
William .... Roy Allen
Jared .... William C. Smith
Alex .... Herbert Coleman
Foreman .... Jerome Shaw
Mrs. Mkize .... Georgette Harvey
Hlabeni .... William Marshall
Eland .... Charles Grunwell
Linda .... Sheila Guyse
Johannes Pafuri .... Van Prince
Matthew Kumalo .... William Greaves
Abaslom Kumalo .... Julian Mayfield
Rose .... Gloria Smith
Irina .... Inez Matthews
Policeman .... Robert Byrn
White Woman .... Biruta Ramoska
White Man .... Mark Kramer
The Guard .... Jerome Shaw
Burton .... John W. Stanley
The Judge .... Guy Spaull
Villager .... Robert McFerrin
Singers: Sibol Cain, Alma Hubbard, Elen Longone, June McMechen,
    Biruta Ramoska, Christine Spencer, Constance Stokes, Lucre-
    tia West, LaCoste Brown, Robert Byrn, Joseph Crawford,
    Russell George, Joseph James, Mark Kramer, Moses LaMar,
    Paul Mario, Robert McFerrin, William C. Smith, Joseph
    Theard.

DARKNESS AT NOON

By Sidney Kingsley
Co-production with
  May Kirshner
Direction: Sidney Kingsley
Scenery: Frederick Fox
Costumes: Ken Barr

Tryout: Philadelphia
New York: Alvin Theatre
        January 13, 1951
        186 performances
Tour: 31 weeks

CAST

Rubashov .... Claude Rains
Guard .... Robert Keith, Jr.
402 .... Philip Coolidge
302 .... Richard Seff
202 .... Allan Rich
Luba .... Kim Hunter
Gletkin .... Walter J. Palance
1st Storm Trooper .... Adams MacDonald
Richard .... Herbert Ratner
Young Girl .... Virginia Howard
2nd Storm Trooper.......................... Johnson Hayes
Ivanoff .... Alexander Scourby

Bogrov	Norman Roland
Hrutsch	Robert Crozier
Albert	Daniel Polis
Luigi	Will Kuluva
Pablo	Henry Beckman
Andre	Geoffrey Barr
Barkeeper	Tony Ancona
Secretary	Lois Nettleton
President	Maurice Gosfield

NOT FOR CHILDREN

By Elmer Rice
Direction: Elmer Rice
Scenery: John Root
Costumes: Mainbocher

Tryout: Bridgeport and New Haven
New York: Coronet Theatre
February 13, 1951
7 performances

CAST

Timothy Forrest	J. Edward Bromberg
Clarence Orth	Alexander Clark
Ambrose Atwater	Elliott Nugent
Theodora Effington	Betty Field
Irma Orth	Natalie Core
Prudence Dearborn	Ann Thomas
Evangeline Orth	Joan Copeland
Digby Walsh	Phil Arthur
Hugh McHugh	Fredd Wayne
Hitch Imborg	John Gerstad
Pensacola Crawford	Frances Tannehill
Pianist	Bud Gregg

THE FOURPOSTER

By Jan de Hartog
Direction: José Ferrer
Scenery: S. Syrjala
Costumes: Lucinda Ballard

Tryout: Wilmington and Boston
New York: Barrymore Theatre
October 24, 1951
632 performances
Tour: 42 weeks

CAST

Agnes	Jessica Tandy
Michael	Hume Cronyn

BAREFOOT IN ATHENS

By Maxwell Anderson
Direction: Alan Anderson
Scenery: Boris Aronson
Costumes: Bernard Rudofsky

Tryout: Princeton and Philadelphia
New York: Martin Beck Theatre
October 31, 1951
29 performances

CAST

Xantippe	Lotte Lenya
Lamprocles	Robert Brown
Lysis	Judson Rees
Phoenix	Robin Michael
Socrates	Barry Jones
Crito	Daniel Reed
Phaedo	William Bush
Critobulus	Stratton Walling
Theodote	Helen Shields
Anytos	David J. Stewart
Meletos	Bruce Hall
Lykon	William Hansen
Crassos	Karl Light
Satyros	Bart Burns
Guards	Edward Groad, John McLiam
Critias	Philip Coolidge
Pausanias	George Mathews
Magistrate	Joseph Warren

THE GRAND TOUR

By Elmer Rice
Direction: Elmer Rice
Scenery: Howard Bay
Costumes: Motley

New York: Martin Beck Theatre
December 10, 1951
8 performances

CAST

Mr. Montgomery	John Rodney
A Female Traveler	Claire Justice
Nell Valentine	Beatrice Straight
A Male Traveler	Maury Tuckerman
Raymond Brinton	Richard Derr
A Deck Steward	Sam Bonnell
Professor Coogan	William A. Lee
Harvey Richman	Edwin Jerome
Adele Brinton	Louisa Horton

MR. PICKWICK

By Stanley Young   *New York:* Plymouth Theatre
Direction: John Burrell   September 15, 1952
Scenery: Kathleen Ankers   61 performances

CAST

Mr. Pickwick .... George Howe
Mr. Tupman .... Earl Montgomery
Mr. Snodgrass .... Anthony Kemble Cooper
Mr. Winkle .... Derek Tansley
Mrs. Bardell .... Norah Howard
Mrs. Cluppins .... Lucie Lancaster
Sam Weller .... Clive Revill
Tommy .... Richard Case
Mr. Buzfuz .... Jacques Aubuchon
Mrs. Weller .... Philippa Bevans
Mr. Weller .... Louis Hector
Mr. Stiggins .... Basil Howes
Mr.Jingle .... Nigel Green
Mary .... Sarah Marshall
Mrs. Leo Hunter .... Estelle Winwood
Joe .... C. K. Alexander
Mr. Wardle .... Neil Fitzgerald
Miss Emily Wardle .... Jean Cooke
Miss Isabella Wardle .... Dolores Pigott
Miss Rachel Wardle .... Nydia Westman
Mr. Perker .... Kurt Richards
Wilberforce .... Wallace Acton
Bailiff .... Wallace Acton
Justice .... William Podmore
Turnkey .... C. K. Alexander

THE EMPEROR'S CLOTHES

By George Tabori   *Tryout:* Wayne University,
Co-production with   Detroit, Mich.
  Robert Whitehead   *New York:* Ethel Barrymore
Direction: Harold Clurman   Theatre
Scenery: Lester Polakov   February 9, 1953
Costumes: Ben Edwards   16 performances

CAST

Elek Odry .... Lee J. Cobb
Bella .... Maureen Stapleton
Ferike .... Brandon de Wilde
Peter .... Anthony Ross
Granny .... Tamara Daykarhanova
The Baron .... Esmond Knight
1st Rottenbiller Brother .... Michael Strong
2nd Rottenbiller Brother .... Mike Kellin
The Fat Hugo .... Philip Rodd
Mr. Schmitz .... Howard H. Fischer
Mrs. Schmitz .... Nydia Westman

The Man Without Shoes .... David Clarke
A Boy .... Richard Case
Milkman .... Allan Rich
Policeman .... John Anderson
Singer .... John Anderson

TEA AND SYMPATHY

By Robert Anderson
Co-production with Mary Frank
Direction: Elia Kazan
Scenery: Jo Mielziner
Costumes: Anna Hill Johnstone

Tryout: New Haven and
    Washington
New York: Ethel Barrymore
    Theatre
    September 30, 1953
    712 performances
Tour: 47 weeks

CAST

Laura Reynolds .... Deborah Kerr
Lilly Sears .... Florida Friebus
Tom Lee .... John Kerr
David Harris .... Richard Midgley
Ralph .... Alan Sues
Al .... Dick York
Steve .... Arthur Steuer
Bill Reynolds................................. Leif Erickson
Phil .... Richard Franchot
Herbert Lee .... John McGovern
Paul .... Yale Wexler

SABRINA FAIR

By Samuel Taylor
Direction: H.C. Potter
Scenery: Donald Oenslager
Costumes: Bianca Strook

Tryout: New Haven, Boston, and
    Philadelphia
New York: National Theatre
    November 11, 1953
    318 performances

CAST

Maude Larrabee .... Cathleen Nesbitt
Julia Ward McKinlock .... Luella Gear
Linus Larrabee, Jr. .... Joseph Cotten
Linus Larrabee .... John Cromwell
Margaret .... Katharine Raht
David Larrabee .... Scott McKay
Gretchen .... Ruth Woods
Sabrina Fairchild .... Margaret Sullavan
Fairchild .... Russell Collins
A Young Woman .... Harriette Selby
A Young Man .... Gordon Mills
Another Young Woman .... Loraine Grover
Another Young Man .... Michael Steele
Paul D'Argenson .... Robert Duke

IN THE SUMMER HOUSE

By Jane Bowles
Co-production with Oliver Smith
Direction: Jose Quintero
Scenery: Oliver Smith
Costumes: Noel Taylor

Tryout: Hartford, Boston, and
Washington
New York: The Playhouse
December 29, 1953
55 performances

CAST

Gertrude Eastman-Cuevas	Judith Anderson
Molly	Elizabeth Ross
Mr. Solares	Don Mayo
Mrs. Lopez	Marita Reid
Frederica	Miriam Colon
Esperanza	Isabel Morel
Alta Gracia	Marjorie Eaton
Quintina	Phoebe MacKay
Lionel	Logan Ramsey
A Figure-Bearer	Paul Bertelsen
Another Figure-Bearer	George Spelvin
Vivian Constable	Muriel Berkson
Chauffeur	Daniel Morales
Mrs. Constable	Mildred Dunnock
Inez	Jean Stapleton

THE WINNER

By Elmer Rice
Direction: Elmer Rice
Scenery: Lester Polakov

Tryout: Buffalo, Cleveland, and
Pittsburgh
New York: The Playhouse
February 17, 1954
30 performances

CAST

Eva Harold	Joan Tetzel
Martin Carew	Tom Helmore
David Browning	Whitfield Connor
Newscaster	P. Jay Sidney
Arnold Mahler	Lothar Rewalt
Irma Mahler	Jane Buchanan
Haggerty	Phillip Pruneau
Dr. Clinton Ward	Charles Cooper
Miss Dodd	Lily Bretano
Stenographer	David Balfour
Judge Samuel Addison	Frederick O'Neal
Hilde Kranzbeck	Vilma Kurer

ONDINE

By Jean Giraudoux
  English version by Maurice
  Valency
Direction: Alfred Lunt
Scenery: Peter Larkin
Costumes: Richard Whorf

Tryout: Boston
New York: 46th Street Theatre
  February 18, 1954
  156 performances

CAST

Auguste .... John Alexander
Eugenie .... Edith King
Ritter Hans .... Mel Ferrer
Ondine .... Audrey Hepburn
The Ondines .... Dran Seitz, Tani Seitz, Sonia Torgeson
The Old One .... Robert Middleton
The Lord Chamberlain .... Alan Hewitt
Superintendent of the Theatre .... Lloyd Gough
Trainer of Seals .... James Lanphier
Bertha .... Marian Seldes
Bertram .... Peter Brandon
Violante .... Anne Meacham
Angelique .... Gaye Jordan
Venus .... Jan Sherwood
Matho .... Barry O'Hara
Salammbo .... Lily Paget
A Lord .... William Le Massena
A Lady .... Stacy Graham
The Illusionist .... Robert Middleton
The King .... William Podmore
A Servant .... James Lanphier
1st Fisherman .... Lloyd Gough
2nd Fisherman .... Robert Middleton
1st Judge .... Alan Hewitt
2nd Judge .... William Le Massena
The Executioner .... Robert Crawley
Kitchen Maid .... Stacy Graham

ALL SUMMER LONG

By Robert Anderson
Direction: Alan Schneider
Scenery: Jo Mielziner
Costumes: Anna Hill Johnstone

Tryout: Washington
New York: Coronet Theatre
  September 23, 1954
  60 performances

CAST

Willie .... Clay Hall
Don .... John Kerr
Mother .... June Walker
Dad .... Ed Begley
Ruth .... Carroll Baker
Harry .... John Randolph
Theresa .... Daniela Boni

THE TRAVELING LADY

By Horton Foote
Direction: Vincent J. Donehue
Scenery: Ben Edwards
Costumes: Ben Edwards

Tryout: Princeton, Cincinnati, and
Cleveland
New York: The Playhouse
October 27, 1954
30 performances

CAST

Mrs. Mavis	Mary Perry
Slim Murray	Jack Lord
Judge Robedaux	Calvin Thomas
Georgette Thomas	Kim Stanley
Margaret Rose	Brook Seawell
Clara Breedlove	Helen Carew
Sitter Mavis	Katherine Squire
Mrs. Tillman	Kathleen Comegys
Henry Thomas	Lonny Chapman
Sheriff	Tony Sexton

THE BAD SEED

By Maxwell Anderson
Adapted from the novel by
William March
Direction: Reginald Denham
Scenery: George Jenkins
Costumes: Sal Anthony

Tryout: Springfield, Mass., Wash-
ington, and Baltimore
New York: 46th Street Theatre
December 8, 1954
334 performances
Tour: 31 weeks

CAST

Rhoda Penmark	Patty McCormack
Col. Kenneth Penmark	John O'Hare
Christine Penmark	Nancy Kelly
Monica Breedlove	Evelyn Varden
Emory Wages	Joseph Holland
LeRoy	Henry Jones
Miss Fern	Joan Croydon
Reginald Tasker	Lloyd Gough
Mrs. Daigle	Eileen Heckart
Mr. Daigle	Wells Richardson
Messenger	George Gino
Richard Bravo	Thomas Chalmers

CAT ON A HOT TIN ROOF

By Tennessee Williams
Direction: Elia Kazan
Scenery: Jo Mielziner
Costumes: Lucinda Ballard

Tryout: Philadelphia
New York: Morosco Theatre
March 24, 1955
694 performances
Tour: 33 weeks

CAST

Lacey	Maxwell Glanville
Sookey	Musa Williams
Margaret	Barbara Bel Geddes
Brick	Ben Gazzara
Mae	Madeleine Sherwood
Gooper	Pat Hingle
Big Mama	Mildred Dunnock
Dixie	Pauline Hahn
Buster	Darryl Richard
Sonny	Seth Edwards
Trixie	Janice Dunn
Big Daddy	Burl Ives
Reverend Tooker	Fred Stewart
Doctor Baugh	R. G. Armstrong
Daisy	Eva Vaughan Smith
Brightie	Brownie McGhee
Small	Sonny Terry

ONCE UPON A TAILOR

By Baruch Lumet
Co-production with George Boroff
Direction: Joseph Anthony
Scenery: Boris Aronson
Costumes: Paul Morrison

Tryout: Philadelphia
New York: Cort Theatre
May 23, 1955
8 performances

CAST

Sheindel	Anita Cooper
Sòrelle	Anne Hegira
Frenzl	Oscar Karlweis
Leibel	Jimmy Oster
Chana Bayle	Adelaide Klein
Bertzi	Peter Fernandez
Elka	Rebecca Darke
Mechel	Milton Selzer

TIGER AT THE GATES

By Jean Giraudoux
  Translated by Christopher Fry
Co-production with Henry M.
  Margolis
Direction: Harold Clurman
Scenery: Loudon Sainthill
Costumes: Loudon Sainthill

New York: Fulton Theatre
October 3, 1955
217 performances

CAST

Andromache	Barbara Jefford
Cassandra	Leueen MacGrath
Laundress	Judith Braun
Hector	Michael Redgrave
Paris	Leo Ciceri
1st Old Man	Howard Caine
2nd Old Man	Jack Bittner
Priam	Morris Carnovsky
Demekos	John Laurie
Hecuba	Catherine Lacey
Mathematician	Milton Selzer
Lady In Waiting	Jacqueline Brookes
Polyxene	Ellen Christopher
Helen	Diane Cilento
Messenger	Ernest Graves
Troilus	Peter Kerr
Abneos	Howard Caine
Busiris	Wyndham Goldie
Ajax	Felix Munso
Ulysses	Walter Fitzgerald
A Topman	Nehemiah Persoff
Olpides	Jack Bittner
Senator	Tom McDermott
Sailor	Louis Criss

A QUIET PLACE

By Julian Claman
Direction: Delbert Mann
Scenery: Donald Oenslager
Costumes: Anna Hill Johnstone

Tryout: New Haven (November
23, 1955), Boston, Cleve-
land, Pittsburgh, and
Washington
(Closed out of town)

CAST

Biagina	Susan Kohner
Maria	Ernestine Perrie
Rico	Dino Terranova
Frances Lucas	Leora Dana
Oliver Lucas	Tyrone Power
Mr. Metcalfe	Halliwell Hobbes

THE PONDER HEART

By Joseph Fields and
  Jerome Chodorov
  Adapted from the story by
  Eudora Welty
Direction: Robert Douglas
Scenery: Ben Edwards
Costumes: Frank Spencer

Tryout: Boston
New York: Music Box
  January 4, 1956
  149 performances

CAST

Jacob	Theodore Browne
Sarah	Vinie Burrows
Mr. Springer	David Leland
Edna Earle Ponder	Una Merkel
De Yancey Clanahan	Don Hanmer
Big John	John Marriott
Narciss	Juanita Hall
Purdel Peacock	Edwin Buckley
Bruce Peacock	Richard Klein
Treva Peacock	Helen Quarrier
Johnnie Ree Peacock	Jeanne Shelley
Mr. Peacock	Harold Grau
Mrs. Peacock	Charlotte Klein
Eloise	Barbara Jean Gilliam
Uncle Daniel Ponder	David Wayne
Dorris R. Gladney	Will Geer
Bonnie Dee Ponder	Sarah Marshall
Sam	Noel Williams
Rodney	Johnny Klein
Willie	Junior Marshall
Teacake Magee	Ruth White
Judge Waite	John McGovern
Dr. Eubanks	Donald Foster
Truex Bodkin	Dwight Marfield
Mrs. Bodkin	Mary Farrell
Al	J. Talbot Holland
Clyde	William Dwyer
Clerk	James Karr
Bailiff	Tony Kraber
Foreman	Alan Manson

Jurors and Spectators: Daniel Bergin, Joseph Bishop, Tom Geraghty, Jim Holden, Richard Rothrock, Lieselotte Singer.

THE LOVERS

By Leslie Stevens
Co-production with Gayle Stine
Direction: Michael Gordon
Scenery: Charles Elson
Costumes: John Boyt

Tryout: Detroit and Chicago
New York: Martin Beck Theatre
  May 10, 1956
  4 Performances

CAST

Grigoris	Hurd Hatfield
Clothilde	Vivian Nathan

Sextus .... Earl Montgomery
Xegan .... Norman Rose
Mattiew .... Robert Jacquin
Simon .... Harry Bergman
Volc Sturmer .... William Bramley
Marc .... Mario Alcalde
Douane .... Joanne Woodward
Chrysagon De La Crux .... Darren McGavin
Blaise .... Gerald Hiken
Draco De La Crux .... Robert Burr
Austrict De La Crux .... Pernell Roberts
Herstal De La Crux .... Robert Lansing
Probus .... Morris Carnovsky
Tomas .... Gayne Sullivan
Saul .... George Ebeling
Lisanne .... Kathe Snyder
Mairese .... Frances Chaney
Ironsmith .... George Tyne
Millwright .... George Berkeley
Wheelwright .... Bert Conway
Escavalon .... Lester Rawlins
Clement of Metz .... Bramwell Fletcher
Stewards .... Byron Mitchell, Kurt Cerf
Friars .... Edward Setrakian, Charles Chaucer
Knights Escavalon .... Robert Dowdell, John Carter,
    Grant Eastham, John MacKay
People of St. Omer .... Peggy Richards, Flori Waren,
    Lena Romano, Edith Martin, Patricia Allaben, Emily Mc-
    Laughlin, Page Johnson, Norman Wigutow

BUILD WITH ONE HAND

By Joseph Kramm
Direction: Joseph Kramm and
    Warren Enters
Scenery: Howard Bay
Costumes: Dorine Ackerman

Tryout: New Haven (November 7,
    1956), Philadelphia, and
    Baltimore
    (Closed out of town)

CAST

Tom .... Johnnie Doyle
Dr. Brothers .... Elliott Nugent
Myra Brothers .... Geraldine Fitzgerald
Marilyn .... Jada Rowland
Mr. Maguire .... William E. Tierney
Logan Harvey .... Larry Gates
Orr .... Tom Emlyn Williams
Lambrides .... Peter Xantho
Heffernan .... Stanley Tackney
Mrs. Noesting .... Claire Waring
Mrs. Maguire .... Anne Ives
Edward Whitlock .... Paul Lipson
Mr. A. .... Robert W. Stewart
Mr. B. .... Clarence Nordstrom
Mr. C. .... Earl George
Henry Wilkins .... Russell Hicks
Lucy Harvey .... Iris Whitney
Herman Klinger .... Anatol Winogradoff
Arlene .... Genevive Griffin
Arthur Harrison .... Arthur Jarrett

SMALL WAR ON MURRAY HILL

By Robert E. Sherwood
Direction: Garson Kanin
Scenery: Boris Aronson
Costumes: Irene Sharaff

Tryout: New Haven and Boston
New York: Ethel Barrymore
Theatre
January 3, 1957
12 performances

CAST

Lt. Lord Frederick Beckenham	Daniel Massey
Major Clove	Nicholas Joy
Orderly	Peter Foy
Sentry	Bill Becker
Sam Pieters	Harry Sheppard
Gen. Sir William Howe	Leo Genn
Hawley, Batman to Gen. Howe	William Strange
Hessian	Michael Lewis
General Graf Von Donop	Stefan Schnabel
Robert Murray	Joseph Holland
Mary Murray	Jan Sterling
Captain Dupont	Nicholas Probst
Daisy	Jonelle Allen
Susan Lindley	Patricia Bosworth
Sergeant Galway	Elliott Sullivan
Corporal Mullet	Allan Stevenson
Amelie	Vinnette Carroll
Samuel Judah	Francis Compton
Mrs. Torpen	Sally Walker
Abigail Torpen	Susan Oliver
John	George Francis
Cora	Sharon Porter
Soldiers	Warner LeRoy
A Girl	Jan Jarrett
A Boy	Marc Sullivan

THE SATURDAY NIGHT KID

By Jack Dunphy
Co-production with Oliver Smith
Direction: George Keathley
Scenery: Oliver Smith
Costumes: Noel Taylor

Tryout: Westport, Conn. (September 9, 1957), and
Philadelphia
(Closed out of town)

CAST

Mrs. Topaz	Shelley Winters
The Young Man	Alex Nicol
The Driver	Joseph Wiseman

TIME REMEMBERED

By Jean Anouilh
  English version by Patricia Moyes
Co-production with Milton
  Sperling
Direction: Albert Marre
Scenery: Oliver Smith
Costumes: Miles White

Tryout: New Haven, Washington,
  and Boston
New York: Morosco Theatre
      November 12, 1957
      248 performances

CAST

Amanda, a milliner .... Susan Strasberg
The Duchess of Pont-Au-Bronc .... Helen Hayes
Theophilus, a butler .... Frederick Rolf
Lord Hector .... Glenn Anders
The Ice Cream Man .... LeRoi Operti
The Taxi Driver .... George Ebeling
Prince Albert .... Richard Burton
Ferdinand, head-waiter .... Sig Arno
The Singer .... Stanley Grover
The Pianist .... Edmund Horn
The Violinist .... Seymour Miroff
The Cellist .... Emil Borsody
The Landlord .... Frederic Warriner
Germain, a ghilly .... Truman Gaige
Footmen and Waiters .... E. W. Swackhamer,
    Fred Starbuck, George Landolf

NUDE WITH VIOLIN

By Noël Coward
Co-production with Lance
  Hamilton and Charles Russell
Direction: Noël Coward
Scenery: Oliver Smith
Costumes: Frank Thompson

Tryout: Wilmington and
  Philadelphia
New York: Belasco Theatre
      November 14, 1957
      86 performances
Tour: 7 weeks (in repertory with
    Present Laughter)

CAST

Sebastien .... Noël Coward
Marie-Celeste .... Therese Quadri
Clinton Preminger, Jr. .... William Traylor
Isobel Sorodin .... Joyce Carey
Jane .... Angela Thornton
Colin .... John Ainsworth
Pamela .... Iola Lynn
Jacob Friedland .... Morris Carnovsky
Anya Pavlikov .... Luba Malina
Cherry-May Waterton .... Mona Washbourne
Fabrice .... Robert Thurston
Obadiah Lewellyn .... Cory Devlin
George .... Robert Wark
Lauderdale .... Bobby Alford

THE ROPE DANCERS

By Morton Wishengrad
Co-production with Gilbert Miller
Direction: Peter Hall
Scenery: Boris Aronson
Costumes: Patricia Zipprodt

Tryout: New Haven, Boston, and
    Baltimore
New York: Cort Theatre
    November 20, 1954
    189 performances

CAST

Lizzie Hyland .... Beverly Lunsford
Margaret Hyland .... Siobhan McKenna
The Moving Man .... William Edmonson
Mrs. Farrow .... Joan Blondell
Clementine .... Barbara Ellen Myers
James Hyland .... Art Carney
Lameshnik .... Joseph Julian
The Cop .... Joseph Boland
Dr. Jacobson .... Theodore Bikel

THE COUNTRY WIFE

By William Wycherley
Co-production with Malcolm Wells
    and Daniel Blum
Direction: George Devine
Scenery: Motley
Costumes: Motley

Tryout: Wilmington and Wash-
    ington
New York: Adelphi Theatre
    November 27, 1957
    45 performances

CAST

Mr. Horner .... Laurence Harvey
Quack .... George Tyne
Boy .... Willie Wade
Sir Jasper Fidget .... Ernest Thesiger
Lady Fidget .... Pamela Brown
Mrs. Dainty Fidget .... Ludi Claire
Mr. Harcourt .... Richard Easton
Mr. Dorilant .... Peter Donat
Mr. Sparkish .... John Moffatt
Mr. Pinchwife .... Paul Whitsun-Jones
Mrs. Margery Pinchwife .... Julie Harris
Alithea (sister of Pinchwife) .... Maureen Quinney
Mrs. Squeamish .... Colleen Dewhurst
Lucy (Alithea's maid) .... Joan Hovis
Old Lady Squeamish .... Cynthia Latham
Parson .... David Vaughan

SUMMER OF THE 17TH DOLL

By Ray Lawler   *New York:* Coronet Theatre
Co-production with   January 22, 1958
   The Theatre Guild   29 performances
Direction: John Sumner
Scenery: Anne Fraser

CAST

Pearl Cunningham	Madge Ryan
Bubba Ryan	Fenella Maguire
Olive Leech	June Jago
Emma Leech	Ethel Gabriel
Barney Ibbot	Ray Lawler
Roo Webber	Kenneth Warren
Johnnie Dowd	Richard Pratt

PRESENT LAUGHTER

By Noël Coward   *New York:* Belasco Theatre
Co-production with Lance   January 31, 1958
   Hamilton and Charles Russell   6 performances
Direction: Noël Coward   *Tour:* 7 weeks (in repertory with
Scenery: Oliver Smith   *Nude with Violin*)
Costumes: Frank Thompson and
   Scaasi

CAST

Daphne Stillington	Angela Thornton
Miss Erikson	Avril Gentles
Fred	Robert Thurston
Monica Reed	Mona Washbourne
Garry Essendine	Noël Coward
Liz Essendine	Joyce Carey
Roland Maule	William Traylor
Morris Dixon	John Ainsworth
Henry Lyppiatt	Winston Ross
Joanna Lyppiatt	Eva Gabor
Contesse de Vriae	Therese Quadri

HOWIE

By Phoebe Ephron
Co-production with James M. Slevin and John Gerstad
Direction: John Gerstad
Scenery: Frederick Fox
Costumes: Patton Campbell

Tryout: Boston
New York: 46th Street Theatre
September 17, 1958
5 performances

CAST

Edith Simms	Peggy Conklin
Walter Simms	Leon Ames
Sally Sims	Patricia Bosworth
Barbara Dickerson	Patricia Smith
Howie Dickerson	Albert Salmi
Jimmie Keefe	Nicholas Pryor
Martha Robinson	Abby Lewis
Joe Robinson	John D. Seymour
Sylvia	Maggie Grindell
Victor	Robert Paschall
Martin	Stephen Gray
Joseph McNish	Conrad Fowkes
Announcer	Charles McDaniel
Wendy	Barbara Wilkin
The Professor	Gene Saks
Bill Pfeiffer	John Fiedler

A HANDFUL OF FIRE

By N. Richard Nash
Co-production with David Susskind
Direction: Robert Lewis
Scenery: Jo Mielziner
Costumes: Lucinda Ballard

Tryout: Washington and Philadelphia
New York: Martin Beck Theatre
October 1, 1958
5 performances

CAST

Mariachis	Jesus De Jerez, Thomas E. Infante, Alex Hassilev
Rodolfo	Robert Nieves
Bullfighter	Neil Laurence
Tamale Vendor	Jorge Gonzales
Padre	Angel Rigau
Tourist Wife	Jeanne Barr
Tourist Husband	Jake Sitters
A Woman	Scottie MacGregor
Rodolfo's Mother	Thelma Pelish
Pepe	Roddy McDowall
Alonso	Leonardo Cimino
Matias	Louis Guss
Ruben	William Edmonson
Policemen	Irving Winter, Dario Barri
Manuel	James Daly

Vargas .... Gene Gross
Sylvi .... Kay Medford
Maria .... Joan Copeland
Carmelita .... Myriam Acevedo
Young Man .... Mark Rydell

THE PLEASURE OF HIS COMPANY

By Samuel Taylor and Cornelia
    Otis Skinner
Co-production with Frederick
    Brisson
Direction: Cyril Ritchard
Scenery: Donald Oenslager
Costumes: Edith Head

Tryout: New Haven and Boston
New York: Longacre Theatre
    October 22, 1958
    474 performances
Tour: 25½ weeks

CAST

Toy .... Jerry Fujikawa
Biddeford Poole .... Cyril Ritchard
Jessica Poole .... Dolores Hart
Katharine Dougherty .... Cornelia Otis Skinner
Jim Dougherty .... Walter Abel
Mackenzie Savage .... Charlie Ruggles
Roger Henderson .... George Peppard

EDWIN BOOTH

By Milton Geiger
Co-production with José Ferrer
Direction: José Ferrer
Scenery: Zvi Geyra
Costumes: Edith Head

Tryout: La Jolla, Calif., Los
    Angeles, and San Francisco
New York: 46th Street Theatre
    November 24, 1958
    24 performances

CAST

William Winter .... Lorne Greene
Junius Brutus Booth, the elder .... Ian Keith
Edwin Booth, the boy .... Stephen Franken
Junius Brutus Booth, the younger .... Sydney Smith
Edwin Booth .... José Ferrer
Asia Booth .... Marion Ross
John Wilkes Booth .... Richard Waring
Mary Devlin .... Lois Smith
Edwina Booth .... Anne Helm

CUE FOR PASSION

By Elmer Rice
Co-production with Franchot
  Productions
Direction: Elmer Rice
Scenery: George Jenkins
Costumes: Dorothy Jenkins

Tryout: New Haven and
  Philadelphia
New York: Henry Miller's Theatre
  November 25, 1958
  39 performances

CAST

Lucy Gessler .... Joanna Brown
Grace Nicholson .... Diana Wynyard
Mattie Haines .... Anne Revere
Carl Nicholson .... Lloyd Gough
Tony Burgess .... John Kerr
Lloyd Hilton .... Robert Lansing
Hugh Gessler .... Russell Gaige

THE GAZEBO

By Alec Coppel
  From a story by Myra and Alec
  Coppel
Co-production with Frederick
  Brisson
Direction: Jerome Chodorov
Scenery: Jo Mielziner
Costumes: Virginia Volland

Tryout: Wilmington, Philadelphia,
  and Atlantic City
New York: Lyceum Theatre
  December 12, 1958
  218 performances
Tour: 9 weeks

CAST

Elliott Nash .... Walter Slezak
Harlow Edison .... Edward Andrews
Mathilda .... Jane Rose
Nell Nash .... Jayne Meadows
Mrs. Chandler .... Ruth Gillette
Mr. Thorpe .... Ralph Chambers
The Dook .... Michael Clarke-Laurence
Louie .... Don Grusso
Jenkins .... Leon Janney
Dr. Wyner .... Richard Poston
Druker .... John Ford
Potts .... Pat Patterson

LISTEN TO THE MOCKING BIRD

By Edward Chodorov
  Based on *Tabitha* by Arnold
  Ridley and Mary Cathcart
  Borer
Co-production with Saul Gottlieb
Direction: Edward Chodorov
Scenery: Leo Kerz
Costumes: Guy Kent

Tryout: Boston (December 27,
  1958), Cleveland, and
  Washington
  (Closed out of town after
  a backstage fire)

CAST

Martin McKenrick	Biff McGuire
Mary Trellington	Angela Thornton
Faith Borrow	Una Merkel
Mr. Fawcett	Felix Deebank
Mrs. Trellington	Cavada Humphrey
Hope Begg	Billie Burke
Lavinia Prendergast	Eva Le Gallienne
Sergeant	Sheppard Kerman
Detective Inspector Bruton	Donald Moffat
Chief Inspector	Francis Compton
Coroner	Anthony Kemble-Cooper
Constable	Phil Bruns

LOOK AFTER LULU

By Noël Coward
  Based on *Occupe-toi d'Amelie*
  by Georges Feydeau
Co-production with Gilbert Miller,
  Lance Hamilton, and Charles
  Russell
Direction: Cyril Ritchard
Scenery: Cecil Beaton
Costumes: Cecil Beaton

Tryout: New Haven
New York: Henry Miller's Theatre
  March 3, 1959
  39 performances

CAST

Lulu d'Arville	Tammy Grimes
Bomba	Rory Harrity
Valery	Craig Huebing
Emile	Bill Berger
Gaby	Barbara Loden
Yvonne	Sasha Von Scherler
Paulette	Grace Gaynor
Philippe de Croze	George Baker
Adonis	Paul Smith
Gigot	Eric Christmas
Claire	Polly Rowles

Marcel Blanchard	Roddy McDowall
General Koschnadieff	Ellis Rabb
Herr Van Putzeboum	Jack Gilford
Florist's boys	David Faulkner, David Thurman
Prince of Salestria	Kurt Kasznar
Rose	Reva Rose
Oudatte	Earl Montgomery
Cornette	John Alderman
Mayor of the District	Arthur Malet
Photographer	William Griffis
Aunt Gabrielle	Philippa Bevans
Little Girl	Ina Cummins
Inspector of Police	David Hurst

JUNO

Book by Joseph Stein
  Based on Sean O'Casey's *Juno
  and the Paycock*
Music by Marc Blitzstein
Co-production with Oliver Smith
  and Oliver Rea
Direction: José Ferrer
Scenery: Oliver Smith
Choreography: Agnes de Mille
Costumes: Irene Sharaff

Tryout: Washington and Boston
New York: Winter Garden
  Theatre
  March 9, 1959
  16 performances

CAST

Mary Boyle	Monte Amundsen
Johnny Boyle	Tommy Rall
Juno Boyle	Shirley Booth
Jerry Devine	Loren Driscoll
Mrs. Madigan	Jean Stapleton
Mrs. Brady	Nancy Andrews
Mrs. Coyne	Sada Thompson
Miss Quinn	Beulah Garrick
Charlie Bentham	Earl Hammond
Foley	Arthur Rubin
Sullivan	Rico Froehlich
Michael Brady	Robert Rue
Paddy Coyne	Julian Patrick
"Captain" Jack Boyle	Melvyn Douglas
"Joxer" Daly	Jack MacGowran
Molly	Gemze de Lappe
"Needle" Nugent	Liam Lenihan
I.R.A. Men	Tom Clancy, Jack Murray
Mrs. Tancred	Clarice Blackburn
Mrs. Dwyer	Betty Low
I.R.A. Singer	Robert Hoyem
Furniture Removal Men	George Ritner, Frank Carroll
Policeman	Rico Froehlich

Singers: Anne Fielding, Cleo Fry, Pat Huddleston, Gail Johnston,
     Barbara Lockard, Pat Ruhl, Diana Sennett, Joanne Spiller,
     Frank Carroll, Ted Forlow, Rico Froehlich, Robert Hoyem,
     Jack Murray, Julian Patrick, George Ritner, Robert Rue,
     James Tushar.

Dancers: Sharon Enoch, Mickey Gunnersen, Pat Heyes, Rosemary
Jourdan, Annabelle Lyon, Marjorie Wittmer, Jenny Workman,
Chuck Bennett, Ted Forlow, Curtis Hood, Scott Hunter,
Eugene Kelton, James Maher, Eurique Martinez, Howard
Parker, Jim Ryan, Glen Tetley.

CHERI

By Anita Loos
   Adapted from the novels *Cheri*
   and *The Last of Cheri* by Colette
Co-production with Robert Lewis
Direction: Robert Lewis
Scenery: Oliver Smith
Costumes: Miles White

Tryout: Washington
New York: Morosco Theatre
October 12, 1959
56 performances

CAST

Charlotte Peloux	Edith King
Madame Valerie Aldonza	Frieda Altman
Baroness de Berche	Lucy Landau
Count Anthime Berthellmy	Jerome Collamore
Madame Lili	Jane Moultrie
Prince Guido Ceste	Angelo del Rossi
Butler	Byron Russell
Léa de Lonval	Kim Stanley
Patron	John Granger
Frédérick Peloux (Chéri)	Horst Buchholz
Rose	Margot Lassner
Edmée	Joan Gray
Coco	Lili Darvas
Fanchette	Ginger

FLOWERING CHERRY

By Robert Bolt
Co-production with Don Herbert,
   Don Sharpe Enterprises,
   H. M. Tennent Ltd., and
   Frith Banbury, Ltd.
Direction: Frith Banbury
Scenery: Boris Aronson
Costumes: Theoni V. Aldredge

Tryout: Baltimore and Washington
New York: Lyceum Theatre
October 21, 1959
5 performances

CAST

Isobel Cherry	Wendy Hiller
Tom	Andrew Ray

Cherry	Eric Portman
Gilbert Grass	George Turner
Judy	Phyllis Love
David Bowman	Roy Poole
Carol	Susan Burnet

FIVE FINGER EXERCISE

By Peter Shaffer
Co-production with Frederick
   Brisson and H. M. Tennent Ltd.
Direction: John Gielgud
Scenery: Oliver Smith

Tryout: Wilmington and Washington
New York: The Music Box
   December 2, 1959
   337 performances
Tour: 29 weeks

CAST

Louise Harrington	Jessica Tandy
Stanley Harrington	Roland Culver
Clive Harrington	Brian Bedford
Pamela Harrington	Juliet Mills
Walter Langer	Michael Bryant

SILENT NIGHT, LONELY NIGHT

By Robert Anderson
Direction: Peter Glenville
Scenery: Jo Mielziner
Costumes: Theoni V. Aldredge

Tryout: New Haven and Boston
New York: Morosco Theatre
   December 3, 1959
   124 performances

CAST

Katherine	Barbara Bel Geddes
Mae	Eda Heinemann
John	Henry Fonda
Janet	Lois Nettleton
Philip	Bill Berger
Jerry	Peter De Visé

MOTEL

By Thomas W. Phipps
Co-production with Kenneth
   Wagg and James M. Slavin
Direction: Herbert Machiz
Scenery: Ben Edwards
Costumes: Ben Edwards

Tryout: Boston (January 6, 1960)
(Closed out of town)

CAST

Wally	Myron McCormick
Nancy	Sandy Dennis
Frank Lilly	George Mathews
Ruby	Vicki Cummings
Mrs. Dretz	Virgilia Chew
David	Richard Easton
Isobel	Siobhan McKenna
Al	Joe Ponazecki
Mr. Leffler	Jack De Lon

THE BEST MAN

By Gore Vidal
Direction: Joseph Anthony
Scenery: Jo Mielziner
Costumes: Theoni V. Aldredge

Tryout: Wilmington and Boston
New York: Morosco Theatre
March 31, 1960
520 performances
Tour: 20 weeks

CAST

Dick Jensen	Karl Weber
First Reporter	Howard Fischer
William Russell	Melvyn Douglas
Mike	Martin Fried
Second Reporter	Tony Bickley
Third Reporter	Barbara Berjer
Fourth Reporter	Tom McDermott
Alice Russell	Leora Dana
Assistant to Dick Jensen	Ruth Maynard
Mrs. Gamadge	Ruth McDevitt
Arthur Hockstader	Lee Tracy
Mabel Cantwell	Kathleen Maguire
Bill Blades	Joseph Sullivan
Joseph Cantwell	Frank Lovejoy
Senator Carlin	Gordon B. Clarke
Dr. Artinian	Hugh Franklin
Sheldon Marcus	Graham Jarvis
Reporters, Delegates, etc.	John Dorrin, Mitchell Erickson, Ruth Tobin

APPENDIX C

Two Plays in Which the Company

Had Only an Indirect Interest

MISS LIBERTY

Book by Robert E. Sherwood
Music and lyrics by Irving Berlin
Produced by Irving Berlin, Robert
  E. Sherwood, and Moss Hart
Direction: Moss Hart
Scenery: Oliver Smith
Choreography: Jerome Smith
Costumes: Motley

Tryout: Philadelphia
New York: Imperial Theatre
  July 15, 1949
  308 performances

CAST

Maisie Dell	Mary McCarty
The Herald Reader	Rowan Tudor
James Gordon Bennett	Charles Dingle
Horace Miller	Eddie Albert
Police Captain	Evans Thornton
The Mayor	Donald McClelland
French Ambassador	Emile Renan
Carthwright	Sid Lawson
Joseph Pulitzer	Philip Bourneuf
The Sharks	Bill Bradley, Allen Knowles, Kazimir Kokic, Robert Pagent
Bartholdi	Herbert Berghof
The Models	Stephanie Augustine, Trudy DeLuz, Marilyn Frechette
Monique DuPont	Allyn McLerie
The Boy	Tommy Rall
The Girl	Maria Karnilova
The Acrobats	Virginia Conwell, Joe Milan, Eddie Phillips
Strong Man	Kazimir Kokic
The Countess	Ethel Griffies
A Lover	Ed Chappel
His Girl	Helene Whitney
A Gendarme	Robert Penn
A Lamplighter	Johnny V. R. Thompson
Another Lamplighter	Tommy Rall
A Socialite	Marilyn Frechette
An Actress	Helene Whitney
A Minister	Ed Chappel
An Admiral	Robert Patterson

The Boys .... Bob Kryl, Ernest Laird
The Mother .... Elizabeth Watts
The Policeman .... Evans Thornton
The Brothers .... Lewis Bolyard, David Collyer
The Train .... Eddie Phillips, Erik Kristen, Joseph Milan
Reception Delegation .... Dolores Goodman, Virginia Conwell,
      Fred Hearn, Bob Tucker, Allen Knowles
A Maid .... Gloria Patrice
The Dandy .... Tommy Rall
Ruby .... Maria Karnilova
A Sailor .... Eddie Phillips
His Girl .... Dolores Goodman
Richard K. Fox .... Donald McClelland
The Judge .... Erik Kristen
A Policeman .... Robert Patterson
Immigration Officer .... Evans Thornton
A Boy .... William Calhoun

SECOND THRESHOLD

By Philip Barry
   with revisions by
   Robert E. Sherwood
Produced by Alfred de Liagre
Direction: Alfred de Liagre
Scenery: Donald Oenslager

Tryout: New Haven and Boston
New York: Morosco Theatre
January 2, 1951
126 performances

CAST

Toby Wells .... Hugh Reilly
Malloy .... Gordon Richards
Miranda Bolton .... Margaret Phillips
Josiah Bolton .... Clive Brook
Thankful Mather .... Betsy Von Furstenberg
Jock Bolton .... Frederick Bradlee

Index

NOTE

Page numbers in italics indicate references to captions.
From Appendices B and C only production credits are cited.
Subentries are chronologically listed.